If you knew that you would die at age twenty-five, what would you do with your life? William Borden did not have that knowledge, but in his brief life he greatly impacted the world for Christ. I was deeply moved as I was reminded of the impact of his life. I wish every Christian college student would read this book. Life does not begin after college and graduate school. Life is now! The world awaits your impact!

GARY D. CHAPMAN
Author of the New York Times No. 1 bestseller *The 5 Love Languages*

Although he died at a remarkably early age, William Whiting Borden had an enduring impact on all who knew him, and on the course of Christianity in the twentieth century. Now, in this engaging new biography by Kevin Belmonte, 'Borden of Yale' comes to life again for another generation. A book to inspire and encourage followers of Jesus everywhere.

TIMOTHY GEORGE
Founding Dean of Beeson Divinity School,
Samford University, Birmingham, Alabama

William Borden was a name well known in the past; and it is good that his life story will continue to be remembered into this new century. Kevin Belmonte's book is superbly documented, and very well written.

KENNETH HENKE
Curator of Special Collections and Archivist,
Princeton Theological Seminary, Princeton, New Jersey

William Borden's life and example hearken back to earlier figures in the Christian tradition: he was a latter-day David Brainerd, motivated by a self-sacrificial missionary zeal ...

KENNETH P. MINKEMA
Jonathan Edwards Center, Yale University, New Haven, Connecticut

William Borden's s  us to go into all the world ... to prea ..

BLE JIM RYUN
Congress, 3 Time Olympian,
and recipient of the Presidential Medal of Freedom

These pages give a vivid, cinematic telling of William Borden's life, his deep compassion, and the large circle of his friendships. Faith illumined his brief but vibrant life. In the ivy halls of college, and beyond, he knew the True North of belief.

Here, we see the power of youth wisely focused, and the beauty of truth written in personality. Like a voyage, this biography charts the reasons for hope which marked and guided Borden's passion to share the gospel at home and abroad.

This is a book that can help today's generation of students—and believers and seekers alike—re-discover evangelism and the abiding joy of following Jesus Christ. It will delight and inspire ...

KELLY MONROE KULLBERG
Editor and co-author of *Finding God at Harvard*,
founder of The Veritas Forum

William Borden tells of a Christian life richly and profoundly lived, one greatly respected and revered in his own time.

Like a note sung and reverberating through a great cathedral space, his short life continues to reverberate into the modern missionary movement. There is no better biographer than Kevin Belmonte to keep Borden's beautiful song continuing.

JEFF JOHNSON
Award-winning musician

William Borden had the whole world open to him; but risked everything to follow the call of God's love and share the gospel with those who needed to hear it. Faith shone for him like a beacon, and he brought hope to many lives, though he only lived to age twenty-five. We are excited to see author and historian Kevin Belmonte tell William Borden's story again, with new insights. Our hope is that this book will lead each of us to consider God's call, and what He may ask us to undertake.

JAMES AND LISA DOUGHERTY
Co-Directors, Overseas Missionary Fellowship (US)

William Borden graduated from The Hill School, a private preparatory school in Pennsylvania, in 1904. A person of privilege, as were many of his classmates, he went on to Yale University and Princeton Theological Seminary.

Yet he never lost sight of how 'the other half lived,' founding the Yale Hope Mission, and embarking on a trek to China in 1913 that cost him his life.

No one represented The Hill School motto, 'Whatsoever Things Are True' more than William Borden. His life, sacrifice, and many contributions unfold in this excellent biography.

LOUIS E. JEFFRIES
Archivist and Librarian,
The Hill School (William Borden's prep school),
Pottstown, Pennsylvania

The life of William Borden has inspired my faith and walk with God since I first read his story as a young girl. I pray that this biography will inspire a new generation to follow in the steps of Borden's whole-hearted, single-focused devotion to Christ, to choose Him above all this world has to offer, and to live their lives with eternity always in view.

NANCY DEMOSS WOLGEMUTH
Author and founder/host of Revive Our Hearts

An insightful, beautifully written, inspiring account of a remarkable life. It's simply outstanding!

TRENT SHEPPARD
Author of *God on Campus* and *The Jesus Journey*

In the tradition of *Chariots of Fire* and Eric Liddell, William Borden's story reveals the hand of God at work in a remarkable way ... Kevin Belmonte has brought to life another story from history that we desperately need today.

CHRIS FABRY
Moody Radio, host of 'Chris Fabry Live'

For readers in the UK and places beyond, Kevin Belmonte's well researched and stirring narrative of William Borden's life will inspire a new generation to follow Christ courageously, and without reserve.

ALAN TAYLOR
Church Leader, England

This book is an Olympian achievement: biography at its best, a very compelling and inspiring read.

DAVID NAUGLE
Author of *Worldview: History of a Concept*,
Dallas Baptist University, Dallas, Texas

It was said of William Borden, 'thousands will thank God that he lived.' But how will the thousands of our own time be able to thank God for someone whose name they may not know? That is where Kevin Belmonte comes in. He rescues exemplary saints from the shadows of history. He gives us the lives of people like Borden for us to savor, and most especially, to join the thousands in thanking God for. This is a masterful book.

MICHAEL CARD
Author and song-writer,
composer of 'El Shaddai' and 'Immanuel'

In the pages of this book, it's wonderful to see how much Kevin Belmonte has uncovered regarding this extraordinary man.

GAIL BORDEN
Member of the extended Borden family

Kevin Belmonte's marvelous portrait of William Borden, 'the millionaire missionary,' not only inspires, but wistfully captures the time of a faith-prompted generation: one that modeled a decency, decorum, and dedication for which our hearts so yearn.

LAGARD SMITH
Former Professor of Law,
Faulkner University, Montgomery, Alabama

Kevin Belmonte has done something remarkable. He's taken a figure history had virtually forgotten, and revealed a man whose commitment and actions literally transformed the world around him. This is a life changing story that our culture today needs to know.

PHIL COOKE
Filmmaker, media consultant, and author of *The Way Back*

Beacon-Light

The Life of
William Borden
(1887–1913)

KEVIN BELMONTE

One ship drives east, and another drives west,
with the self-same winds that blow.
'Tis the set of the sails, and not the gales,
that tell them the way to go ...

– Ella Wheeler Wilcox (1904)

CHRISTIAN
FOCUS

Copyright © Kevin Belmonte 2021

paperback ISBN 978-1-5271-0719-9
ebook ISBN 978-1-5271-0786-1

10 9 8 7 6 5 4 3 2 1

Published in 2021
by
Christian Focus Publications Ltd,
Geanies House, Fearn, Ross-shire,
IV20 1TW, Great Britain.

www.christianfocus.com

Cover design by
Daniel van Straaten

Printed and bound by Bell & Bain

Contents

Dedication

*To the memory of William Borden, and the schools
that shaped his character:*

The Hill School, Yale, and Princeton – with gratitude to historians
Edmund S. Morgan and David McCullough, whose studies of
Benjamin Franklin and the Wright Brothers
have been a guiding inspiration …

Memories of a Legacy

Be strong. Strong with a strength
that the world may not at first recognize.[1]
– Dr John Timothy Stone's pastoral charge to
William Borden (September 1912)

And already, not a few friends are saying that a book must be written
which will tell the story of [William Borden's] life ...[2]
– Henry Weston Frost (May 1913)

He seemed like a fixed beacon-light in moving waters,
by which others could safely steer their course ...[3]
– Dr Samuel Zwemer (September 1913)

To live, as [William Borden] lived, is to enrich the world;
and to leave behind ... things that are true ...[4]
– Francis J. Grimké (Summer 1927)

---

1. See 'Borden Ordained for Chinese Post,' on page 3 of the Sunday, September 22, 1912 edition of *The Chicago Tribune*. Dr Stone spoke these words at The Moody Church in Chicago on Saturday, September 21, 1912.

2. Henry Weston Frost, in the May 1913 issue of *China's Millions* magazine (Toronto: China Inland Mission, 1913), p. 49.

3. See page 71 of Samuel Zwemer's biography *William Whiting Borden*, dated September 1913, and housed at the Presbyterian Historical Society in Philadelphia. It is cited as a published text in J. L. Murray and F. M. Harris, *Christian Standards in Life* (New York: Association Press, 1915), page 85, and Volume 29 of *The Encyclopedia Americana* (1920), lists *A Life of William Borden* (1916) among Samuel Zwemer's works. See also J. W. Cochran, *Heroes of the Campus* (Philadelphia: Westminster Press, 1917), p. 168, which cites this 1916 book in its Bibliography. The PHS manuscript bears this citation: National Council of the Churches of Christ in the United States of America Division of Christian Education Records, 1897–1974. 103.00 cubic feet, including 'Borden, William Whiting, Biography, Sept 1913' in box 73, folder 12. (Call number: NCC RG 9).

4. See C. G. Woodson, ed., *The Works of Francis J. Grimké*, v. 3 (Washington: Associated Publishers, 1942), p. 211. A hero of African-American history, Grimké was a former slave who was educated at Princeton, and later became a prominent clergyman in Washington, D.C.

Acknowledgements

Many have been a friend to this book-writing journey. I wish to thank Christian Focus Publications Ltd. of Scotland, for their commitment to William Borden's story. To have such a distinguished publisher, from my ancestral home, is a true privilege. Working with Editorial Manager Rosanna Burton, and her colleagues at CFP, has been rewarding at every turn.

Gail Borden, a friend whom I met at Oxford, wrote with an unexpected, but very welcome invitation to undertake a new biography of William Borden. That has been a gift.

I am very greatly indebted to Dr Os Guinness (D.Phil. Oxford), the great-nephew of Geraldine Guinness Taylor, the author of William Borden's classic biography, *Borden of Yale, '09*. Early on, as I considered this project, I wrote to Os—a treasured friend of many years—and asked his thoughts. He told me about his great-aunt, and ardently commended this new book. To have the blessing and kind prayers of Mrs Taylor's nephew has been a special gift. Os also encouraged me to contact the publishers at Christian Focus regarding Borden's story. His wise counsel, and personal commendation, opened a door of opportunity.

Louis Jeffries, Senior Archivist at The Hill School, has been indefatigable in finding key research items for William Borden's life. I am deeply grateful to him, and The Hill School, for countless marks of kindness to this book. To use a phrase William Borden would have known from his study of Latin at The Hill School, *gratias tibi valde.*

Kenneth Henke, Curator of Special Collections and Archivist at Princeton Theological Seminary, has taught me much about Borden's years at Princeton, his family's time at Westland, President Grover Cleveland's former home, and 'the way-station of hospitality' that developed there. I wish to thank the Presbyterian Historical Society, Philadelphia, for sending a digitized copy of Samuel Zwemer's biography of William Borden. To Ms Charlene Peacock, Reference Archivist, and her PHS colleagues, my abiding thanks for such sterling assistance. Camden Public Library kindly sent images of the Borden family cottage. And Ken Gross of the Walsh History Center helped me identify Borden's great friend Captain Fremont Arey. As a native Mainer myself, this kindness was especially welcome; and lends fine memories of the sea.

Finally, I cherish the memory of William Borden and his remarkable family. People all over the world owe them a great debt for philanthropy and faith – and so many lives have been touched through the schools, hospitals, universities, and charitable institutions remembered in William Borden's will. He has walked 'the home above,' as he called it, for over 100 years as we mark time: yet his gifts still endow streams of blessing.

But the greatest gift was his life; and the resplendent way he lived it.

Tributes from the Famous

Dr Kenneth Latourette was one of William Borden's finest friends at Yale, and in his *Autobiography,* he penned these words of recollection and tribute—

A potent influence in 1909 was William Whiting Borden. He was from a wealthy Chicago family, [and] entered Yale purposing to be a missionary.

He planned to go to a real frontier, the Moslems in West China, and to seek appointment under the China Inland Mission. He was an able student, president of Phi Beta Kappa in his senior year. He was athletic, of great energy, handsome, and a born leader of men …

After Yale, he entered Princeton Theological Seminary and graduated. Then he went to Egypt to study Arabic, planning to go from there to China … While in Cairo, he was taken with spinal meningitis and died. His biography, *Borden of Yale, '09,* written by Mrs Howard Taylor at his mother's request, has had a profound influence on successive generations of students.[1]

Added to this, Latourette had also written: 'William Borden was one of my dearest friends … I look back on his friendship as one of the richest I have known.'[2]

---

1. See *Beyond the Ranges: The Autobiography of Kenneth Scott Latourette* (Grand Rapids: Eerdmans, 1967), pp. 35-36. Latourette was one of the most eminent church historians in 20th century academia, and Sterling Professor at Yale. His *History of Christianity* is a widely-acknowledged classic.

2. Part One of this quote (pre-ellipsis) is from Kenneth Scott Latourette to Bernard R. DeRemer, 8 October 1956, a letter housed at Moody Bible Institute. Part

Some years later, speaking before an audience of several thousand collegians at the Urbana Conference of 1981, Dr Billy Graham spoke of Borden's legacy—

> Many people had difficulty understanding why a young millionaire wanted to spend his life like that, but those who knew Borden for any length of time understood it. The consuming desire of his life was to share the love of Jesus Christ with people wherever he was, whatever he was doing. He loved people, and longed for them to know the God who loved them, and died for them – who had changed his life.[3]

Two of this quote (post-ellipsis) is from *Beyond the Ranges* (Grand Rapids: Eerdmans, 1967), p. 36.

3. Billy Graham, quoted in *Confessing Christ as Lord*, ed. by J.W. Alexander (Downers Grove: InterVarsity Press, 1982), p. 129.

Preface: A Star to Sail Her By

Borden had become a nationally known figure. That a young man of his wealth and remarkable abilities would lay aside a brilliant future to [become a] missionary to north-west China astonished many people.

'I know of no young man in this country, or in England, from whose life I expect greater things,' wrote Dr R. A. Torrey.[1]
– M. R. Bradshaw (1965)

Thousands will thank God that William Borden lived.[2]
– Dr James Martin Gray (1913)

But he abides, and his influence abides ...[3]
– Charles Soutter Campbell (1913)

'The most influential missionary of the early 20th century never made it to the mission field.'[4] So ran the sweeping and astonishing headline of a feature story for *Christianity Today* in February

---

1. See M. R. Bradshaw, *Torch for Islam* (London: China Inland Mission, 1965), p. 26.

2. 'Minute in Memory of William Whiting Borden,' *The Christian Workers Magazine*, Nov. 1913, p. 140. I have attributed this to Dr James Martin Gray because of the great similarity between this tribute and one directly attributed to Dr Gray in *The Missionary Visitor* magazine, June 1913, p. 197.

3. Charles Soutter Campbell, *William Whiting Borden: A Short Life Complete in Christ* (privately printed, c. 1913), p. 30.

4. See Jayson Casper, 'The Forgotten Final Resting Place of William Borden,' a feature *Christian History* article posted online at: http://www.christianitytoday.com/history/topics/missions-world-christianity/forgotten-final-resting-place-of-william-borden.html

2017. And the person to whom these words refer was William Whiting Borden. His life story was told in a classic biography: a book that yielded a phrase once known throughout the world:

'No Reserve. No Retreat. No Regrets.'[5]

For nearly a century these words have given hope, like a welcome freshet of solace and renewal, or a cordial of steadfast virtue. Few phrases over this time have been more dearly treasured, in so many places of the world.

Borden's life, spanning just twenty-five years, was told by a gifted author who was 'the first lady of missionary letters,' Geraldine Guinness Taylor, the daughter of renowned Christian philanthropist H. Grattan Guinness, and the daughter-in-law of missionary pioneer Hudson Taylor.

So as a book, *Borden of Yale* had a rare provenance. Its sales were no less noteworthy. Published in 1926, it 'went through eight printings in nine years.'[6] Its power to inspire, in telling the story of a young man who embodied the idea of dedication and sacred purpose, seems always renewed.

And here, there are timeless things in William Borden's story. One of them, the most telling, was his quest to live a faithful life.

Many assay that quest now, as they always will do. Geraldine Taylor's book vividly explored the reasons why William Borden was resolute in seeking the call of God on his life, and how he kept that call with sterling fidelity. He has been gone many years, but his story lives on: a beacon-light still.

---

5. See Geraldine Guinness Taylor, *Borden of Yale '09* (London: China Inland Mission, 1926), p. 260. Here, this credo is given as 'no reserve, no retreat, no regrets.' And this is its authoritative text. However, these are Geraldine Taylor's words, not William Borden's. Tradition holds that these words were written in Borden's personal Bible. But to date, this Bible has not come to light, and all that can be confirmed is that Geraldine Taylor wrote these words. Tellingly, she makes no reference of any kind to finding them in Borden's Bible.

6. See J. A. Carpenter, *Sacrificial Lives* (New York: Garland, 1988).

Yet notwithstanding …

One hundred years have passed since William Borden's time, and we might well wonder, how do we enter his world at this remove?

Images are a key, and one photo captures the theme of Borden's odyssey. In the pages of *Borden of Yale*, a picture shows Borden sailing a 'friendship sloop,' *Tsatsawassa*, off the coast of Camden, Maine.[7]

It's a telling image, and time falls away to look at it. The sloop moves into the wind, across a wide bay. Borden stands at the helm, a silhouette in the foreground. He is a fine mariner, setting out on a voyage: and knowing well his destination.

These are reveal-ing moments of Wil-liam Borden's life. Few young men of his time charted their course more ably. And he won many friends on the way.

He was a young man of deep spiritual conviction; and left the world phrases that speak to the ardent place faith held as the centerpiece of his life.

A photo of the *Tsatsawassa*, the 'friendship sloop' where Borden spent so many cherished hours at sea (from the author's 1st British edition copy of *Borden of Yale*, 1926).

One of them was: 'The true Christian is one who has caught a vision … of the risen Christ.'[8] It's an eloquent, compelling phrase, and recalls words from C. S. Lewis that mark his memorial in

---

7. For confirmation of the Bordens' sloop design, see the online site: https://www.mysticseaport.org/galleries/ranger-friendship-sloop/

8. 'What Does It Mean To Be A Christian?' a tract by William Whiting Borden, (New York: The National Bible Institute, c. 1912).

Westminster Abbey: 'I believe in Christianity as I believe that the Sun has risen, not only because I see it, but because by it, I see everything else.'[9]

The sea holds hidden depths, it is true. But the depths of William Borden's character were seen by everyone who knew him. He died young, but the compelling sides of his nature, burnished by vibrant belief, lived on in their memory.

In the decades to follow, their recollections filled books and magazines.

The pages of this book chart Borden's journey, and delve into the ways 'vital truth,' as he called it, was the star he reckoned by. He described this by invoking the faith of the sage from ancient Tarsus who'd written many books in the Bible.

'And what Paul taught others,' he stated, 'was but the vital truth that gripped his own heart and made him exclaim: "For me, to live is Christ."'[10]

That truth guided and shaped William Borden's life.

The following pages show why.

---

9. See C. S. Lewis, *The Weight of Glory* (New York: HarperCollins, 2001), p. 140.
10. W. W. Borden, 'What Does It Mean To Be A Christian?' (1912).

CHAPTER 1

First Pages of the Story

To begin this book, it's helpful to set the stage with two vignettes showing William Borden during his graduate student days at Princeton.

For if his life was one that now verges on legend, it's the more important to remember that any such legend comes only from the life that inspired it. We need to know what William Borden was like on days when he navigated his sloop at sea, was profiled in newspapers alongside stories of the Wright Brothers,[1] or spoke with those who knew him. As far as possible, we need to see him as he really was.

For there is where the best story lies.

In summer 1910 William Borden, age twenty-two, sailed for Europe to spend three weeks in Hanover, for intensive study of German to aid his linguistic studies at Princeton Theological Seminary. During this time, he visited Berlin and his good friend from Yale, Kenneth Latourette (later an eminent scholar of church history). Latourette described Borden as 'an able student,'[2] but during their weekend visit, all studies were set aside for the sights and sounds of Berlin, good conversation, and very likely bicycling,

---

1. See page 2 of *The Mariposa Gazette,* Saturday, 31 July 1909.
2. See *Beyond the Ranges* (1967), pp. 35-36 and p. 39.

as Borden was an avid cyclist during his stays in Europe – ever the student athlete he'd been at Yale.[3]

To hear this story recalls a wistful reflection, expressed by Edmund Morgan when writing of Benjamin Franklin; but it is no less true of William Borden—

> But we may be permitted a small regret … for having been born too late to enjoy his company. We can never catch the warmth of his smile, the tone of his voice, the little gestures, the radiant presence that drew people to him wherever he went.[4]

Some figures from history prompt a wish that we'd met them.

Around the time of Borden's visit in Germany with Latourette, he wrote a prescient and haunting letter to his friend and mentor, Dr Henry Weston Frost, a much-respected leader of China Inland Mission. Taking up his pen on Wednesday, July 20th, Borden said that during his stay, 'people talk about peace (in Peace Congresses), but in reality, here in Europe, they are preparing for a great struggle, I believe. The opinion seems to be that Germany will soon be ready to make a grab for more territory, which she badly needs, etc.'[5]

Even then, four summers before August 1914, Borden saw gathering storm clouds of war. He would not live to see the outbreak of World War I, but he saw worrying signs of a coming conflict: one to afflict so many of his generation.

Borden's sojourn in Europe was revealing in that it showed him to be a keen observer of people and events; but equally so is

---

3. See Taylor, *Borden of Yale* (1926), pp. 181-182. As Borden's close friend Robert Wilder (founder of the Student Volunteer Movement) said of Borden's one-time visit with Wilder and his family in their Norwegian home: '[William] took a real interest in our home-life and all our doings. He helped [my] children to learn to ride their bicycles, running by each of them in turn.'

4. See the Preface to *Benjamin Franklin*, by E. S. Morgan (New Haven: Yale University Press, 2002), p. ix.

5. See Taylor, *Borden of Yale* (1926), pp. 182-183. The last sentence of this quote is from a letter Borden wrote to H. W. Frost from Hanover, Germany, Wed., July 20, 1910, housed at The Billy Graham Center, Wheaton College.

an account that comes to us from a very different place: the coast of Maine in New England.

Among the many revealing postcards taken of Camden, Maine from the time that William Borden and his family summered there, one stands out. It seems less a postcard than it does an artist's wish to capture a moment and place.

A close look at the picture shows the photographer had set out early to get a photo of the inland sea as the morning mist lifted from the waters of a small cove. Small clusters of white effervesce and rise; and smoke swells lazily from a chimney in the distance. A sailboat stands out to sea; getting underway for an early cruise.

It's a 'friendship sloop' just like the one the Borden family owned – in fact, the photographer may well have taken a photograph, unaware, of the *Tsatsawassa*, the name the Bordens gave their sloop – one possibly taken from the fine, sonorous Native American name of a lake in Rensselaer County, New York state.

An early 1900s scene from Camden, Maine, where a fine sloop like the Borden family's *Tsatsawassa* stands out to sea (from the author's photo collection, postcard dated 1906).

'The Bordens,' one family member has said, 'loved the water, and yachts.'[6] All his life, William Borden kept that abiding love of sailing and the sea.

6. Author email correspondence with Gail Borden, Thursday, August 31, 2017.

His friend Captain Arey knew this better than most.[7] 'I've known him ever since he first come to Camden,' the Captain remembered fondly, and with more than a trace of a native Mainer's accent and speech:

> When he came up in the spring, he always shook hands with everybody. All the summer people don't do that. If 'twas a stranger or a fisherman, didn't make no difference. He always spoke to everybody – like as if he wanted to, and shook hands with them.
>
> [Aboard ship,] he was always singing ... He'd climb away up the riggin' ... He did everything well he tried to do. He was so strong, too!
>
> When he'd go out and work at the riggin' I'd be afraid he'd break the sail, he was so strong ... [But] he could take a chart, and go anywhere with it. Of course, he'd studied into it, and learned it ...
>
> William was a nice hand to sail a boat. You didn't need no one else when he was along ... Sometimes he'd steer, and sometimes he'd help with the sails, but he was an expert on the boat.[8]

Notwithstanding differences in their backgrounds—Captain Arey a native Mainer, Camden born and bred, and Borden the cultured son of a wealthy, prominent Chicago family—like recognized like in their friendship. Arey respected Borden as a gifted and dedicated mariner. In a word, he was a born sailor.

'If we was out all night on the boat,' Arey said, 'he'd roll in the blanket and sleep on deck. The others would be in the cabin. There might be a bed to spare, but he'd take the deck. He liked it better.'[9] There were other memories too:

---

7. Capt. Fremont Arey, as the *Santa Barbara News-Post* refers (Apr. 12, 1912) to John Borden 'and his captain, Fremont C. Arey, Camden, Maine.' John Borden was William Borden's elder brother. Further, page 21 of the 1902–3 *Camden [Phone] Directory* lists 'Arey, Fremont C., yachtsman.' Author correspondence with Ken Gross of Camden Public Library, on Friday, 26 Oct. 2018, confirms F. C. Arey (b. 1863) was a 'master mariner.'

8. See Taylor, *Borden of Yale* (1926), p. 162.

9. ibid., p. 163.

It was blowin' awful heavy one night – dark and rainy. Two other fellers was out with us, [William's] friends. About two o'clock in the morning, the bran' new boat we was towin', the steam-launch, rolled over and sunk, the rope parted. I remember what he said.

'The boat's gone,' he called down to the other fellers—

'We can go faster now!'

Lots and lots of boats that night that was about as big as the *Tsatsawassa* was wrecked – that is, the sails were torn, and the spars broke, so that they had to be towed in. The storm commenced about eleven o'clock. James Perry and another of William's friends was with us. I don't think any of us slept. I know I didn't, and know William didn't.

It was about six o'clock next morning when we got into Beverley Farms and anchored (after a record run of nearly two hundred miles in eighteen hours). When all was made safe, William said:

'Now we'll have family prayers, and give thanks for gettin' in.'[10]

This pointed to another side of who William Borden was: for he possessed a faith that ran deep, strong, and abiding – like the waters of the sea he so loved.

Captain Arey had seen that too, and he remembered:

When he and I'd go out alone sometimes, I'd ask where he'd like to go.

'Anywhere,' he'd say, 'so as to get out where it's quiet.'

And he'd go down into the [ship] cabin with his Bible, or some other book, and study all the time we was out.

It might be three hours or so. And when we'd come in, he'd seem to be kind of refreshed in his mind.[11]

For Borden, it was a time to contemplate, and consider things of eternity.

---

10. ibid., pp. 163-164.

11. ibid., pp. 163-164.

'What is your goal?' he once wrote, 'and Who is in the boat with you? May each one of us be able to say ... He is not only on board, but at the helm.'[12]

It was an eloquent phrase, summoning images of a pilgrim's voyage.

A journey of faith.

89 Bellevue Place, Chicago, the handsome late-Victorian residence where William Borden was born (from the author's 1st British edition copy of *Borden of Yale*, 1926).

But all journeys have their beginnings, and though Camden would always hold a special place in Borden's life, he was born in Chicago, America's great city of the Midwest, where he and his consequential family had important ties.

William Borden's story began on Tuesday, November 1, 1887. Outside the walls of 89 Bellevue Place, Chicago, strong winds blew in a gale from the north.[13] But within the durable walls of blue Bedford Stone that graced the stately French Chateau William Borden Sr. built for his family,[14] the forceful winds were scarcely more than a rumor of sound. And there, a new son was born in the Borden family.

---

12. W. W. Borden, 'The Origin of the Student Volunteer Movement for Foreign Missions,' in *The Christian Workers* magazine, March 1913, p. 456.

13. See the weather forecast for November 1st given on page 15 of the October 30, 1887 edition of *The Chicago Tribune*.

14. 'A permit was issued last week to Mr William Borden for the erection of a three-story residence at 87 and 89 Bellevue Place. It was designed by E. M. Hunt of New York, and will be a very handsome structure. The exterior will be constructed of Blue Bedford stone and the interior will be furnished in an elaborate manner. It will cost $50,000.' See the May 8, 1886 issue of *The Sanitary News* (Chicago: The Sanitary News, 1886), p. 26.

William Borden, Sr. and Mary Whiting had married in Detroit on Friday, December 28, 1883, at the Jefferson Avenue Presbyterian Church. They set out, thereafter, for a one-year honeymoon. When they'd met, Mary Whiting had been an art college student in Chicago, and those who had seen her work thought she had 'considerable talent as a painter.'[15] During their one-year honeymoon in Europe, the Bordens took time, therefore, to study 'the work of the great masters.'[16]

Five children in all were born to this couple: Frederick (who died in infancy), John, a noted adventurer and explorer;[17] Mary, a poet, novelist, and heroine of World War I as a nurse on the front lines; and the youngest, Joyce, a gifted singer who married the Croatian violinist Zlatko Balokovic, and toured Europe.

William Borden was the fourth child. As a younger boy, he enjoyed playing with his elder siblings, John and Mary, and at the age of nine, he welcomed the birth of this younger sister, Joyce, who was born when he was nine.

Their home, 89 Bellevue Place, was one of the great homes of Chicago in the late 19th century.[18] He and his family called it, with

---

15. See Jane Conway, *A Woman of Two Wars: The Life of Mary Borden*, (Chippenham: Munday Books, 2010), pp. 7-8. Mary Borden was a descendant of Pilgrim leader William Bradford, who paid tribute to the author's ancestor, Richard Masterson, as 'an anciente friend.' The author is grateful to return this kindness to William Borden and his family in writing this biography.

16. See Conway, *A Woman of Two Wars* (2010), pp. 7-8.

17. *The Rudder* magazine (March 1913) states John Borden commissioned B. B. Crowninshield to design the 101-foot schooner *Adventuress*, built in East Boothbay, Maine, for sailing high latitudes in the Pacific Ocean. See also page 83 of *Wooden Boat* magazine May/June 2013.

18. Here it's important to dispel the persistent myth that Borden family money came from 'the Borden milk' dairy interests. It didn't. Two definitive sources confirm this. In an October 8, 1956 letter, Borden's close friend K. S. Latourette stated: 'I distinctly remember that William denied being related to the Borden milk people.' This letter is from Latourette to Bernard R. DeRemer, housed in the Archives of Moody Bible Institute. But the most authoritative statement comes from William Borden himself, who told a friend: 'People often mistake us for the rich Condensed Milk firm that bears the name of Borden.' See Taylor, *Borden of Yale* (1926), p. 256.

picturesque simplicity, '89,'[19] and a remarkable home it was: a genuine Chicago counterpart to the kind of home setting young Theodore Roosevelt once knew during his childhood in New York City.

It was an architectural gemstone, with handsomely furnished, high ceilinged rooms. And its library was a place where an intellectually curious child, like William Borden, could lose himself in books of fine literature, travel narratives of faraway places, and classic works by famous writers of the Christian tradition.

He was uniquely favored to grow up in such a home.

Borden's father, William Sr., saw to the building of the grand chateau at 89 Bellevue Place that Borden knew in youth. With its high turrets and Normanesque arched windows, this four-story home must have seemed like a castle to the Borden children. And their father had commissioned it.

Writing of this caring man of presence and drive, Samuel Zwemer said:

> Borden's father was a man of sterling character, [with] reverence for other people's conscience, and high esteem for Christian character. He had wonderful business capacity, a brilliant mind, and was a great reader. He gave much time to his children, planning for them the best possible education and taking them frequently on journeys into the country, which were wonderfully stimulating … He had simple although cosmopolitan tastes, and cared most for the 'comforts of home,' in the best sense of both words.
>
> He spent most of his evenings helping the children with their lessons, playing after dinner games with them. A lady who knew William Whiting Borden from earliest childhood speaks of his loving fellowship with his father 'whose name he bore …'[20]

Moving verse, written later by Borden's elder sister Mary, adds to the picture, showing a father whose love of books was welcomely interrupted by his children—

---

19. See Taylor, *Borden of Yale* (1926), pp. 54 and 224.
20. See Samuel Zwemer's biography, *William Whiting Borden* (September 1913), p. 10.

... long hours he spent apart in thought,
until a word of love would start a deep sweet
look behind his eyes,
and he would sit with us, and talk from his great
store of beauty, poetry, and of great men.[21]

Last of all, William Borden greatly resembled his father in appearance, and they were much alike in terms of temperament.[22] Both were early risers, and loved the outdoors.[23] They shared more than a first name, and people took note.

And what of Borden's mother Mary?

She was, as Geraldine Taylor wrote in her biography, 'a devoted mother,'[24] and her son William shared a close bond with her, present from his youngest years. For about age three, as he would play quietly in her room, so as 'not to disturb her writing,' he would leave his toys, 'steal up behind a chair to raise the wavy hair at the back of her neck, and kiss her without a word.'[25]

So a picture emerges that complements the portrait of William Borden Sr. given in Samuel Zwemer's memoir: that of a close-knit family. And Mary Borden's influence became more far-reaching and meaningful when her son William 'was about seven years old.' For it was then that she 'entered upon a new experience spiritually,' a conversion to evangelical Christianity that brought a deep and abiding 'peace with God.'[26]

---

21. See Taylor, *Borden of Yale* (1926), p. 12.

22. See Zwemer, *William Whiting Borden* (1913), pp. 10-11.

23. ibid., pp. 10-11.

24. See Taylor, *Borden of Yale* (1926), p. 15.

25. ibid., p. 7. This story is also recounted in Zwemer, *William Whiting Borden* (1913), p. 13.

26. ibid., p. 15. Henry Weston Frost, a close Borden family friend, recalled: '[Mrs Borden] had been converted, as she herself believes ... under the influence of some Salvation Army special meetings in Chicago, conducted by Mrs Ballington Booth. At a very early date, she took her William to those meetings, to sit beside her and to listen to all that passed ... At a later time Mrs Borden transferred her connection to the Chicago Avenue

The character of Mary Borden's faith was the kind of belief that wrought a transformation for good in the life of D. L. Moody: an ardent faith set in the love of God and others – which led him to found schools for the underprivileged, serve those in need, and evince a deep concern for Christian missions in foreign lands.

So it was natural for Mary Borden to transfer her church membership to the Chicago Avenue Church founded by Moody, where she 'found opportunities for service,' and the 'Bible teaching she coveted.'[27] She began to bring her children there, with important consequences for her son William especially.

In other ways, young Borden was very much a boy of his time and place—thoughtful and active, much like his father—he loved 'a good roughhouse … running round, and having a good time,'[28] his 'brown eyes shining with excitement.'[29] This, friends and family thought, foreshadowed a devotion to active sports: football, baseball, golf, and sailing among them. He took to these quickly, and did well.

Borden, along with his cousin John Whiting, 'attended successive schools in Chicago':[30] The University School, the Chicago Manual Training School, and The Latin School. They were fine schools, though different in character.

The University School, Chicago, was a 'feeder' academy for the University of Chicago, founded by John D. Rockefeller in 1890. Rockefeller's ties to The University School doubtless had great appeal for William Borden, Sr., who wanted his son and namesake to have the best.[31]

Church, commonly known as the "Moody Church."' See *The Princeton Seminary Bulletin*, May 1913, (Princeton: Princeton University Press, 1913), p. 12.

27. ibid., p. 15.

28. ibid., p. 4.

29. See Zwemer, *William Whiting Borden* (1913), p. 16.

30. See Taylor, *Borden of Yale* (1926), p. 4.

31. See *The School Review* (Hamilton: C. H. Thurber, 1895), p. 440. See also *Register of the University of Chicago, 1905–1906* (Chicago: Univ. of Chicago, 1906; and page 165

The Chicago Manual Training School was created between 1882 and 1884 by the Chicago Commercial Club to offer both academic and vocational education for boys at the high school level. And in 1903, it became part of the University of Chicago Laboratory Schools.[32]

As for The Latin School, today it's 'one of the oldest independent schools in the city of Chicago.' It was formed in 1888 when a group of parents in Chicago asked Mabel Slade Vickery, a teacher from the East Coast, to take charge of 'a new, parent-owned school.' The first class began modestly, comprised of '10 boys approximately 10 years old.' The intent of this educational venture was 'to provide students with a rigorous college-preparatory education in the classical tradition, with a curriculum that was heavily influenced by Classical studies and the study of the Greek and Latin languages, hence the name Latin School.'[33]

So prior to his time at The Hill School in Pottstown, Pennsylvania, William Borden was given a varied and academically challenging set of experiences.

His father had chosen wisely and well.

As to the spiritual side of Borden's youth, going to Chicago Avenue Church services spoke meaningfully to this part of his life. When he was eight, about the time he started at the Chicago Manual Training School, his mother one Sunday asked that he and his siblings take up a piece of paper and write about 'what they wanted to be when they grew up.' Borden set his name across the top, 'W. Borden, Jan. 19, 1896,' thought for a few moments,

---

of the book *Annual Register, 1904-1905* (Chicago: Univ. of Chicago, 1905); and page 17 of the book *Circular of Information* (Chicago: Univ. of Chicago, 1901). Last, see *A Handbook of the Best Private Schools* (Boston: P. E. Sargent, 1915), page 72, which states: 'University School, Dearborn Ave. & Elm St., is a college preparatory school.'

32. Information online from the University of Chicago: https://www.lib.uchicago.edu/e/scrc/findingaids/view.php?eadid=ICU.SPCL.CMTS

33. This formation is posted online by The Latin School at: http://www.latinschool.org/about-us/mission-history

and wrote: 'I want to be an honest man when I grow up; a true and loving and kind and faithful man.'[34]

These words were partly prescient in their way, but more than anything they were an aspiration born of things young Borden had been hearing from Sunday to Sunday at the Chicago Avenue Church. For about one year, perhaps a little more, he'd been hearing of Christ's redeeming love. He'd seen the transformation in his mother's life, and her growing love for things of eternity, as they were so often called then. That counted for much.

Something in all that he'd been hearing, and seeing, called to him. Geraldine Taylor recreated the scene when young Borden took his first step toward things of faith. It was under the preaching ministry of Dr R. A. Torrey (a graduate of Yale, Class of 1875), who was then Pastor of The Chicago Avenue Church.[35]

'One Sunday morning,' Geraldine Taylor wrote, 'young Borden heard Dr R. A. Torrey …

> give the invitation to the communion service about to be held. 'Is it not time that you were thinking about this yourself, William?' his mother whispered.
>
> 'I have been,' was the unexpected reply.
>
> When the [communion] elements were handed from pew to pew, to Mrs Borden's surprise, William quietly took the bread and wine as did those about him. Rather than be taken aback at this interpretation of her question, Mrs Borden mentioned the matter to Dr Torrey, who smiled and said:
>
> 'Let him come and see me about it tomorrow.'

---

34. See Zwemer, *William Whiting Borden* (1913), p. 18.

35. After Geraldine Taylor's biography of Borden appeared, R. A. Torrey told Borden's mother: 'This life of your son is wonderful; it is one of the most interesting and helpful biographies that I have ever read. Not only is the life itself of great importance but the record of it is written with great skill, both in the choice of material and in the way in which it is put. I know something of Mrs Taylor's ability to write biographies from her life of Hudson Taylor and from "Pastor Hsi," but I am inclined to think that she has done the work upon this book with even wiser judgment and greater skill …' See page 320 of the April 1927 issue of *The Missionary Review of the World*.

Young though he was, his answers to Dr Torrey's questions [about Christ's gift of redemption] made it evident that he was ready for the step he had taken, and [this] led to his joining the church in the regular way.[36]

About this time Dr Torrey offered an opportunity one Sunday 'for all who wished to dedicate their lives to the service of God to indicate this purpose by rising for prayer.' It was simply, clearly stated; but a momentous step for all who listened to consider. Torrey urged them to take 'a step of life-consecration,' the affirmation of an ardent wish to serve Christ, and follow the ways of faith always. As others prayed and stood to their feet in assent, Mary Borden saw her son, just eight years old,[37] stand without a word, and remain standing until Torrey closed the invitation. Several long moments went by, while others stood.

But Mary Borden always treasured the sight of her son, resolved to serve and follow Christ as Savior – to seek His plan and purposes.

It was a child's step, it is true, but it pointed to the future.

Thereafter, Mary Borden saw a discernable change in her son. He began to pray with her and read the Bible. Even as he would set out each morning for school, books strapped on

The Moody Church in Chicago, which Borden attended in his youth, and where he was ordained on 21 September 1912 (from the author's 1st British edition copy of *Borden of Yale*, 1926).

---

36. See Taylor, *Borden of Yale* (1926), p. 16.

37. This is a best estimate of Borden's age, based on the strong contextual evidence given in Taylor and Zwemer's biographies.

his back, cap and lunch-box in hand, and be in 'a tearing hurry,' he sought time each morning for a brief word of prayer with his mother.

Many times also, Mary Borden saw her son pick up his Bible and go read on his own in his room. At moments, she recalled, he would look up from his reading in a way that spoke of his fondness for what he read.

Faith's call to him was growing deeper, and he warmed to it.[38]

Young Borden's burgeoning commitment to faith coincided with still other memories of this time that his mother cherished ever after. She loved, for example, to see her active, energetic son win friends, or watch him go along with them to do 'stunts,' and see him take part in athletics: especially 'tennis, riding, sailing and mountain climbing.' Horseback riding might have been a bit worrisome at times, but he soon became a skilled rider. And as for the 'stunts' he so often performed, he could 'stand on his head and drink a glass of water, or bend his body backward in a bow, and invite someone to sit on him.'[39]

Not long before Borden started at The Hill School, or when he was 'about fourteen and a half,' his mother remembered a summer 'we all spent at Estes Park, Colorado.' One scene was vivid from that time:

> He and I used to do mountain climbing together. I well remember climbing one small mountain called 'Old Man,' and William's loving care of me; going ahead of me and then calling me to come on, or else running back where he thought his help was needed and stretching out his hand to help me over the hard places, then pointing out a lovely view for me to look at, or finding a rock for

---

38. See *The Princeton Theological Seminary Bulletin Necrological Report*, August 1914, p. 320. Here it's stated that Borden 'made a public confession of his faith in The Moody Church, Chicago ... at the age of fourteen.' NOTE: this is the only source of this information, likely from Borden's mother.

39. See Zwemer, *William Whiting Borden* (1913), pp. 22-23.

me to rest on, and encouraging me all the way along. He thus got me with very little fatigue to the top of the mountain.

He was always ahead of me.

I thought at the time what a perfect illustration it was of our Saviour's care of us in this life. And now, again, [as I think of his passing,] William has reached the top first.[40]

Nor was Mary Borden alone in seeing changes in her son, and the deepening of things that spoke memorably of his spiritual qualities. Writing in 1913, Captain Arey of Camden, the Borden family's seaside summer residence, recalled:

I've known [William] ever since the first summer he come – that must have been nine years ago. And if anyone showed on their outside the happiness of being a Christian, it was Mr Borden. When he talked, it seemed just as if you could feel his earnestness … He was always singing, and a splendid swimmer.[41]

It was one thing for a mother to speak of her son's faith, and what she saw of it in a family setting. That had a special place, and an important one.

But that a sea captain in a rustic New England port should say that a young man's faith had winsome ways, was no less important than what Mary Borden saw. Over time Captain Arey became very fond of Borden, and it might well have been otherwise. As a master mariner retained by the family to help care for the family sloop, the *Tsatsawassa*, his dealings with the Borden family might have been rather cursory and business-like. But they weren't. In terms of age, he was old enough to have been young Borden's father; yet despite such an age gap, they were friends.

In some people, even young people, expressions of faith can be off-putting. The character of William Borden's faith, in

---

40. ibid., p. 23.

41. ibid., pp. 23-24. Selection edited.

his teens, was something far removed from that. It drew other people to him and won him close friends.

That telling pattern would be repeated often in the years to come.

CHAPTER 2

The Hill School

Hill, dear old Hill,
We'll always be
Loyal forever,
Ties that will never sever.

Bind us to you
Faithful and true,
To you forevermore,
Old Hill, Dear Old Hill.[1]

– The Hill School Fight Song

William Borden's arrival at The Hill School in Pennsylvania brought the fine and handsome sight of one of America's premier preparatory schools into view.

In 1910, within a few years after Borden's student days, The Hill School was featured at great length in *Scribner's Magazine*, alongside detailed profiles of Exeter, Andover, Groton, and St Paul's.[2] The article's author, Arthur Ruhl, reported that 'The Hill School is a family school, like Groton and St Mark's ... and in its present form, with its two hundred and fifty boys, is a continuation of the school started in 1851 by the Rev. Matthew

---

1. The text of this song is posted online by The Hill School at: http://www.thehill.org/SchoolSongs

2. Arthur Ruhl, 'Some American Preparatory Schools,' *Scribner's Magazine*, June 1910 (New York: Scribner's, 1910), pp. 681-700.

Meigs.' Under his son and successor, John Meigs, Hill became famous for academic rigor, and 'boys prepared thoroughly for college.' As Rhul stated emphatically: 'It is a matter of record that Hill boys rarely fail to pass their entrance examinations.'[3] It was a sterling choice for William Borden.

An aerial photo of The Hill School, the prestigious preparatory school Borden attended (from the author's 1st British edition copy of *Borden of Yale*, 1926).

And under the learned aegis of renowned instructor Alfred Grosvenor Rolfe, The Hill School had a genuine 'Mr Chips' among its faculty, noted for his 'fine influence for truth, honor, and appreciation of the beautiful in literature; above all, a cheerful, genial, kindly, helpful humor.'[4]

Athletics were also highly encouraged at The Hill School, and its programs were at once innovative and successful.

The Hill School was famed for its standout football program, led by one of America's leading coaches, Michael Sweeney: a storied athlete himself, and a former world record holder in the high jump. Here, Arthur Ruhl said of Sweeney's team—

---

3. Ruhl, 'Some American Preparatory Schools,' *Scribner's*, (1910), p. 694.

4. Boyd Edwards and Isaac Thomas, *Mr Rolfe of the Hill* (Pottstown: Feroe Press, 1920), p. 12.

I suppose there is not a better trained eleven in any of the preparatory schools, and it is said that the plays worked out by Mr Sweeney and the boys at Hill are sometimes used by next season's Yale team. They looked, indeed, like … Yale men in the bud when they came swinging on to the field the day of the Hotchkiss game, in sailor hats and blue and white sweaters, and one wasn't surprised to hear that a majority of them go to Yale.[5]

Sweeney was William Borden's coach on the 2nd Eleven at The Hill School, and given Borden's strong, sturdy build, it is not surprising to learn that he played center for the team. To judge from a team photo taken in autumn 1903, one can see why Borden was a standout on the offensive line.

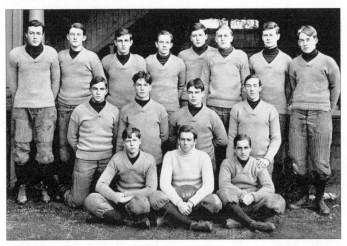

Borden in fall 1903, shown 3rd from left in the 2nd row, with his football teammates at The Hill School (photo courtesy of The Hill School).

He stood about five feet ten, and weighed about 180 pounds. Not many prep school opponents from this early era were going to get the better of Borden on the gridiron. To call the names of his teammates was to call a roll of stalwart friends: Hildreth, Houghteling, Barker, Harvey and Pierce.[6]

5. Ruhl, 'Some American Preparatory Schools,' *Scribner's* (1910), p. 695.

6. See the team roster and photo in *The Dial* yearbook, 1904. Provided courtesy of Hill School Archivist, Louis Jeffries.

Second Team

MR. LORD } MR. HAYNES }	. . .	Coaches
Left End	HILDRETH	
Left Tackle . . . :	DAUB	
Left Guard	HOUGHTELING	
Center	BORDEN	
Right Guard . . .	{ BARKER { SMITH, J.	
Right Tackle . . .	{ BUTLER, W. M. { GILBERT	
Right End	HERRESHOFF	
Quarter	HARVEY	
Left Half	PUTNAM (Captain)	
Right Half	WATSON	
Fullback }	PEIRCE DOLPH, S. E.	

Substitutes

AUGUR	NOYES	WODELL

The Second Team football roster for The Hill School. Borden was
a standout at center (photo courtesy of The Hill School).

Other elements of life at The Hill School recall a bygone era
and the patterns of 'a family school,' a prestigious setting designed
to foster character, fine academic training, and preparation for
life through team play in athletics, with the challenges they
represented. As the article for *Scribner's* went on to say—

Set on the outskirts of a small Pennsylvania manufacturing
town, The Hill School [and its] surroundings are spacious and
restful ...

Its charm is [also present] in the busy family atmosphere
enclosed by its compact walls, and spread over its playgrounds.
Except for the chapel, a gift of the alumni, the gymnasium,
masters' club [a venue for teachers], and a few detached cottages
nearby, nearly all the school's life, as at St Mark's, is carried on
under one roof. And in this family atmosphere the headmaster's
wife—a lady of strong religious feeling—has had an important
part. Mrs Meigs came to the school as a bride, and she has
[become] a part of that little courtyard life.

At eleven each morning, when the boys are [eating] crackers,
just as they do at Groton, the masters drift into [Mrs Meigs']

24

cheerful drawing-room for tea or coffee, and some of her famous cinnamon buns.[7]

Away from home, and in true contrast to the unfamilial and cruel conditions so often associated in this era with some British boarding schools, The Hill School presented a better, far different picture. As Arthur Ruhl had also observed:

> [At Hill,] after the game with Hotchkiss, I watched the football team, looking [quite young] in their every-day clothes, learning manners and being fed with tea and cakes and tactful [guidance]. And the discussions about their future which these young men have with the headmaster's wife in the 'sky parlor,' are matters of [cherished] school history.
>
> A [head]master's wife in such a school has a wide field for the exercise of her influence [Ruhl continued]. For several very important years, she and her husband are 'switchmen,' so to speak, turning [many student] ventures from one track to another. She may not be able to follow Dr [Oliver Wendell] Holmes' advice and 'begin the education of children with their grandparents,' but she often can, as I heard Mrs Meigs herself [once] say, turn the advice about, and begin the education of grandchildren.[8]

These were all moments, scenes, and influence that Borden remembered. His parents had chosen well in selecting The Hill School. It fostered good things in the lives of young men.

What were Borden's own thoughts, on arriving at his new prep school?

Many are relayed in a letter he wrote to his mother within days of starting his time there. He was particularly thankful he was shown kindness because a trail had been blazed at Hill by his elder brother John, who preceded him there as a student. As a younger fifth former, Borden was one month from turning fifteen, and there was much to tell—

---

7. Ruhl, 'Some American Preparatory Schools,' *Scribner's,* (1910), pp. 694-695.

8. ibid., p. 695.

[Saturday,] September 27, 1902

Dear Mother—

I like the school very much, all the old fellows are nice to the new fellows, asking us to come and see them in their rooms, etc.

My room is in the East Wing, second floor, number 4. My roommate is a very nice fellow, a little older than I am, and two or three inches taller ... A great many of the old fellows here knew John, most of them are sixth formers. All the old teachers are very nice to me, and they seem very jolly, especially Mr Rolfe, Mr Hallock and Mr Weed, whom I suppose you met ... I like Professor and Mrs John [Meigs] very much, from what I have seen of them so far ...

I am taking football for exercise ... trying for the second team; but I don't think there is much chance of my making it.

Last night, they had the first meeting of the Y.M.C.A. Throop Wilder is President, and John Holabird is Vice-President. The meeting was great! Throop spoke first, and then a good many of the old fellows got up and spoke.

Dwight Meigs led in prayer, and then other fellows gave short prayers. This year there are more new fellows than ever ...

[For meals in the dining hall,] I sit at Mr Weed's end of the fifth-form table, which is right at the end of Mrs John [Meig]'s table.

Give my love to ... everybody; and tell them I expect to write soon.

Your loving son,

William[9]

Then followed a letter to his sister Mary, with details of classes he was taking, how he fared in them, and his great interest and involvement with football at Hill. In the classroom and on the field, his days were full and challenging.

---

9. See Taylor, *Borden of Yale* (1926), pp. 23-24.

[Saturday,] Oct. 4, 1902

Dear Sis—

I received your letter yesterday, and thank you for it very much. As my roommate gets about three letters every mail, *I like to get one once in a while.*

Talk about work! I have six studies, Chemistry, English History, French, Greek, English and Bible History.

English Comp. is fierce. We have to make a literal translation of parts of Virgil, or Caesar--and in class change this into idiomatic English. Then again we have to write on the character of people in the Sir Roger de Coverley papers, in the style of Steele.

We have had two Y.M.C.A. meetings, at one of which Boyd Edwards,[10] who was at Northfield, spoke. I have joined, [and so has Eugene Delano, my roommate]. Throop Wilder is fine. He is President of the Y.M.C.A., and of the Athletic Association. I am trying out for the second team [in football], it is pretty hard work. There are a great many Chicago fellows here ...

Hoping you will write soon again, I am,

Your loving brother, Bill[11]

A letter to his father, three weeks later, brought with it one of those references from a life story that brings history to life. Borden had a later-to-be-famous friend at The Hill School, Harry Widener, who would tragically lose his life in the *Titanic* sea disaster of April 1912. To honor Widener's memory, and his great love of books, Harvard's famous Widener Library was built.

But when Borden wrote his letter home, ten years before the *Titanic* sank, far more pleasant thoughts of the Borden summer

---

10. 'The guest speaker at the Y.M.C.A. meeting in the school room on Wednesday, October 28, 1903, was Boyd Edwards, who was a frequent guest minister, and later became headmaster of Hill from 1922–1928. He then became headmaster of Mercersburg Academy in Mercersburg, PA, in 1928 (just after James Stewart, the future Hollywood actor, graduated).' Research information provided by Hill School archivist Louis Jeffries via email correspondence with the author, Tuesday, 23 January 2018.

11. See Taylor, *Borden of Yale* (1926), p. 24. Edited for clarity.

home in Camden, Maine, then in the planning stages, were uppermost. Athletics came in for discussion too:

[Sunday,] Oct. 26, 1902

Dear Father—

Mother says you are working over the plans of our Camden house ...[12]

I haven't noticed any pictures of summer houses in the magazines. Harry Widener is the son of the man who owns that house you liked so much. You remember you were looking at it in a magazine at Camden last summer ...

The Borden family summer cottage in Camden, Maine, a treasured scene for so many hours of sailing, and time with family and friends (photo courtesy of the Camden Public Library).

We have had three football games so far. The first two were with the Haverford Grammar School and Princeton Freshmen, the score in each game was 0 to 0. The third game was a perfect cinch for us, the score being 41 to 0 in favour of Hill. Only one

---

12. As it is now, Borden Cottage, on outer Bay View Street 'sits on a 14-acre parcel.' See the April 17, 2018 article detailing this at: https://www.penbaypilot.com/article/camden-lines-2018-warrant-bella-point-congregate-housing-borden-cottage-beds-signage-/100632

[field] goal was missed. Monday the annual interclass track will
be held. I am going into the shot-put ...

With lots of love,
Your son, William[13]

After this, Borden wrote a letter to his mother detailing social
life at The Hill School, and the visit of a Christian leader he much
admired: Robert Speer, who'd worked closely with D. L. Moody.
Borden would later read Speer's writings avidly.

[Sunday,] Oct. 26, 1902

Dear Mother—

Last Saturday we only danced for a little while, and all sat around
on the floor and sang songs. I liked it much more than dancing,
and hope we will do it again ... I suppose you are waiting until
Nov. 1 [and my birthday] to send down anything, but when you
do I wish you would send plenty of fruit and cake ...

[Robert] Speer was here today and preached,[14] he was fine ...
I will have to stop now, as the Prep bell for bed[time] has rung.

With lots of love,
William[15]

And here, a word should be said of Borden's roommate, Eugene
Delano.

He was, as one might surmise, a cousin of future President
Franklin Delano Roosevelt. But 'Gene' Delano, as Borden called
him, later became troubled. Borden saw nothing of this, nor did
anyone else, seemingly, during these years. But tragically, he took
his own life – not long after graduating from Yale. Thankfully,
the years of their friendship at Hill were happy ones; and Borden
always spoke well of his friend in letters home.

---

13. See Taylor, *Borden of Yale* (1926), pp. 24-25.

14. 'One of the guest ministers was Robert E. Speer, who taught full time at Hill
from 1899–1901.' Research information provided by Hill School archivist Louis Jeffries
via email correspondence with the author, Tuesday, 23 January 2018.

15. See Taylor, *Borden of Yale* (1926), pp. 25-26.

As his first year at The Hill School drew to a close, Borden found its rigorous academic training a source of challenges that he worked hard to meet. His years of college and graduate school would always be remembered by professors and mentors as years of academic achievement. But there was a time, during these days at Hill, when he developed the character, discipline, and determination to excel.

One letter home, from early in 1903, opens a window on this time:

[Sunday,] January 18, 1903

We have had good weather lately, and today is simply fine … The air is cool and bracing. I intend to take a long walk this afternoon with some fellows.

About my examinations. I passed Algebra easy enough, and got a 100 in it, I think. But I did not pass Geometry. However, Mr Shephard let me go into the class, and I will try again to pass it Monday … He will help me, [with a] sort of tutoring, and I hope to pass it tomorrow.

I took an exam in *Lorna Doone,* [R. D. Blackmore's novel,] and the result was rather surprising. I got a 95 in it. There wasn't a single mistake in spelling or punctuation, [and not] a single mark of correction anywhere. It was quite long, taking me nearly two hours of steady writing.

I have a terribly hard time … I scarcely do anything but study. [I] study at night, [and] every spare minute from the time I get up until school begins … After lunch, I have about 1 hour & a 1/2 spare time. Then I have to prepare my lessons for the afternoon session; and begin the same program again after supper.[16]

Borden's hard work and perseverance brought the result he hoped for. His academic work improved markedly where it needed to. His fondness for Mr Rolfe, The Hill School's very own 'Mr Chips,' was also growing.

---

16. ibid., p. 26.

Borden told his mother:

> I am getting to like Mr Rolfe more and more all the time. He is
> simply great. Always happy and cheery, [he is] never harsh or
> gruff, except when he has to stop fellows from rough-housing;
> and even then he is nice, and makes a joke out of it, or does
> something else ...[17]

In such a setting, it's not surprising to learn that the Head of
School, John Meigs, wrote to Borden's parents, praising his winter
term 1903 academic record. It was a welcome letter, with news of
a well-earned reward:

> [Tuesday,] March 31st, 1903
>
> My dear Mr Borden—
>
> I am very happy to congratulate you on William's excellent
> record for the past term, and to inform you that he is one of
> twenty members of the school who have been excused from all
> of their examinations.
>
> Faithfully yours,
>
> John Meigs[18]

As the fall term of 1903 began, Borden's love of football showed
itself in letters home. One spoke of The Hill School's great rival
Lawrenceville, and a game played less than a month before the
Wright Brothers flew at Kitty Hawk.[19] Borden's thoughts were full
of gridiron exploits; and competition against skilled opponents.

Borden's avid interest in competition of another kind showed
itself in a letter written early in the start of his last half-year at The
Hill School. He had joined the school Debating Club. Football and
gridiron competition would always have a first place among the things
he was most keenly interested in, but he developed genuine fondness

---

17. ibid., p. 27.

18. ibid., p. 28.

19. A happenstance noted in email correspondence with Mr Louis Jeffries, Archivist
of The Hill School, Tuesday, 30 January 2018.

for the thrust and parry of this type of public speaking. It was, after all, a 'team' endeavor, and many young men like Borden have relished a chance to test their ideas and arguments against others in a setting where skill in public speaking was prized and admired.

As spring drew near, Borden's thoughts centered on Class Orations and an upcoming Class Dance. He looked forward to the dance; but felt some trepidation over giving his Class Oration, and was honest enough to say so. One senses his feelings were a mix of wanting to test his mettle, and wondering if he would be able to come up to the standard others had shown. Then too, he told his mother also of his great interest in the fortunes of the Russo-Japanese War:

> [Wednesday,] February, 3, 1904
>
> Gene [Delano] delivered his oration the other night, and it went off very well. In fact, all the orations so far have been remarkably good, and it's up to us who come later to do as well. As I have told you, mine comes Friday, the second speaker. I get scared, off and on, by spells.
>
> I am very much interested in watching this war between Russia and Japan ... We rush over to the reading room after breakfast for a glimpse at the morning papers, before going to study. The newsboy who sells papers here in the evening does a flourishing business ...[20]

Regrettably, this is the last glimpse of Borden's letters from The Hill School. But a brief summary here says much: he graduated in spring 1904, with an average of 83.6; or fourth among forty-eight boys, of whom he was the youngest student.

As a reward for his excellent performance, Borden's parents had a special gift planned for him – one that will be the focus of the next chapter. It would bring many new and important experiences for him.

---

20. See Taylor, *Borden of Yale* (1926), p. 34.

CHAPTER 3

God's Kingdom and England's Summer

In June of 1904 Bill graduated from The Hill School; in scholarship rating as one of the first four in his class. Before entering Yale, he took a year's trip around the world with an older friend. They started from the Borden summer home in Maine, in early August of 1904. Japan was the first country reached, after crossing the United States and the Pacific.

Here, Bill first saw missionaries at work ...[1]

> – Charles Soutter Campbell (circa 1913)

I made up my mind to become a missionary during a trip I made around the world in '04 and '05, just after I was graduated from my preparatory school.

Before that, I had not thought much of, [or rather, very often of] foreign missionaries. But when I was in the Orient, I stayed at the home of several missionaries, and I changed my mind.[2]

> – William Borden, quoted on page one of the
> Saturday, September 21, 1912 edition of
> *The Chicago Tribune*

---

1. See Charles Soutter Campbell, *William Whiting Borden: A Short Life Complete in Christ* (privately printed, c. 1913), p. 6.

2. See 'Young Millionaire Renounces World To Become Missionary,' page one of the Sat., 21 Sept. 1912 edition of *The Chicago Tribune* newspaper.

Following two years of study and achievement at The Hill School, Borden's parents, William and Mary, felt that a year spent on a trip around the world would be 'well worthwhile before he entered college.'[3]

So, at sixteen, he began a railroad trip from Maine, across the United States, for the port of San Francisco. His feelings, on hearing the first whistle and clatter of the steam engine, mingled anticipation and excitement.

Just how excited he was showed itself in a bit of foolhardy bravado. For after fond, prolonged family farewells, Borden decided to swing up onto the train when it was already in motion. At this, his father called out—

'William, don't do things like that! It isn't fair to Mr Erdman.'[4]

As was the custom of the time, Borden would be traveling in company with a trusted companion of integrity and culture. For this task, all expenses paid, his parents chose Walter Collins Erdman, an accomplished graduate of both Princeton University and Princeton Theological Seminary.[5] This choice was carefully made, and following a visit and interview with Borden's parents 'in the pine grove' of the family summer home at Camden, Erdman was chosen.[6]

As it happened Erdman had come highly recommended, by way of a trusted family friend, Dr Henry Weston Frost, Director of China Inland Mission in North America. For some time, Frost had known Borden's mother Mary, and she turned to him as an advisor. Frost long remembered how it all unfolded:

> My acquaintance with [William] began [when he'd] just graduated from The Hill School in Pottstown, and was intending to make a tour around the world. Thus, his mother had written

---

3. See Taylor, *Borden of Yale* (1926), p. 35.

4. ibid., p. 36.

5. See *The General Catalogue of Princeton University* (Princeton: Princeton University Press, 1908), p. 321.

6. See Taylor, *Borden of Yale* (1926), p. 35.

to me, asking if I would suggest a suitable companion for him, and I had named the Rev. Walter Erdman as such ...

From that time on ... I counted it a privilege to see [William] frequently.[7]

Just ten years older than Borden, Walter Erdman was described as 'scholarly, brilliant, [and] full of humour.' With such qualities, he would prove 'a delightful companion;' but 'his chief recommendation,' for Borden's parents, rested 'in his fine Christian character.'[8] In short, Erdman was just the kind of young adult they hoped their son would be, and what better way to foster that hope, than in choosing a chaperone of Erdman's qualities?

Borden and Erdman began their cross-country trip from the Borden summer home in Maine in early August 1904.[9] Taking the journey in slow stages, and likely stopping in places of interest for a day or so along the way—for a sixteen-year-old needed to exit the train for a stretch of the legs every now and again—the two friends arrived in San Francisco. They took lodgings, and confirmed that all was in readiness with the travel agent who booked passage for them on the *S.S. Korea,* a two-funneled steamer of 18,000 tons which operated on 'the Sunshine Belt to the Orient, between San Francisco, Honolulu, Japan, China and Manila.'[10]

She was a ship with a storied history.

The *S.S. Korea* was one of the largest and finest ships on the Pacific. It carried accommodation for 300 first class passengers, and there was 'no expense spared in their equipment. The *Korea* was capable of 20 knots (23 MPH) but maintained a service speed of 16 knots (18.4 MPH).'[11]

---

7. See the June 1913 issue of *The Bible To-Day* magazine, p. 132.

8. See Taylor, *Borden of Yale* (1926), p. 35.

9. See Campbell, *William Borden* (1913), p. 6.

10. Advertisement text on a 1909 postcard of the *S.S. Korea* purchased by the author.

11. See Jonathan Kinghorn, *The Atlantic Transport Line, 1881–1931* (London: McFarland & Company, 2012), pp. 180-181.

The *S.S. Korea* had an open deck on its port side, but on the starboard side, the lower of these decks 'was plated over to provide a sheltered corridor to the best cabins.' On one run of 'the Sunshine Belt,' the *S.S. Korea* kept an average speed of eighteen knots, setting a new record in 1905 of ten days, ten hours, and twenty-eight minutes.[12]

So Borden and Erdman, with their fellow passengers, would have a fast and well-appointed voyage across the Pacific. And Borden's first sight of the *S.S. Korea*, standing in at the pier, must have been impressive.

The *S.S. Korea*, the steamship on which Borden sailed for a year-long tour of the world in the summer of 1904 (from the author's photo collection, postcard circa 1903).

Fog hung over the Golden Gate on the grey, chilly September day when the *S.S. Korea* put out from San Francisco.[13] Tug boats and other craft let out whistles in farewell; shouts of *Bon Voyage* filled the air from well-wishers on the pier. The two friends were on their way: a whole world, and a year's travel awaited.

Several days out to sea, Borden penned the first of his letters home, and he had his first sight of people from China, sailing for home. He wrote a young man's letter, brim-full of curiosity over folkways and customs he'd never seen before:

12. ibid., pp. 180-181.

13. See Taylor, *Borden of Yale* (1926), p. 35.

[Tuesday,] September 20, 1904

Dearest Mother,

We are off at last; and so far, it seems quite nice ...

Our fellow passengers are mostly married people, in fact there aren't more than half a dozen young folk that I have noticed.

[The Chinese sailors and crew] are by far the most interesting ...

There is an open space between the promenade deck and the poop [deck] where they [are;] some with grey queues, and others with black.

I watched them eating this afternoon with their chopsticks. About ten of them squatted around one pot of rice, and a pot of some sort of meat. Each man had a little tin pan, which he filled with rice. They ate by holding the pan up to the mouth, and then shoving in the rice with their chopsticks, which they held in one hand. They picked up the pieces of meat with their chopsticks, and smeared them round in a common bowl of gravy ...[14]

Just one day later came a more conventional and vividly detailed letter home, evoking the sights and sounds of shipboard life, and new acquaintances made:

[Wednesday,] September 21, 1904

Dear Mother,

Today we have gotten pretty well settled and have had a chance to look around a bit. Our chairs are located on the port side, near the forward end of the promenade deck. Our neighbours are a couple of young men starting out as missionaries ... Jones and Gibb ... on the train with us [out] to San Francisco.

Then there is a Mr [J. H.] Lamb and his wife [Martha] and little boy. Mr Lamb is a classmate of Walter's, and he and his wife are going to the Philippines as missionaries.[15] They are very nice,

---

14. ibid., p. 37.

15. John Henderson Lamb, born November 27, 1872, graduated from the College of Emporia and Princeton Theological Seminary (Class of 1901, see p. 50 of *Princeton Seminary Bulletin*, June 1921). He was a missionary and teacher for a theological seminary in Manila, spending nine years there, and was also treasurer of The Presbyterian Mission Board. Returning to America in 1915, he was pastor of the Presbyterian Church

and awfully jolly. Mr Lamb and I got permission from the chief engineer and went all through the engine-room ...

The colour of the water out here, as it surges away from the ship is remarkable. It is a deep indigo blue ...

A day at Honolulu, where the water was like melted opals in colouring, and clear as crystal, was welcome. Native boys, eager to dive for money, swam out to meet the ship, [and] some [dove] off, even from ... the hurricane deck.

The Aquarium, with its rainbow-coloured fish, bathing, surf-riding, and a drive to various points of interest made the time pass quickly; until a [group] of passengers came on board, wearing wreaths of flowers after the custom of the island; and the journey was resumed toward the setting sun.[16]

In another letter, dated Tuesday, October 4, Borden talked more about the passengers of the *S.S. Korea*. His letter showed a sailor's curiosity, and a traveler's eye about conditions at sea. 'I often wish to be sailing out here,' he said—

where the trades blow steadily, and the sea is comparatively smooth.

Going round the world may be quite a trip, but it isn't anything uncommon among these passengers. There are three or four who are on their fourth trip around, and several on their third and second.

So we sink into insignificance. We have a couple of German and Austrian Counts and Countesses, an Italian doctor, and also several German university men ... Then there is an Admiral of the U.S. Navy, and a Bishop. So you see, we have quite a few celebrities.

We have only seen the smoke of one boat since we left San Francisco. The Pacific is quite large.[17]

---

at Waverly, Kansas. See *A Standard History of Kansas and Kansans*, vol. 3, by W. E. Conelley, (Chicago: Lewis Publishing Co., 1918), p. 1406.

16. See Taylor, *Borden of Yale* (1926), pp. 38-39.

17. ibid., p. 39.

Borden's admiration for the immensity and power of the Pacific was further increased 'by encountering a typhoon' before making port in Japan, as he recorded in his journal: a description that spoke of how the typhoon came on—

[We had a] strong breeze from the south-east, and fairly big sea running. Life-lines [were] put up on the lower deck and all awnings taken down. [The] wind developed to a gale in the afternoon. [We] hove to about seven, and rode [out the] typhoon during the night.

[Then it] rained hard early in the morning, with [the] wind still blowing a gale. [The] engines [were] started and [the ship] kept a half speed from 5:30 a.m. to 4:30 p.m. [She] shipped big seas over the prow. [The] sea quieted down in the afternoon, and full speed was put on.[18]

Since later accounts of Borden at sea reveal that he never suffered from sea-sickness, it is unlikely that he did in the midst of this dangerous weather. Quite the contrary, he seems to have reveled in it all. One wonders if Walter Erdman and the other passengers were so fortunate. Very likely, most were not.

The day after the typhoon subsided, the *S.S. Korea* arrived in Yokohama.

This brought a first railway journey: a short one, 'south from Yokohama to the shrines of Kamakura,' about which Borden wrote to his mother:

[Sunday,] October 9, 1904

[Dear Mother,]

At the station, we took rickshaws and went first to see the Dai Butsu ...

It is a very impressive and remarkable piece of work, [and] dates from A.D. 1243. Around the image, foundation stones may be seen in the ground. These supported the temple that once covered the statue.

[Sadly,] it has been gone a long time, as a result of tidal waves ...[19]

---

18. ibid., p. 39.

19. ibid., p. 42.

Less than one month into his travels in Japan, Borden wrote a momentous letter home to his mother. She'd sent gifts and a letter for his seventeenth birthday, which had taken place on November 1st:

Kyoto, [Thursday,]
November 3, 1904

[Dear Mother,]

I have received your birthday note with all the others ... a very pleasant surprise. Your request that I pray to God for His very best plan for my life is not a hard thing to do ... I have been praying that very thing for a long time.

Although I have never thought very seriously about being a missionary until lately, I was somewhat interested in that line as you know, [when I was Chairman of the Mission Study Band at The Hill School].

I think this trip is going to be a great help in showing things to me in a new light ... I met such pleasant young people on the steamer who were going out as missionaries, and meeting them influenced me ... Walt has so many friends here, whom we meet in nearly every city, that I have seen a great deal of the [missionary] work that is being done ... Talking with them, we learn of the work and the opportunities ... so that I realize things as I never did before ...

I look ahead, [and] it seems as though the only thing to do is to prepare for the foreign field. Of course, [I'll need] a college course, [and] perhaps some medical study, and certainly Bible study – at Moody Institute perhaps.

I may be a little premature; but I am beginning to think a little different. I don't know what you will think of this; but ... I know you can help me.

With lots of love,
William[20]

This is the first letter where Borden expressed a thought of any kind to be a missionary. Written two days after his seventeenth

---

20. ibid., pp. 47-48.

birthday, it was a first unfolding of a calling he would later pursue so prominently. His world tour was helping him see that the world beyond America's shores just might be his parish.

All that transpired heretofore in Borden's round the world journey had been of absorbing interest, and affirming. But then, shortly after he and Walter Erdman reached China, Borden contracted a worrying case of typhoid fever, and he spent 'his first Christmas away from home in a hospital in Hong Kong.'[21]

Thankfully his illness was not severe, nor of long duration. He was soon out of hospital, and able to continue with the trip.

As one early biographer, C. S. Campbell, wrote, it was a journey filled with rich cultural opportunities, breathtaking scenery, and a memorable encounter with new technology on the roads of France. 'The travelers,' Campbell said—

> moved on from China to India and to Egypt. [Borden's] interest in missions kept growing as he saw more distinctly the destitution [in] these countries and [spiritual need in] the hearts of the people.
>
> In Egypt, they saw Cairo, the Nile, the Pyramids and Karnak, and then passed on to Constantinople, Athens, Syria and Palestine. They spent some time in Switzerland and Paris. In Switzerland, [young Borden] climbed some of the mountains, and was from that time an enthusiastic mountain climber. On a later visit, he climbed a number of the highest mountains in the Swiss Alps.
>
> In Paris, he took automobile lessons and became proficient in driving a machine – though one day, he ran into a motor-cyclist and had to pay a fine.[22]

During this part of his European tour, Borden had written to his father from Naples, Italy. Linguistic misadventures took up much of the letter:

---

21. See Campbell, *William Borden* (1913), p. 6.

22. ibid., pp. 6-7.

[Saturday,] May 13, 1905

[Dear Father,]

I have been enjoying myself [here] … French is certainly more useful here in Italy, although a great deal of English is spoken.

I can understand French, when not spoken at express speed; and some Italian, but the difficulty is to make oneself understood! It is really quite amusing. You ought to hear my attempts in Italian and French and English all at once.

I hope to have my [study of] Homer pretty well in shape by the time I get back, so as to not be bothered with it at Camden. I suppose you will be going up there soon. Have my golf clubs ready; I am longing for a whack at the ball.[23]

In a much longer letter, Borden discussed a mutual love of classical antiquity, especially the store of famous relics on the Palatine, and kindred hills of Rome:

Florence, [Sunday,]
May 28, 1905

[Dear Father,]

We were nearly two weeks in Rome, and saw a great many interesting things. I am curious to know how long you and Mother spent there on your wedding trip. There is an awful lot to see, isn't there?

I wrote to Mother telling her about some of the places and pictures we had seen, but not nearly all.

So I will tell you what we did and enjoyed most.

The afternoon of our first day we drove by the Colosseum, through the Arch of Constantine, around across the Tiber and back to our hotel, stopping at the Pantheon on the way. Horatius must have been a pretty good swimmer to cross the Tiber, if it flowed as swiftly then as it does now.

The Colosseum is very interesting, I think. We went all over it from top to bottom. They have excavated some since you

---

23. See Taylor, *Borden of Yale* (1926), pp. 71-72. Borden would have played golf at the Megunticook Golf Club of Camden, where his father was one of its Board of Governors. See *Glimpses of Camden* (Newtonville: J. R. Prescott, 1904), p. 39. Its club-house was 'the social centre of cottagers' with a main assembly room, ladies parlor, and a reading room.

were in Rome, and have laid bare the old pavement outside the amphitheatre on the side opposite the Forum ...

The Pantheon, you remember, is the only building of ancient Rome in anything like perfect preservation. Its dome is very large and has a hole, thirty feet across, in the centre ... Dr Forbes ... says that the Pantheon was [once] the caldarium of the baths of Agrippa, son-in-law of Augustus.[24]

Here, Borden's reference to 'Dr Forbes' warrants explanation.

For S. Russell Forbes had written the well-known guidebook, *Rambles in Rome* (1882), a standard text that went through many editions. Of this book, none other than C. H. Spurgeon had written:

'If you are visiting Rome, you will find in this book a high-class companion and guide. Try it and see the difference between the mere guidebook produced by the trade to sell, and the chatty, masterly production of a writer of ability and taste.'[25]

This is a fine connection between the life of Borden and C. H. Spurgeon, the famous preacher at London's Metropolitan Tabernacle. Spurgeon's commendation appeared in the Thomas Nelson and Sons edition of *Rambles in Rome* that Borden carried with him as he walked the streets of Rome.

Soon after this, Borden wrote a set of letters to his mother:

[Thursday,] June 1, 1905

We are now in [Venice,] the city of watery streets and gondolas, having arrived last night. After dinner we strolled over to St Mark's, heard the band play, and had some ice cream. I expect to enjoy our stay here.[26]

Much of this enjoyment came from the warm June weather. Each day there was 'a swim at the Lido,' then afternoon-tea, most

---

24. ibid., p. 74.

25. See *The Sword and the Trowel* magazine, May 1882 (London: Passmore & Alabaster, 1882), p. 245; and the epigraph quotation from C. H. Spurgeon facing the title page of *Rambles in Rome* (London: Thomas Nelson & Sons, 1892).

26. See Taylor, *Borden of Yale* (1926), p. 74.

welcome 'after the sight-seeing of the morning.' Evenings were 'spent in a gondola, meeting friends, listening to music, and watching the lights over the water.'[27]

And then there were more experiences – those a young man would remember with an air of romance, in subsequent letters home, as Borden did.

'In the Doges' Palace,' he 'met an American party of seven young ladies, with a chaperone, who proved to be friendly [and] interesting, and they had already joined company with a "Mrs A." and her daughter, [a] graduate of Bryn Mawr under appointment as a missionary to India.'[28]

Their company did much to make Borden's time in Venice memorable. He told his mother about it all, in words that must have brought a smile to her as she read them. Her world-traveling son was growing up:

[Sunday,] June 4, 1905

[Dear Mother,]

Mrs A. invited us to go out in their gondola last night.

It was simply great! The lights on the Grand Canal, and the little dark Rios were a picture. We went way up to the north-eastern corner of the city; to the Three Bridges, and then out by the Guidecca, and back down the Grand Canal.

We lay alongside one of the singing barges; and listened to the music for an hour or so. It was fine! I suppose you know all about it, for you and father must have enjoyed just such nights here together. I think I would like to come here in my wedding trip, if I ever have one.

Walt and I were remarking the other day that we had only met three American girls on our whole trip, until now. There's nothing like a real true American girl; [those who are] French, German, English or Irish aren't in it!

[that is, in the running] ...[29]

---

27. ibid., p. 74.

28. ibid., p. 74.

29. ibid., p. 74. Selection edited.

Amid these bright scenes and festive meetings, Borden was still reflecting, in quieter moments, on deeper things. He'd written about them from Rome, at some length: centered on his thoughts of becoming a missionary:

[Wednesday,] May 17, 1905

Darling Mother,

I am glad you have told Father about my desire to be a missionary. I am thinking about it all the time, and looking forward to it …

I know that I am not at all fitted or prepared yet, but in the next four or five years I ought to be able to prepare myself.

I have been reading [Robert] Speer's book on *Missionary Principles and Practice*. It is very good, in my opinion. He takes up the different kinds of missionary work, educational, medical and evangelistic, and discusses them with regard to the different countries.

You may have read it; and if you haven't, I think you would like it …

I would like some medical skill [as a missionary,] enough so as to not be absolutely helpless and ignorant. But I really oughtn't to try and form plans of my own, but let God do it for me; and then it's sure to be right …

I will be mighty glad when I can talk things over with you.

Lots and lots of love,
William[30]

After several days' stay in France, and notwithstanding the mishap with a motorcyclist referred to above, Borden and Walter Erdman crossed the channel to England, and went straightaway to London.

A vivid letter home followed soon after, with news of the Henley Regatta, the fortunes of the 'American Eight,' St Paul's Cathedral, and tracing the steps of the 'great Cham,' the man of letters and celebrated lexicographer, Samuel Johnson:

---

30. ibid., p. 74.

London, [Friday,]
July 7, 1905

We have been having delightful weather here for a week and have enjoyed ourselves very much. We went out to Wimbledon, and saw some fine tennis last Tuesday.

Tomorrow, we will go and see some of the finals, which will be very good. Wednesday we went to the Henley Regatta, at Henley-on-Thames. It was a fine sight. We got a canoe, and paddled around among the crowd.

The very first boat we went alongside had [our cousin] Barbara in it.

The Henley Regatta in summer 1905, when Borden saw the skill of great competitors on display (from *The Sketch* magazine, July 1905).

It was rather remarkable, considering there were ten thousand people there. We only stayed for the morning races and returned to London about two. We saw the American Eight, defeated by the famous Leander crew.

[We also] went to St Paul's Cathedral the other day, and climbed up to the whispering gallery, and down into the crypt to the tombs of Wellington, Nelson and others ... On the way back, we went down a little court off Fleet Street, and saw the Church of the Knight Templars ...

Oliver Goldsmith's Tomb was just outside.

The most interesting thing we did was to take lunch at the Cheshire Cheese. This is the original Inn at which Dr Sam Johnson, and others, used to meet: 'Ye Olde Cheshyre Cheese.'

In the afternoon, we went over to Lord's Cricket Grounds to see the Cambridge-Oxford match. It was evidently quite a social event, as everyone was there and in their best. The field also was fine, but after watching the match for a while we had had enough of cricket, and retired. Today we spent our morning at the Tower [of London,] which I found very interesting.[31]

Beyond the absorbing visits described in this letter, Borden also went to tour 'museums and picture galleries,' and walked through 'the Houses of Parliament, Westminster Abbey, and Hampton Court.' He boated on the Thames, and came home 'in the long summer evening, by four-horse coach.' There were shopping excursions, calls on family friends living in England, 'and more than one visit to Shepherd's Bush, where "the finest tennis in the world" was being played.'[32]

And there was yet something more ...

Dr R. A. Torrey 'was then holding evangelistic meetings in the Grand Hall on the Strand.'[33] Borden and Walter Erdman knew of this, and wished to be part of gatherings they heard described as a source of blessing to many.

Here in England, the second transforming experience of Borden's world tour unfolded. It was one of the most carefully detailed events ever described in his diary and letters; and for that reason, it is important to closely follow what he wrote.

---

31. ibid., p. 78.

32. ibid., pp. 78-79.

33. See Campbell, *William Borden* (1913), p. 7.

He began with a letter home to Chicago:

> Hotel Russell, London,
> Friday, July 7, 1905
>
> Dear Mother ...
>
> Dr Torrey, as you know, has been holding meetings here in London for five months. This last month or so, they have been in a specially constructed hall on the Strand, seating about five thousand. Sunday was the last day of these meetings. Walt and I went [to one] in the afternoon ...
>
> Dr Torrey spoke about being 'born again,' and mentioned some of the foolish ideas people have about it. His sermon was meant to straighten things out. I know that my own ideas were somewhat hazy, and I wasn't at all sure about it. But I am now ... Dr Torrey gave five proofs by which we can tell whether we are 'born again' ... Every proof was a verse of Scripture ...
>
> The five proofs were very convincing and plain.[34]

What Borden heard stirred him so deeply and compellingly that he 'missed dinner at the hotel,' and 'hastened back to the evening meeting' on the Strand.

His letter home to his mother about this was written with a keen sense of immediacy and urgency, as though he wished she could have been there to see all that unfolded. Borden's recollections were of such a vivid nature that they seem to be what he regarded ever after as sacred moments.

During the evening meeting, Borden told his mother:

> Dr Torrey called for decisions. Fifty or sixty came forward, and confessed Christ. Dr Torrey told us to speak to those [near] about us. I had an awful tussle, and almost didn't, for I thought the people around me were all Christians.
>
> However, I wasn't sure, and so decided [to do so].
>
> I spoke to a lady next to me, and [some] others, but they were all saved. However, I felt much better; and know it will be easier to do next time.

---

34. See Taylor, *Borden of Yale* (1926), p. 79.

In the After Meeting Miss Davis, [the evening soloist,] sang the song, 'I Surrender All', and an invitation was given to those who had never publicly done so, whether Christians or not, to do so then [and surrender all].

I stood up with several others, and we sang the chorus …[35]

I surrender all, I surrender all;
All to Thee, my blessed Saviour, I surrender all.[36]

These moments of spiritual realization had taken place five days earlier than Borden's letter of July 7. For under the date of Sunday, July 2, he had written in his diary: 'I went back to [the] Grand

Dr R. A. Torrey and song-leader Charles Alexander, shown on the dais of the hall where 'gospel gatherings' were attended by thousands each day in the summer of 1905 (from the book *Torrey and Alexander*, by J. Kennedy McLean, 1905).

Hall, Strand, at 6:30 when it was already quite well filled. [I heard a] fine address. I was much helped, and surrendered all to Jesus at the invitation, while Miss Davis was singing …'[37]

---

35. ibid., pp. 81-82.

36. See the text of hymn number 36 in Ira Allan Sankey, ed., *Hallowed Hymns, New and Old* (New York: Biglow & Main Co., 1908).

37. See Campbell, *William Borden* (1913), p. 7.

Following this, Dr Torrey gave a brief talk on 'The Way of Life,' and spoke also about 'How to keep on with the Christian Life.'[38] Borden listened carefully, as he seemingly never had before. Eternal truth went home to his heart and mind.

Something had called to Borden, like deep calls unto deep. His feelings were not unlike the stirring words D. L. Moody had spoken once to young people: 'Give yourself up fully, wholly, and unreservedly to the Lord.'[39]

Borden had resolved to do just that. For days of college to come, and all the days to follow, he had given himself 'fully, wholly, and unreservedly to the Lord.'

---

38. See Taylor, *Borden of Yale* (1926), p. 82.

39. D. L. Moody, quoted in *Northfield Echoes* (East Northfield: E. S. Rastall, 1896), p. 113.

CHAPTER 4

Now to New Haven

William Borden prepared for Yale in Chicago at the
University School, Latin School, and Manual Training
School, and [then] in Pottstown at The Hill School. He was
president of Phi Beta Kappa. In athletics, he was active
in football, baseball, crew, and wrestling, rowing on the
winning 1909 club crew in the fall of Junior Year, and playing
on the winning Philosophical and High Oration baseball
team and on the Phi Beta Kappa team. He served on the Class
Book committee, and on the Senior Council. Elected a Class
Deacon, he devoted himself largely to religious work.[1]
– Yale Alumni Weekly (April 25, 1913)

His ideals, as to a variety of matters in college work,
were higher than those of even very strong Christian men.[2]
– Dr Harlan Page Beach, Yale Divinity School (1913)

Few men at Yale have left so strong an impress[ion]
on the character of men of their time as William Borden did ...[3]
– Dr H. B. Wright of Yale (1915)

---

1. See the *Yale Alumni Weekly*, April 25, 1913 (New Haven: Yale Publishing Association, 1913), p. 816.

2. See Zwemer, *William Whiting Borden* (1913), pp. 70-71. In 1906, H. P. Beach (1854-1933) became the first Professor of Missions at Yale Divinity School.

3. Quoted in J. L. Murray and F. M. Harris, *Christian Standards in Life* (New York: The Association Press, 1915), p. 82. J. Lovell Murray was Educational Secretary of the Student Volunteer Movement, and Frederick M. Harris was Secretary of the Publication Department for the international Committee of Young Men's Christian Associations.

It was certain, by January 18, 1904, several months before he graduated from The Hill School, that William Borden would be attending Yale.[4] There was little surprise in this, for his elder brother John was already attending Yale, and an uncle, H. A. Worcester, had graduated from Yale in 1884.[5]

Attending Yale was something of a tradition by the time Borden began his college career there, although his paternal grandfather John had attended Harvard. One wonders if this might have caused a bit of friction at family gatherings, since grandfather John Borden (a forceful man in his own right) lived until 1918, and was in his late seventies when his grandson William's choice was made.

Moreover William Borden was, with his three siblings, a partial heir to his grandfather's considerable estate. But in the end, there seems not to have been any problem with the choice of Yale over Harvard, since no word of any contention, or anything close to it, survives in key source documents.

Yale had other things in its favor. Borden knew that both of D. L. Moody's sons, Will and Paul, attended Yale. He'd spoken very highly, and very prominently in *The New York Times*, of the benefits his sons gained while they were there. Moody had done so in February 1898, and these words from near the end of his life were the more carefully remembered because of that:

> 'I have been pretty well acquainted with Yale for twenty years,' Moody said, 'and I have never seen the university in as good condition, religiously, as now. My oldest son graduated here, and if my other son, who is now in the freshman class, gets as much good out of Yale as his brother did, I shall have reason to thank God through time and eternity.'[6]

---

4. Borden's choice of Yale as his college was announced on page 1 of *The Hill School News*, January 18, 1904.

5. George Starkweather Fowler, ed., *History of the Class of 1906: Yale College, v. 1* (New Haven: Yale University, 1906), p. 78.

6. See the article, 'Mr Moody Defends Yale,' in the February 14, 1898 edition of *The New York Times*, p. 7.

Borden, for many years, had attended what was now The Moody Church (formerly Chicago Avenue Church). He was well aware of D. L. Moody's ties to Yale, and Moody's keen approval of the university.

And lastly, Borden knew of many friends from The Hill School who chose to attend Yale. Indeed, The Hill School Yale connection was so strong, and so prolific, there was a club at Yale called The Hill School Club. Borden could look forward to joining that club; with a ready circle of friends he already knew.

These things, and his family's ties to Yale, guided his choice to go there.

The Phelps Gate at Yale, a glimpse of one way Yale was much like Oxford or Cambridge during Borden's years there (from the author's photo collection, postcard from 1905).

Three months before going up to Yale, on Sunday, June 4, 1905, Borden had written to his mother with a special request for guidance and wisdom—

'Do pray for me. College is so near, and there will be such a lot of things to do, tremendous opportunities! Pray that I may be guided in everything, small and great.'[7]

So, only 'a month or so after his return to America,' Borden arrived at Yale, to begin four years of study. His fine academic record at The Hill School served well by way of admissions requirements. The only other indication of scholarly standing was clearly one from a bygone era, as Borden wrote on September 28, 1905:

---

7. See Taylor, *Borden of Yale* (1926), p. 76.

Dear Mother,

I am here, as you know, and the [admissions] crises have passed …

Yesterday I took my *Iliad* examination and this afternoon learned that I had successfully passed it. As this was my only condition, I am now a member in full standing of the class of 1909 …[8]

Proficiency in Homer's *Iliad* was then a key basis for admission to Yale: it was a different era indeed: a time when skill in classical languages, Greek and Latin, stood prominently in prep school education and collegiate life.

As for Borden's new lodgings at Yale, his family wisely advised him to room alone during his freshman year, at 242 York Street. He would have enough to adjust to in the rigorous academic schedule he was about to begin, so a single room it was.

242 York Street was home to 'Garland's,' at this time 'one of the sweller dormitories for freshmen.' Pierson Hall 'was just opposite, while on both sides of York Street were a number of private dormitories.' Borden's quarters were 'a second-floor rear room, which served as both bedroom and study.'[9]

'My room,' Borden told his mother in the letter above from September 28, 'is at the back, and has a large bay-window in three sections, with an immense window-seat.'[10] He could tell, on first sight, that it was the kind of room which lent itself to study and reflection. He would be looking out through that bay window in the early hours, when he had his 'Morning Watch,' or time of Bible study. It was a fine room to have, on all counts. He would fit in well at Garland's.

Then, after he'd settled in to his 'new digs' a bit, his brother John came by. Borden closely recounted the interesting evening that followed to his mother—

---

8. ibid., p. 88.

9. See Campbell, *William Borden* (1913), p. 7.

10. See Taylor, *Borden of Yale* (1926), p. 88.

Borden, seated at left, in front of the fireplace in his dormitory room at Yale (photo courtesy of The Billy Graham Center, Wheaton College, Illinois).

John took [a friend and me] down to Mory's to dine.[11]

This is a little place, quite historic, where the [Yale] fellows feed, more or less. The tables have initials carved all over them, and in one room there is a special table on which seniors leave their trademarks.

After dinner, I went back home and John left ...

About 8:30, some sophomores came in, and made me do a few foolish stunts, which didn't amount to much. I sang them a song, and attempted to 'scramble' like an egg, a very difficult thing to do, I assure you! However, they went after a few minutes, and I was left in peace ...

The next morning I passed my *Iliad* examination, and in the afternoon registered at Alumni Hall ... We were assigned to divisions, and given study schedules ... In the afternoon I went out and watched the football practice ... There [I] met Bob Noyes, a Hill fellow, who very kindly invited me to dinner.[12]

---

11. Mory's, thriving today, is a famous tavern, established circa 1849 and 'run in the style of a homey English pub.' See https://www.morys1849.org/Default.aspx?p=Dynami cModule&pageid=23&ssid=100037&vnf=1

12. See Taylor, *Borden of Yale* (1926), p. 88.

In the pages of Samuel Zwemer's biography of Borden a picture of Borden in these first days at Yale emerges: through the recollections of a friend whom Zwemer quoted anonymously.

'I first met Bill Borden in the fall of 1905,' this friend remembered—

> at the beginning of my freshman year in Yale. What struck me then ... and during my entire acquaintance with him, was the amazing maturity of his character. Though almost a year older than he [was], I felt that in character, self-control, and [measure] of purpose, he was many years my senior.
>
> In many ways, I should say, he was the most mature man of his class.
>
> I do not mean to imply ... that he was 'oldmannish' in the least. He had a keen sense of humor, could let out a most uproarious war whoop of a laugh, and was a famous 'rough-houser.' I remember [one] occasion, in a confused melee on the top floor of 250 York Street, he got a 'scissors-hold' on my head, and I thought, for a second, he would crack it in two.
>
> His interest and [gifts] in athletics [would soon become evident.] He was one of the strongest men physically that I have ever known ...[13]

One classmate who met Borden early at Yale, and whose name we do know was Charles Soutter Campbell, or 'Charlie Campbell,' as Borden liked to call him. The two became good friends; and in time, best friends.

Campbell later recalled his early acquaintance with Borden:

> As we left [a Y.M.C.A.] meeting, [Bill] joined me, and we walked back together to [242] York Street. [He] told me then ... of his trip around the world, [and] his interest in [Christian] missions. This was the beginning of the friendship which has meant so much to me.[14]

---

13. See Zwemer, *William Borden* (1913), pp. 68-69.

14. See Taylor, *Borden of Yale* (1926), p. 97.

At Yale, Charlie Campbell earned a fine record. He received a Philosophical Oration appointment, and was a member of the Phi Beta Kappa academic honor society.

He was also a member of the University track team for three years, and won his letter 'Y' in the pole vault, during an intercollegiate meet in his sophomore year.[15]

As for Borden himself, his fervent devotion to football had only grown since his days at The Hill School, where his prowess was such that he'd been 'a first team substitute before he left school.'[16]

'Old School Football' at Yale, a sport then played much like rugby (from the author's copy of *The Yale Banner and Pot-Pourri* yearbook, 1913-1914).

For Borden to do so well, on a talented team coached by Michael Sweeney, whom Yale had tried to hire away from Hill, and whose gridiron players were sought after by Yale, says much for Borden's gifts as a football player.[17]

---

15. This information about Charlie Campbell is taken from *The History of the Class of 1909, Yale College.*

16. See Campbell, *William Borden* (1913), pp. 4-5. Borden himself told his mother on Sunday, Nov. 22, 1903: 'We have been to Lawrenceville … I was taken with the [varsity] team as a sub.'

17. 'It is said that the plays worked out by Mr Sweeney and the boys at Hill are sometimes used by next season's Yale team.' See Ruhl, 'Some American Preparatory

Among teams that The Hill School competed against in Borden's time were college squads like the Freshman Team from Princeton. Thus he'd been a part of hard-fought games, against high caliber competition. He'd played center at Hill, and looked to continue as a lineman at Yale.

It was a storied era for football, for the Varsity Squad at Yale would become National Champions in 1905. Yale was a true powerhouse in football at this time: home to gridiron legends like Amos Alonzo Stagg, Walter Camp and Jack Owsley, the standout halfback for Yale from 1901 to 1904. The following year, Owsley would coach Yale's undefeated 1905 football team.[18]

In such a setting, William Borden 'went out for the freshman football team, and played very good ball.' He 'came very near' making the active roster, becoming 'a first substitute for a line position.' In fact, during 'the game with the Princeton Freshmen, he was told to warm up to go in,' but 'time was called, or something of that sort' keeeping him from taking the field.[19] Charlie Campbell and other classmates among Borden's new set of friends saw first hand what a talented athlete he was.

One good friend in Borden's class, Maxwell Parry, cast his memories in prose that Theodore Roosevelt would have relished. Parry became Class Orator at Yale:

Schools,' *Scribner's*, (1910), p. 695. See also 'Michael Sweeney,' an online article at: http://www.thehill.org/FoundersHall3

'Mike Sweeney was hired in 1896 to develop an athletic program. His program became well known and was copied by many other schools. Yale University tried to hire him away, but he remained loyal to Hill, though the School did give him a year off to go and set up a similar program at Yale. When [Sweeney] came to The Hill, he was well known for track, as he was the holder of the world record for the running high jump at the time. Many students came to The Hill just to be coached by [him]. [He] also made a name for himself as a football coach ... and it did not take long for him to establish a successful program. In his approximately 15 years of coaching football, seven of his teams finished undefeated, and two of them were un-scored upon.'

18. See page 233 of *The Yale Banner* magazine for 1904. See also pages 42, 44-45 of the Dec. 1905 *Yale Banner and Pot-Pourri* yearbook.

19. See Taylor, *Borden of Yale* (1926), p. 97. See also Campbell, *William Borden* (1913), p. 9.

There was one thing nobody at Yale ever questioned, [Bill Borden] was strong. He was red-blooded, and he had the punch. He played hard ... When he bucked the football line, every ounce of his hundred and seventy-five was back of him.[20]

But while football prompted keen interest and involvement with sports, the one thing above all others that stirred Borden most deeply was faith. It would always be so. Faith shaped the unfolding of his first year at Yale, and the three years that followed. In time, others saw it as his guiding beacon too.

And what of his first year at Yale?

It was marked by a true flurry of activity: a year of welcome challenges, some difficulties, but largely a rich store of memories and transforming moments.

Academically, he'd good news to send home to his father and mother, and a letter from Monday, March 26, 1906 spoke of his performance for the year.

'My marks for this term are all A's,' Borden said, 'except Greek, which is C; my general average is A. We have to pick our courses for sophomore year soon, and I will send a book giving courses of study; so that you and father can look it over.'[21]

This was a helpful summary, but Borden's letter didn't convey a full picture of his first year's academic performance. In *The Yale Banner and Pot-Pourri* yearbook, Borden made the list of those who won 'honors in the studies of freshman year,'[22] alongside gifted friends like Harvey Hollister Bundy (whose son, McGeorge

---

20. See Taylor, *Borden of Yale* (1926), p. 149. See page 1028 of the 1918 edition of *The Obituary Record of Graduates of Yale University*: Maxwell Parry 'wrote a number of plays including "Boys of Gettysburg," "The Lie Beautiful," "The Flower of Assisi" (in memory of his classmate, William Whiting Borden).' See also page 951 of the May 30, 1913 issue of *Yale Alumni Weekly*: 'At a service recently held at the First Baptist Church, Indianapolis, Ind., Maxwell O. Parry read from the pulpit a play which he had written in memory of William W. Borden and called "The Flower of Assisi".'

21. See Taylor, *Borden of Yale* (1926), p. 111.

22. See *The Yale Banner and Pot-Pourri* yearbook for 1907, (New Haven: Yale University Press, 1907), p. 164.

Bundy, would later serve in President Kennedy's cabinet).[23] Others on this Honor Roll were Charlie Campbell and Malcolm Burt 'Mac' Vilas.

Writing home, Borden spoke of exams 'in Ruskin and Byron … in which I am quite sure I did well.' Also, he said, 'my standing in Analytical Geometry is nearly as good as in Trigonometry. In fact, everything goes well – but my Greek.'[24]

Borden would have fared better in Greek, but for the misfortune of having a professor who had taken an unreasonable dislike to him. We learn more of this from another of Borden's close friends at Yale, Kenneth Latourette, later to become one of the world's most distinguished historians, with a legacy treasured at Yale.

As Latourette had written:

> My first recollection of Bill is in a Greek class in which we both recited to Prof. [Thomas Day Seymour,][25] a rare scholar and … Christian gentleman; but he had a quick temper, and at times was subject to [strange] dislikes. For some reason I could never account for, he seemed totally to misunderstand and thoroughly to dislike Bill. For one who prepared as conscientiously as [he,] it was very galling to be systematically, openly, and unjustly berated. Although very indignant, he never retorted in any way; and I cannot now remember that he ever spoke of the experience, except when someone else mentioned it. [Even] then, he only said a few words of apology for Professor [Seymour].[26]

---

23. During his college years, the author kept the grounds of the summer home owned by McGeorge Bundy, in Manchester-By-The-Sea. Mr Bundy showed the author much kindness, which he here wishes to acknowledge.

24. See Taylor, *Borden of Yale* (1926), p. 115.

25. Almost certainly Thomas Day Seymour, listed in 1904 as a 'Professor of the Greek Language and Literature.' He died in 1907. Since 'Thomas Day and [his wife] Sarah Hitchcock Seymour [were] both descendants of old and distinguished Yale families [and] there were numerous alumni in Seymour's family tree, including two Presidents of Yale,' one can easily see how he might have been staid, stuffy, and full of himself. He was said to be a man of 'strong likes and dislikes' and he would at times 'criticize qualities in the abstract with vehemence.' This dovetails with Latourette: 'but he had a quick temper, and at times was subject to queer [i.e. strange] dislikes.'

26. See Taylor, *Borden of Yale* (1926), pp. 111-112.

Down the years, many undergraduates have known a similar situation.

Academia is not always an ideal setting of caring, accomplished pedagogues. Professorial dislikes are sometimes without foundation and capricious. Borden saw this first-hand; but as Latourette recalled, he acquitted himself well in very trying circumstances. It was a sign of character.

As for athletics, Borden's friend Charlie Campbell said: 'Bill was soon in the thick of ... the play of college life.'[27] He could be proud of many things about his first year's performance in football. Trying to make 'the freshman football eleven,' he discovered he was one of 'ninety-nine others doing likewise.'[28] Against such keen competition, to win a spot as 'first substitute for a line position,' and to suit up for the game against Princeton's freshman squad meant he'd done well indeed.

He'd taken part in other sports too. Wrestling was one of them.

When the winter season came, Borden spent hours in the gymnasium as a dedicated and able competitor. As his friend Campbell recalled: '[Bill] was a hard man to [get] down, and, though he never made the [college] wrestling team, he was well up with the best of his weight [class].'[29] Yet Borden did take part in the club tournaments, or 'intramural competition,' and told his father all about it:

> 'I am keeping up my wrestling,' he wrote home to Chicago, 'and like it very much. It certainly is a science! [He added a little later in another letter:]'
>
> 'Yesterday I wrestled in the tournament and got beaten ...
> My class is "middle heavy-weight." My opponent was about a head taller ... but the same weight. He is a senior ... We had two

---

27. See Campbell, *William Borden* (1913), p. 8.
28. See Taylor, *Borden of Yale* (1926), p. 89.
29. See Campbell, *William Borden* (1913), p. 9.

bouts of five minutes each, and neither succeeded in putting the other down. So after the rest we went at it again, and [wrestled] till one of us was thrown ... After forty-nine minutes ... he succeeded ... I lost [several] pounds ... but [had no] injuries, and feel fine now.'[30]

'Wearers of the Y,' showing rowing and football, in which Borden was a fine student-athlete at Yale (from the author's copy of *The Yale Banner and Pot-Pourri* yearbook, 1913-1914).

In spring 1906, Borden took part in horseback riding and track. He was also an avid fan of Yale's baseball team, and a member of the freshman rowing crew. He was a talented baseball player, hence his keen interest there; and he now began to practice and row competitively. It was soon a favorite pastime, and he showed much promise in a sport with a rich, storied tradition at Yale.

The boat-house at Yale during Borden's time, part of a storied athletic tradition there (from the author's copy of *The Yale Banner and Pot-Pourri* yearbook, 1908-1909).

---

30. See Taylor, *Borden of Yale* (1926), pp. 104-105.

As lines recalling the era when this tradition began read—

> *... at the first stroke, the race was contested to the turn;*
> *then, we were slightly in the lead.*
> *We got about a little quicker than the other boat –*
> *and with a strong wind at our backs ... crossed the line winners.*[31]

Then too, Borden wrote home with fine news of an equestrian day, along with track competition. 'This afternoon,' he told his mother in late April 1906:

> Jim Whittaker and I went off on a glorious horseback ride ...
> We went way out in the country, and then struck down to the
> Sound, and came back to New Haven along the shore. The air,
> and everything, was fine – and I enjoyed it immensely.[32]

One wonders what New Haven was like in a time when such long horseback rides could be taken. With modern urban sprawl, such riding trails and pathways as Borden knew are long gone. But what a fine thing it must have been for him, and good friends, to go outdoors and unwind from long hours of hard study.

As for track, it was intramural competition once more, but with strong indications that if he kept at it, Borden might make Yale's collegiate team.

One track meet was a welcome reunion with friends from The Hill School, as he wrote home to explain:

> Today was the day of the [freshman] track games and the old Hill
> distinguished herself by winning the meet with a margin of ten
> and a half points. I saw [Coach] Sweeney and the fellows [from
> Hill]; most all of whom I knew, [and] it was fine.[33]

Another letter soon followed, with pardonable pride over progress in chosen events:

---

31. A 'found poem' of lines from C. A. Brinley, *Russell Wheeler Davenport: Father of Rowing at Yale* (New York: Putnam, 1905), pp. 32-33.

32. See Taylor, *Borden of Yale* (1926), p. 115.

33. ibid., p. 116.

I am rather enjoying my track work, and as Johnny Mack, the trainer and coach, condescends to say a word now and then, I'm almost getting a 'swelled head,' but not quite. I suppose if I work hard, after two or three years I may be some good. I am working with both shot and hammer, each weighing sixteen pounds.[34]

These events required considerable strength, as well as athleticism.

A last letter about spring sports described the exploits of Yale's baseball nine in competition, and the college freshman crew. Through and through, it was an Ivy League affair:

Today, Yale distinguished herself in many ways. They easily won from Princeton in Track, won the Inter-Collegiate shoot from Penn, beat Holy Cross in Baseball, 10-7 I believe, the Freshmen Crew beat out the Columbia Freshmen, and the Freshman Ball team was also victorious.

Quite a day, was it not?[35]

As for things of a spiritual nature at Yale, Borden's involvement with them began almost as soon as he arrived there in September 1905. As his friend Charlie Campbell recalled: '[Bill] got in touch with the religious work of the college:'

His connection [to Dwight Hall and the Y.M.C.A.] was quickly established ... He soon made friends with others who were interested in the cause of Christ. He served on the committee in charge of the religious work of [our] class, and soon stamped himself as a leader in the Christian activities of the college.

In spite of his [younger] age, he was far more mature in faith than many considerably older. His grasp of the [essentials of faith] was, even at this time, firm and assured. He had already decided to become a foreign missionary.

A fixed purpose of this sort gives a man a great singleness of aim that steadies not only himself, but those [he meets]; and Bill's character had a solidity about it, directly traceable to his surrender to Christ for a life of service ...

---

34. ibid., p. 116.

35. ibid., p. 116.

Interested as he was in football, and [many other] activities ... Bill let it be known ... that his heart was first in the service of [the Savior,] ever watching for opportunities for spreading the faith he believed so firmly himself.[36]

Other things that Borden discovered about Yale, in the first few weeks of his time there, were part of a letter from early October 1905. Some things were a source of concern; others a source of gratitude. He saw things commonplace in college life: some students were devout, and focused on studies; others less so, with dissolute habits that served them poorly.

'Dear Mother,' he wrote home to Chicago:

The opening of College has brought out all sorts of things.

Nearly everyone uses a translation [dishonestly] in his studies, that is in Greek and Latin. The great majority smoke, go to the theatre Saturday night, and do their studying on Sunday. Rather a hopeless state of affairs!

However, there are some fine Christian men ... and in my own class too, I believe. And I hope to be able to do something, by the grace of God, to help in the right direction.

I am taking meals next door, at a table with seven other fellows ...

I am here in a position to give to others a little of what I have received. I am thankful for all the true teaching I have had from you, dear Mother ... Walt [Erdman,] and others. I know you are praying for me ... others also ...

What a thing Christian fellowship is, and what a power prayer! I wish I had that little poem you sent me once, about the ploughman at his work, praying, and the missionaries [who wondered why] their words had such power: *'because they did not see someone unknown, perhaps, and far away, on bended knee.'*

[Today,] President Hadley preached in Chapel, [with] a very good sermon for the opening of a college year. Only in

---

36. See Campbell, *William Borden* (1913), pp. 8-9.

impressing the necessity of having a fixed purpose in life, and distinguishing between right and wrong, he neglected to say *what* our purpose should be, and *where* we should get the ability to persevere ... things which seemed rather essential to me.

I forgot to mention the Dwight Hall reception which was held Friday night [Sept. 29th]. The freshman class was invited ... I went, and after we had all been introduced ... the captains of the [athletic] teams [spoke,] and John Magee, [Vice-President of the Dwight Hall Y.M.C.A.] ...

Oh, I nearly forgot about this evening's meeting!

Dr Henry Wright, son of the Dean [of the Faculty], gave us a splendid address in Dwight Hall. It was the real true thing; and as he dealt with matters closely related to college life, it was very helpful ...[37]

Two things stand out in this letter, so early in Borden's time at Yale. First is his mention of John Magee, with whom he had a close, important friendship.

Magee, Class of 1906 at Yale, was later ordained a minister of the Episcopal Church and set out for China in 1912, where he met and married Faith Backhouse, an English missionary with China Inland Mission.

In the 1930s, Magee played a key role in saving thousands of Chinese from being murdered by Japanese forces, creating a refugee hospital to care for wounded soldiers and refugees, and serving as chairman in Nanking of the International Red Cross. Film footage taken by Magee in Nanking, and sent to the West, gave some of the first available documentation of the 'Nanking Massacre.' He bequeathed a great humanitarian legacy.[38]

Borden's meeting Dr Henry Wright was also a deeply important part of his early days at Yale, and all the years of his time there.

---

37. See Taylor, *Borden of Yale* (1926), pp. 89-91. Magee, Yale Class of 1906, was General Secretary of the Y.M.C.A. in Dwight Hall, 1908–1910.

38. See the Yale University Library article, 'John Gillespie Magee,' at: https://web. library.yale.edu/divinity/nanking/magee

As Geraldine Taylor has written:

Dwight Hall and Henry Wright [had] so large a part in Borden's experiences at Yale that it is important to understand their relation to the life of the University. From the biography of Dr Wright, it is evident that he was in America ... what Henry Drummond had been in Scotland: [a leader of] brilliant scholarship ... spiritual fervour ... and passion for winning men to Christ.

[Wright] had a genius for friendship, and was young enough (twenty-eight when Borden entered Yale) to be closely in touch with student life.

He had taken his Doctor's degree in classics, and had already been two years on the faculty ... as a Tutor in Greek and Latin. He had also been General Secretary of the Yale Y.M.C.A. (from 1898–1901), and it was during [the] period of his post-graduate studies that he came to be a campus figure.[39]

Moreover, when William Borden entered Yale in autumn 1905, Dwight Hall was entering a golden era of its importance and effectiveness. It was, largely, 'what Henry Wright had made it,' and Dwight Hall, the home of the Y.M.C.A. at Yale—

stood for a high type of scholarship, [and] Christian [endeavor]. From the Sunday evening services, often gathering hundreds, to the group meetings and personal talks in the little room on the top floor, it was the scene of much of the best work done in the University.[40]

All of this made a profound impression on Borden, and Geraldine Taylor described this time of his life by saying that he—

was finding such strength in the companionship of the Lord Jesus Christ that he longed to share [its] great realities with others. [A] purpose was forming in his heart of attempting to start a group for Bible study among those who would not avail themselves of the influences of Dwight Hall ...[41]

---

39. See Taylor, *Borden of Yale* (1926), p. 91.

40. ibid., pp. 91-92.

41. ibid., p. 94.

In sum, Borden wished to reach classmates not versed in things of faith. His time at Dwight Hall, and Dr Wright's example, did much to inspire this purpose.

Borden's friend Charlie Campbell recalled all this, and more, from Borden's first autumn at Yale. 'It was well on in the first term,' he said—

> when Bill and I began to pray together in the morning before breakfast. I cannot say positively whose suggestion it was, but I feel sure it must have originated with Bill. We had been meeting only a short time when a third, Farrand Williams, joined us – and soon after a fourth, James M. Howard. These meetings were held in Bill's room, just before we went to breakfast.
>
> The time was spent in prayer, after a brief reading of Scripture. Our object was to pray for the religious work of the class and college; and also for those of our friends we were seeking to bring to Christ.
>
> I remember so well the stimulus Bill gave us in those meetings. His handling of Scripture was always helpful. From the very beginning of the years I knew him he would read to us from the Bible, show us something that God had promised; and then proceed to claim the promise with assurance.[42]

From such humble beginnings, something more widespread and influential emerged. 'This group for prayer,' Campbell said—

> was the beginning of the daily groups that spread to every one of the college classes. From the membership of two at the start, the group in our class grew until it had to be divided in sophomore year ...
>
> By the end of that year, there were similar groups in each of the classes. It was not passed down from the seniors to the juniors; *it came up from the freshmen to the seniors.* And very real blessing was given in answer to our prayers – quite a number were converted.[43]

All this time, Campbell observed, Borden seemed older than his years. There was a kind of wisdom in him, Campbell felt – one

---

42. ibid., p. 97.
43. ibid., pp. 97-98.

born of deep, abiding conviction.

This led Borden to pursue opportunities where few others saw them.

'I remember,' Campbell wrote—

A 'evening fireside' woodcut, with a student looking much like Borden in his rooms at Yale (from the author's copy of *The Yale Banner and Pot-Pourri* yearbook, 1908-1909).

[a friend] with whom Bill worked very hard, a fellow with a scientific turn of mind, who wanted everything proved. Bill must have looked down with joy from the [heaven] to which he has gone when, some years later, this man came out brightly as a Christian. Bill was always picking out the toughest proposition, and going through thick and thin to win him for Christ ...

His life, how true it rang! He came to college far ahead, spiritually, of any of us. He had already given his heart in full surrender to Christ – had really done it. He had formed his purpose to become a foreign missionary ...

All through college and seminary that purpose never wavered ...

His life was determined. We who were his classmates learned to lean on him; and find in him a strength [from] settled purpose and consecration.[44]

A letter home, from this time, added to what Charlie Campbell had shared. Borden's interest in a careful study of the Gospel of John grew as well:

Sunday, October 15, 1905

[Dear Mother,]

Just after chapel service this morning we had our class prayer meeting ...

---

44. ibid., p. 98.

John Magee invited me to come to the Volunteer Band at five this afternoon. There were about ten present, and we had a time of prayer. There are some fine fellows here in the upper classes, I can tell you.

I have talked over the matter of my group Bible Study Class with Arthur Bradford, and decided that paraphrasing Galatians is a [bit much]. The object of these groups is to interest fellows who do not attend the Wednesday evening meeting in Dwight Hall, led by Dr Wright. So I have [reviewed] methods of Bible study suggested by Dr Torrey, and decided upon Chapter Study as the best.

You know the method, giving out questions to be answered.

And I think John is the book to take, because it is written that men might believe that Jesus is the Christ the Son of God, 'and that believing, ye might have life through His name.'[45]

Henry Weston Frost also witnessed Borden's habits of the heart, or what this era commonly called his 'devotional life.' Years later, writing from Borden's room in his home in New York City, Frost remembered:

in the chair [where William] so often sat, before the desk where he so long wrote and studied, surrounded by [his] books ... there lies before me [his personal copy of] James H. McConkey's book, entitled: *The Three-fold Secret of the Holy Spirit,* and it bears unconscious testimony to the owner's life.

The copy is tastefully bound in buff paper, and ... was originally intact and clean. But now it is torn and soiled, both without and within. Evidently, it has seen many journeys, for it used to be a frequent companion in travel, and it has seen much use, for it has been carefully and repeatedly read.

And upon the first page, certain words are underscored – a way [that William] had with all his best loved books – [and the words] are these:

'The supreme human condition of the fulness of the Spirit, is a life wholly surrendered to God; to do His will.'[46]

---

45. ibid., pp. 94-95.

46. See *China's Millions* magazine, May 1913 (London: China Inland Mission, 1913), p. 49. Italics added.

Select books, like McConkey's, enriched Borden's reading of Scripture. He was always careful to ensure time was set aside, each day, for prayer and reading the Bible. During all the years of their friendship, Frost saw the ardent commitment Borden gave daily to seeking 'the living waters,' as Borden liked to phrase it.

So he kept to a schedule, as Frost recalled:

> There was a time for sleep, a time for waking, a time for prayer, a time for Bible study, a time for general study, a time for recreation, and a time for [society]. [William] owned a 'Big Ben' clock, and there was a covenant [with it] …
>
> I have seen him in the evening, in the midst of [fine] company, glance at the time, and then courteously [excuse] himself, away to room, bed, [and] sleep.
>
> He needed much sleep, for he was not as strong as he appeared; [and] his eye was on the next morning, when he purposed to keep the 'Morning Watch.'

And as for 'the living waters,' to re-visit Borden's phrase, he actually wrote a small meditation about them, and why they were important. At the outset, he spoke of two things, 'First,' he stated, 'we must have a knowledge of the Living Waters. Second, we must *have a desire* for the Living Waters.'[47] To this, Borden added:

> the individual Christian is not merely satisfied himself by drinking of the Living Waters, but after he has received the Living Waters himself, he becomes a fountain of Living Waters, from which goes out a stream that gives nourishment and strength to all those around him.
>
> The individual Christian should be a center of life-giving water, to all with whom he comes in contact. Living Waters satisfy the individual … and equip him for service for others.[48]

By the close of October 1905, Borden found there were many enriching opportunities to learn more about the Christian

---

47. See *The Christian Workers* magazine, October 1916 (Chicago: Moody Bible Institute, 1916), p. 133. Italics added.

48. ibid., p. 133.

life in events held at Dwight Hall, the Y.M.C.A. building on campus at Yale.[49]

Dwight Hall (Y. M. C. A.) Yale University, New Haven, Conn.

Dwight Hall, home of the Y.M.C.A. at Yale during Borden's years there (from the author's photo collection, postcard from 1905).

In a letter written home to Chicago on Sunday, October 29, 1905, Borden described the kind of opportunities he so appreciated at Dwight Hall:

> My group [Bible study] work has not commenced yet, but I hope to get it going before long, by the end of the football season. [John R.] Mott was here last Sunday [Oct. 22,] and I had a few moments' talk with him in the afternoon. He wished to be remembered to you.
>
> [Today] also he was here, and gave us a couple of very fine talks, this morning on the required characteristics of leadership, and this evening in Dwight Hall, a distinctly evangelistic meeting, something rather unusual …

---

49. Founded by undergraduates in 1886 as the Yale University Christian Association to serve the destitute through missionary work, Dwight Hall was incorporated 12 years later as an independent, non-profit educational and religious organization. See https://dwighthall.org/about-us/history

After his time was up, he asked the fellows who wanted to learn how to deal with temptation [in college years] to meet in another room. So we met, only about two-fifths having left, and there again he spoke very earnestly ...[50]

By the start of the New Year, 1906, Borden was finding his stride in terms of his involvement with Dwight Hall, the gift of wise hours of mentoring by Dr Henry Wright, and the growing set of friendships he was making. As he told his parents:

Borden, center of photo, with fellow members of the Executive Committee for the Dwight Hall Y.M.C.A. chapter at Yale (from the author's copy of *The Yale Banner and Pot-Pourri* yearbook, 1908-1909).

It seems sort of nice and very natural to be back here again. I am thankful to say that I have been enabled to get up every morning, so far, in time to have Bible study and prayer before beginning the day's work.

I hope with God's help to keep it up ...

The term has started well as far as sermons go. [Robert] Speer was here this morning and evening; and gave us two very good talks.

In the morning he read a part of the 10th [chapter] of Matthew, taking as his text verses 32 and 33, the subject being 'Confession and Denial.'

He spoke on character as essential to strong manhood, and religion as necessary to character; and showed that religion—Christianity—is a question of personal attitude toward Jesus Christ. It is confession – or denial.

---

50. See Taylor, *Borden of Yale* (1926), pp. 98-99. Here, 2nd Timothy 2:15 has been slightly paraphrased.

The Dwight Hall [Y.M.C.A.] meeting, as you know, is voluntary: but the room was packed, some fellows [were] even standing, a thing they wouldn't think of doing in Chapel. I guess there were about five hundred present.

There, too, [Mr Speer] gave a very powerful talk on 'Apart from me ye can do nothing,' and 'I can do all things through Christ who strengthens me.'

I have a regular night now for going to the [New Haven] Boys' Club.[51] I go down every Saturday with Charlie Campbell [and we volunteer there]. He is a corker, and I am glad I'm getting to know him.[52]

Soon, Borden was able to tell his parents that efforts to launch Bible study work among the wider circle of classmates at Yale were well under way. To that end, Borden and several friends were being mentored by Dr Henry Wright, with a view to beginning these study sessions with their peers. Borden wrote:

There is a group of men here in College, it might be called a personal-workers' group, which meets every Tuesday in Dr Wright's room.

James Howard, Charlie Campbell and I were chosen from our class ...

There are about fourteen in the group now.

Dr Wright first reads a short passage, and says a few words. Then there is general discussion, each one bringing up his case [or efforts to reach classmates], and then prayer. It is fine, [and] we get to know some of the best men in college [as well].

I realize here, more than ever before, that a man's *true friends* are his Christian friends ... I am sure these little

---

51. The New Haven Boys Club was founded in 1871 by Mrs Eli Whitney in her home. In 1872, Mrs Whitney Blake named her Club the 'United Workers,' and to this day, the Club maintains that title as its legal name. In 1891, the Club moved to a new location at 200 Orange Street ... The Club remained at this location until it moved into a new facility in 1915 on Jefferson Street. See http://bgcnewhaven.org/who-we-are/history/

52. See Taylor, *Borden of Yale* (1926), p. 100. For clarity, scripture references have been slightly paraphrased.

gatherings will be a help to me; and will accomplish great things here at Yale.[53]

Yet another glimpse of this time in Borden's college life comes courtesy of Dr Benjamin Wisner Bacon, College Pastor at Yale.[54] He stated that the meetings Borden attended were the heart of Christian activity at Yale during this era:

They were held in the little room under the eaves, on the top floor at Dwight Hall: none being asked save the [gathering Henry Wright had requested]. I felt it an honour to be with these 'heart and soul' Christian boys ...

Henry was of course always the leader, richest in experience, wisest in counsel, most indefatigable in effort. It was the very breath of life to him to be about his Father's business, [mentoring these young men].[55]

Such streams of influence were deepening. Writing to his mother, Borden gave a revealing picture of what his daily life was like. Times of Bible study brought richness to a hectic yet fulfilling schedule. Borden's words give a true flavor of the way collegians spoke in the early 1900s.

'Tuesdays are always my hard days,' he said—

that is, busy ones, as you can easily see when I tell you how my time is occupied. I get up about seven [and] have my Morning Watch, which I like to call my 'breakfast' – for 'man doth not live by bread alone, but by every word that proceedeth out of the mouth of God'—

[After that, I] go to breakfast [in the dining hall], and then Chapel.

From eight thirty until four in the afternoon, my studies keep me busy. From four to five, I try and get in an hour's practice [on] piano, and at five we have our meeting for personal workers.

53. ibid., p. 103.

54. Dr Benjamin Wisner Bacon (1860–1932), graduated from Yale (1881), and Yale Divinity School (1884). After serving two pastorates, he was made an instructor in New Testament Greek at Yale Divinity School and became Buckingham Professor of New Testament Criticism and Exegesis in 1897.

55. See Taylor, *Borden of Yale* (1926), 103n.

After that, [there's] supper and study until nine, when my Bible Study Group meets for about an hour.

This has been the program today, so you see that until now, (10 p.m.), I have been kept moving.

But I sort of like it; [and feel] it's just about enough.[56]

Beyond this, a true watershed moment for Borden's Christian activity at Yale centered on the Nashville Student Volunteer Conference of 1906: one of the great missionary conventions of the Student Volunteer Movement. Held in the Ryman Auditorium (now a landmark venue for music performance), it was attended by over 4,000 students. 'The Yale contingent,' wrote Geraldine Taylor, 'was a strong one.'

And little wonder, for contemporary news accounts traced the palpable, keen sense of anticipation gathered round this event. *The Intercollegian* magazine painted a picture of all that Borden and his friends from Yale were looking forward to:

> The Fifth International Convention of the Student Volunteer Movement will be held at Nashville, Tennessee, beginning Wednesday afternoon, February 28, at three o'clock, and closing Sunday night, March 4, 1906. These Volunteer Conventions are held but once in each student generation, that is, once every four years, and constitute the largest, [and] the most representative ... gatherings of the students of North America.
>
> [It is expected that] fully 500 universities, colleges, and seminaries will be represented by leading students ... volunteers and non-volunteers. Professors as well as students are invited. It is expected that at least 200 missionaries will be present from nearly forty of the mission fields of the world. The secretaries of the Foreign Missionary Societies of the United States ... Canada and other leaders of ... North America will be present, [and] fraternal delegates from Europe ...[57]

---

56. ibid., pp. 114-115.

57. See *The Intercollegian* magazine, Dec. 1905, (New York: The Student Volunteer Movement for Foreign Missions, 1906), p. 49.

Reading this, it's clear great student conventions, like the Urbana gatherings famous today, were pre-figured in the International Convention Borden and his friends attended in 1906. Indeed, one might say this *was* 'Urbana,' many years before an actual Urbana gathering took place.

Borden looked forward to this gathering as a place where his understanding of a missionary's call could receive context and direction. So many who had served as missionaries would be in Nashville. There in the aisles of the Ryman Auditorium, he could meet with them and talk. He could hear more about far away places that he had seen on his world tour; and learn more about the unique opportunities each region represented for missionary service.

This Convention, then, was something not to be missed.

In the days before this gathering took place, Borden's kindness to his friend Charlie Campbell was present, for reasons Campbell later recalled with fondness—

'I was not one of those chosen' to attend the Nashville Convention, Campbell said. 'The last night before the delegation was to leave, I was in bed and almost asleep when a number of upper-classmen filed into my room. I believe Bill was with them. They told me that it was financially possible for them to take one more delegate, and wanted me to go. Of course, I went ...

I have always had the conviction that Bill was back of that. [But] if not, it was at any rate the kind of thing he was always doing ...

What a time we had on that long train journey to Nashville!

Bill and others of us would adjourn to the baggage car occasionally, to let off steam in games that usually came from his fertile imagination.

One of his games went by the name of "hot-hand," [it was something he learned from watching sailors on a German steamer during his trip round the world]. The man who was "it" [had to] face the side of the car, with his eyes closed, supporting his head against the car. The rest would then group themselves behind him, and anyone was at liberty to take a whack.

After each impact, he had to guess who it was that had hit him. If his guess was correct, the giver of the blow had to change places with him; if incorrect, another whack was in order.

Bill shone at this game, in both capacities! Then there would be high-kicking contests, and other games – all in the rapidly moving car.

So we reached Nashville, full of life and spirits, where we separated for the different homes in which we were to [stay].

Those were days of wonderful inspiration for us all …

If Bill was [indeed] responsible for my going to Nashville, he was used of God to bring me a step further on in Christian experience; for it was there I gave my life to God, in consecration for any work to which He might call me.'[58]

We learn from none other than Paul Moody,[59] D. L. Moody's youngest son—and a graduate of Yale, Class of 1901—what it was like to be present during the days the Nashville Student Volunteer Convention unfolded.

'It is,' Paul Moody observed, 'an almost hopeless task to put into words the impressions that Nashville created, still [I] essay the task, [in] gratitude to God for the privilege of partaking of the blessings so freely given there.' Nashville, Moody continued, was for him 'a blessed surprise,' and he marveled over the—

> spirit of sanctified commonsense, or saneness, [which] prevailed [and] was the most impressive thing about the Convention.
>
> Every speaker … recognized that while within the sound of his voice there were hundreds to whom the call to go into

---

58. See Taylor, *Borden of Yale* (1926), p. 107.

59. The Nov. 18, 1921 issue of the *Yale Alumni Weekly* states that Paul Dwight Moody (1879–1947) 'was graduated from Yale in the Class of 1901 and the following two years were spent in study in the Free Church Colleges of Edinburgh and Glasgow. He began teaching at Mount Hermon Boys' School in the fall of 1903, the subject being The English Bible. In World War I, [he served with] the 103d Infantry, 26th Division. [After the war,] he was discharged with the rank of Major, and decorated by the French with the Order of University Palms, Grade of Officer of the Academy. He then served the Madison Avenue Church [of New York], remaining until his call to Middlebury [College to become its President, in 1921].'

distant lands might come, there were also hundreds to whom the will of God showed another path altogether – a path to [service at home] ... But for these persons, the Convention had a message.

While God did not ask them for themselves [in foreign service], He asked for their interest in His Kingdom and their gifts, great or small, and their prayers.

No man or woman could leave Nashville and feel that mission interests belonged to a certain class ... Everyone who looked over the vast auditorium must have felt [a sense of] the limitless resources of the Church, as represented by such a gathering of the flower of the youth of America ...[60]

Paul Moody closed with stirring words, saying: 'If the impressions that were made can by the grace of God be conserved, and the resolutions formed in secret in the heart can be converted into actions, [many others may learn to know] the light that comes from the One who said, "I am the light of the world."'[61]

Writing in the April 1906 issue of *The Missionary Herald*, Dr E. W. Capen,[62] later Dean of the Kennedy School of Missions at Hartford Seminary, struck a chord in unison with many things Paul Moody had cited, speaking of recent missionary history, and stirring things accomplished.

Capen told his wide circle of readers:

The convention was marked by a spirit of faith and consecration. During the last twenty years 2,953 volunteers have sailed for the foreign field, 1,000 of them during the four years ending January 1, 1906.

The conference of secretaries of mission boards, which preceded the opening of the convention, unanimously voted that

---

60. See the April 1906 issue of *The Intercollegian* magazine (New York: The Student Volunteer Movement, 1906), p. 167.

61. ibid., p. 167.

62. Edward Warren Capen, D.D., (1870–1947), attended Boston Latin School, Amherst College, Hartford Theological Seminary, and later became Dean of the Kennedy School of Missions at Hartford Theological Seminary.

there was a need of 1,000 new missionaries each year to man the field.

To the task of securing these recruits and challenging the churches to support them the movement has addressed itself, and on Thursday evening the delegates subscribed nearly $90,000, payable in four annual installments, for [fostering] the expanding work.[63]

These elements made a deep impression on Borden, but the high note of the Nashville Convention for him personally centered on Dr Samuel Zwemer's address in the convention hall. As Charlie Campbell described it: 'Out of the many-sided, worldwide pictures, Bill was particularly interested in what he heard of the Moslem [peoples]. S. M. Zwemer of Arabia spoke a number of times on the Mohammedan countries, and Bill was [deeply impressed by what he heard].'[64]

The climax of Zwemer's address came when he declared that vast areas of 'the Mohammedan world' were 'without a single missionary.' Surely, he said—

> if anywhere, then here there is an opportunity for pioneer mission work, and to carry the Gospel banner where it has never been planted. The very dangers and difficulties of such untrodden fields will be an irresistible attraction to men of heroic stamp …
>
> [I ask you to consider]: Raymond Lull's prayers and tears are receiving answer now in Tunis and Algiers. He was the first, but not the last missionary to the Moslems of Africa. Henry Martyn's life did not 'burn out for God;' it became a shining light for all Persia.[65]

Geraldine Taylor described the deep, powerful appeal that Samuel Zwemer's address held for Borden:

---

63. See *The Missionary Herald*, April 1906 (Boston: Beacon Press, 1906), pp. 164-166.

64. See Campbell, *William Borden* (1913), p. 10.

65. See page 224 of *Students and the Modern Missionary Crusade; Addresses Delivered Before the Fifth International Convention of the Student Volunteer Movement for Foreign Missions, Nashville, Tennessee, February 28–March 4, 1906*.

Among the [many fine] speakers, secretaries of [missionary] boards and visitors to the Convention, of whom there were hundreds, and the foreign missionaries representing twenty-six countries, one man stood out for Borden with a burning message: [Samuel Zwemer].[66]

And the most stirring line of all the things said by Zwemer was this:

> ... *it is the call of the Master. Let us answer with the shout: 'Oh, heart of Christ, lead on!'*[67]

William Borden heard that call, and rallied to it in his heart.

The Nashville Convention was transformative for Borden and his fellow collegians. Charlie Campbell described this season of finding purpose, and what it brought to Yale. 'Soon,' Campbell said—

> all the Yale men were back in New Haven, and hard at work making up for lost time. The conference made a very deep impression on the delegates from Yale. Many saw ... something of the world vision that Bill had gained in his trip around the world. Missionary activities in the college took on new life.
>
> The churches of New Haven ... were visited by groups of two or three ... delegates, [describing] the conference and its call to world evangelization. Bill, with two others, [went out to speak at] three of the New Haven churches.[68]

From these scenes of burgeoning hope, it is a somber thing to turn so quickly to the story of a great grief that came within weeks of Borden's return to Yale. By letter, he described a tragic loss that changed his world forever:

[Friday,] April 13, 1906

Father and Mother were east about a week ago, and had a fine visit with us. First, they went to Vassar, and heard the debate

---

66. See Taylor, *Borden of Yale* (1926), pp. 107-108.

67. ibid., p. 109.

68. See Campbell, *William Borden* (1913), pp. 9-11.

in which [my sister] Mary did very well. This pleased Father immensely.

Then they came on to Yale, and John and I had a nice visit with them.

It was the first time Father had visited either John or myself at school or college. After leaving us they went down to New York, got Mary and went to Lakewood ... Mary spent a day or two with them, and had a fine time ...

Back in Chicago, Father was perfectly well apparently, and had nice visits with most of his near relatives and friends. Saturday evening last he was taken sick; and on Sunday, became critically ill.

It was then we were summoned. Mary got here Monday evening, in time to see him, though he was unconscious. John and I arrived on Tuesday morning, three or four hours after he had passed away.[69]

Charlie Campbell witnessed much of this first-hand, and did what he could to comfort his friend. His memories bring home a sense of what Borden had to face in the days just after his father's passing: with all signs pointing to a massive cerebral hemorrhage, or stroke:

In the spring of 1906, Mr Borden died in Chicago. This was a very heavy loss for Bill, who had loved his father greatly.

This sad event also brought new responsibilities into his life. He was only eighteen and a half ... but bore the added cares with great patience.

Mrs Borden was [then] in poor health for a time, which added [much to] Bill's responsibilities. Quietly he assumed all such cares, and faithfully attended to them in addition to his own work at college.[70]

In his biography of Borden, Samuel Zwemer gave a portion of a letter that Borden wrote, touching further on this tragic loss—

---

69. See Taylor, *Borden of Yale* (1926), pp. 113-114.

70. See Campbell, *William Borden:* (1913), p. 11.

His father's death on April 10th [1906], deeply affected Borden [and] he wrote to a friend: *'I have had the lesson driven home repeatedly of the uncertainty of life, and the need for working while it is light. Two of my classmates have lost their fathers, another classmate died; and now father has been called away.*'[71]

In keeping with a cherished custom of the early 1900s, Borden wore a black armband for a year. It was, in its observance, a way to carry his father's memory with him. Nor would he ever forget all that his father had meant to him.

Amid the deep grief he felt, Borden's faith brought solace. The presence of caring friends and professors at Yale did much to help him in difficult days.

And thankfully, he had one very special event to look forward to and plan for, near the close of his first year of study in New Haven.

As Geraldine Taylor wrote:

> Borden's freshman year came to a [stirring] climax in the Yale Summer Conference that followed Commencement [at Yale in 1906].[72]
>
> [Unable to attend] the Student Conference at Northfield on account of its early date that year, they arranged for a gathering of their own under the leadership of Dr Henry Wright, availing themselves of the ground and buildings of the Hotchkiss School at Lakeville, Connecticut [in early July].
>
> One feature of the conference was a special course of training given to men who were to be leaders of voluntary groups for Bible study in the following year, for Borden's plan of small [groups for Bible study] was to be extended to all the classes.

---

71. See Zwemer, *William Whiting Borden* (1913), p. 77.

72. See page 426 of *The Record of Christian Work* magazine (June 1906) which lists the Northfield Student Conference for June 22–July 1. Also, Harry Beal, Yale Class of 1906, said: 'After attending the Yale Y.M.C.A. Conference at Hotchkiss School, I spent the rest of the summer of 1906 at my family's place on Oneida Lake, in Central New York.' See E. R. Embree, ed., *History of the Class of 1906: Yale College*, v. 2, (1911), p. 111.

A canvass had already been made, and out of Borden's class alone, *more than a hundred and fifty men* were reported as willing to take [part].

This meant the preparation of a large body of leaders, [some two dozen in all,] who were keen to get all they could from the full programme of the conference.[73] Half the substantial reporter's notebook Borden had with him in London [during his world tour of 1904 to 1905] is filled with jottings from this Lakeville Conference, showing how very much it meant to him.[74]

Borden's home correspondence also gives a near view of this transformative conference, and what it meant to him. His enthusiasm for it all was palpable:

[Tuesday,] July 3, 1906[75]

[Dear Mother,]

Whom do you suppose we had with us Sunday? S. D. Gordon![76]

Before breakfast, a few of us met in Henry Wright's room for prayer – our personal workers' group. Afterwards we met

---

73. Based on the Lakeville Conference photo given on page 132 of Taylor, *Borden of Yale* (1926), there are 23 Yale delegates shown, including Borden and Charles Soutter Campbell.

74. See Taylor, *Borden of Yale* (1926), p. 121. Italics added. Borden's great friend Kenneth Latourette states: 'During my senior year [i.e. 1905–1906, Borden's freshman year at Yale] a new plan of voluntary Bible study by undergraduates was projected. The basic principle was to have Bible groups led by classmates. This plan was to begin with the Class of 1909 [William Borden's class] ... In my final year, I was made Bible study secretary of Dwight Hall to supervise the entire structure. That year we had about a thousand undergraduates enrolled in the groups.'

75. It looks as though this Lakeville Y.M.C.A. Conference may well have lasted for a week. Borden was there on Sunday, July 1, and he was writing to his mother from Lakeville on Tuesday, July 3. The Yale conferees may have arrived at Lakeville the previous Friday or Saturday (June 29 or 30). He was clearly already there all day on Sunday, and the Yale conferees may have stayed until Friday or Saturday (July 6 or 7). This seems most likely.

76. *Quiet Talks About Jesus*, S. D. Gordon's most famous book, was published in 1906. His talks at the Yale Y.M.C.A. Conference at Hotchkiss were almost certainly taken from this book. And Borden's great friend at Camden, Maine, Captain Arey, said of S. D. Gordon and Borden: 'He lent me two books by [S. D.] Gordon, *Talks on Prayer* and *Talks on Power*.' See Taylor, *Borden of Yale* (1926), p. 162. This is the only time source materials to say Borden bestowed two gift books by the same author: showing the depth of his respect for S. D. Gordon.

with Mr Gordon. At 10 a.m. he gave us a talk on Power. It was wonderful. I will tell you more about it later. In the afternoon, down by the brook, he spoke on John 7:37-39 in his quiet way.

[As for] study on Student Summer Missions, Dr Wright is outlining for us ten studies on Traits of Manhood. We had 'Honesty' this morning, and it was splendid. I must get some boys together [for a similar study, when] I get back to Camden. I must close now, as I am to play [baseball] on The Hill team against the Grads. Until just a moment ago, I forgot that you were praying for me. The recollection has given me strength ...[77]

In his notebook, Borden had written after Sunday, July 1st's talk:

Say 'No' to self, 'Yes' to Jesus every time. A steep road – hard work? But every man, on this road, has One who walks with him in lock-step. His presence overtops everything that has been cut out ...

In every man's heart, there is a throne and a cross. If Christ is on the throne, self is on the cross; and if self, even a little bit, is on the throne, Jesus is on the cross in that man's heart ... If Jesus is on the throne, you will go where He wants you to go. Jesus on the throne glorifies any work or spot ...

If you are thirsty, and He is enthroned, *drink*. Drinking, the simplest act there is, means taking. 'He that believeth on Me, out of him shall flow rivers of living water. This spake He of the Spirit.' To 'believe' is to know, because of His Word. How shall I know ... I have power to meet temptation, to witness for Him? Believe His Word: it will come.

Lord Jesus, I take hands off, as far as my life is concerned. I put Thee on the throne in my heart. Change, cleanse, use me as Thou shalt choose. I take the full power of Thy Holy Spirit. I thank Thee.[78]

Borden's friend Charlie Campbell penned vivid recollections of the summer following Borden's first year at Yale. He was there to see it:

---

77. See Taylor, *Borden of Yale* (1926), pp. 121-122.

78. ibid., pp. 122-123.

The summer of freshman year was spent in Camden, Maine, where the Borden summer home is located. The house stands well up above the water, overlooking Penobscot Bay, with its many islands ...

Golf, tennis, fishing, swimming, boating and especially sailing the sloop, *Tsatsawassa* – all had their share in making the vacation a happy and healthy one. Bill enjoyed particularly a two or three days' cruise.

Once he sailed to Deer Island to pick up a classmate, and cruised with him from there to Bar Harbor. Coming by Mount Desert, an off-shore squall struck the boat, with all sail set, and threatened to tear out the mast. It was a sight to see Bill throwing every ounce of his truly unusual strength on the wheel in his endeavor to keep the boat pointing far enough off-shore.

The result of all this was that the boat heeled over so far that his classmate, who was trying to get the jib down, went up to his waist in water.

[Yet] even in this vacation time, following ... freshman year, Bill showed a sense of balance that was further evidence of unusual maturity.

He had decided to anticipate a French course, and stuck to the summer work this necessitated with a perseverance that all who had tried such summer work can appreciate.

Nor did Bill take a holiday [at Camden in] work for Christ. He spoke at open-air Y.M.C.A. services, and at Christian Endeavor and other church meetings.

He told the drunken gardener [who tended his family's cottage] about Christ, and had the joy of seeing the man finding peace and respectability in Him. Bill's faith was deepened [when he] returned from his vacation ...[79]

Looking ahead to his sophomore year at Yale, Borden knew he'd much to be thankful for: he had wealth in the gift of friends, a wise, caring academic mentor in Dr Henry Wright, and memories of many Yale classmates who sought the hope of heaven. Faith had brought these good things near.

---

79. See Campbell, *William Borden* (1913), pp. 11-12.

CHAPTER 5

The City's New Rescue Mission

William Whiting Borden of Chicago, who recently completed
his course at Yale, leaves behind him in New Haven a well
established [rescue mission] costing upward of $20,000. This,
so far as known, is the only instance of an undergraduate of
any college who ever established a project of the kind and
conducted it himself ...

[Yale Hope Mission] has become a headquarters for
homeless men ... no charge has ever been made for
either food or lodging ...[1]

– page three of *The Chicago Tribune*,
Tuesday, July 20, 1909

He would tell you to hope again; tell you of the God who'd
made the universe and held you in the hollow of His hand, and
could help you, if you'd only ask. That's the way he talked ... I
went forward and kneeled down, and Bill came and kneeled
down beside me, and he explained as much as he could the
power of Jesus Christ, and how it was only
Him who could help me ...

About two years after I was converted, I was re-married right
in this building, right up-stairs. [Bill] knew I was going to
be married. He met my wife and family – seemed tickled to

---

1. See 'Project of William Whiting Borden A Success,' on page 3 of the Tuesday,
July 20, 1909 edition of *The Chicago Tribune*. $20,000 in 1907, the year the Yale Hope
Mission was founded, would now be worth $500,000 dollars.

death, too, to meet 'em. We've got a home now in Yalesville,
Connecticut, and a big garden, plenty of land, lots of chickens,
and a piano in the house: makes quite a change from when I
first came to the Mission, drunk, with
no prospects but whiskey![2]

– 'Jack' Clark (1913)

The building so many knew as Yale Hope Mission, once 'situated
on Court Street, about half a mile from the Yale campus,' wrought
a transformation for good in tens of thousands of lives.[3] And
William Borden was at the center of it all.

That story, the story of the founding of Yale Hope Mission,
went west, far across America to the *Mariposa Gazette*, the
newspaper of the Mariposa Yosemite region of California. And it
was told alongside a story of the Wright Brothers.

This speaks to the kind of celebrity status William Borden
knew in his lifetime. He hadn't sought it, but word of what he
and several peers from Yale had accomplished in creating the Yale
Hope Mission captured the public's attention.

All were young men of privilege; but faith had prompted them
to care for the downtrodden. Tales of dissolute college life, and
the squandering of family fortunes were common enough. Many
people had heard of such things.

But the story of a young man of great fortune, parting with
funds equivalent to half a million dollars today to help the
homeless, and those with lives ravaged by drunkenness – that
was something one didn't hear about every day.

Newspapers and magazines across the country carried the
story.

～ ～ ～

---

2. See Taylor, *Borden of Yale* (1926), pp. 152-153. Samuel Zwemer writes that this
was the testimony of 'Jack' Clark, as 'recorded by a stenographer.' See Zwemer, *William
Borden* (1913), pp. 99-100.

3. See 'Project of William Whiting Borden A Success,' on page 3 of the Tuesday,
July 20, 1909 edition of *The Chicago Tribune*.

Borden was always quick to take on a project that he knew first-hand to be a deserving one. So, when he heard from John Magee, his friend at Yale, about the idea for creating a rescue mission in New Haven, he warmed to the idea and gave it his full support. It was the kind of project that he thought would do Yale collegians, as well as the destitute, a world of good. A faith endeavor to help the less fortunate could be a godsend: to bring heaven's hope to the homeless and collegians alike.

Geraldine Taylor set the scene when Borden and Magee first spoke together about the project that would become Yale Hope Mission:

> It was on [Borden's] nineteenth birthday, the first of November [1906], that John Magee, the graduate Secretary of the Y.M.C.A., stopped him in Dwight Hall and asked for a few minutes' conversation. There were matters in which he needed help, that he felt Borden could give.
>
> New Haven, a seaport town midway between New York and Boston, was a place where vagrants of all sorts were apt to congregate. Work was to be had on the docks, and it was a half-way house for tramps and hoboes moving from one city to the other. It was also the location of the county jail, from which prisoners were constantly being discharged: with no one to give them a helping hand. For while drinking saloons and infamous resorts were to be found in abundance, there was no Rescue Mission with its doors always open to those who needed [help].
>
> This state of things appealed to John Magee from a double point of view. He saw the need of the down-and-out; he saw also the possible influence of such a mission upon the college community, as a witness to the living, saving power of Christ. And he believed Borden would see and feel it too.[4]

Borden described it all in a letter packed full of news to his mother:

---

4. See Taylor, *Borden of Yale* (1926), pp. 128-129.

[Thursday,] November 1, 1906

Dear Mother ...

John Magee is trying his best to do just what we have wanted done – to develop the evangelistic element and spirit here at Yale ...

The present head of the McAuley Mission in New York is a college graduate who went down, down, and was converted about two years ago, Edward C. Mercer. They had him at Princeton recently, and John has been enquiring to see how it went down there. He found that it was fine, and he is going to invite him here to speak at Dwight [Hall].

That's just what I've been hoping for, and I think you have too. John is really a corker; and is doing a lot. [We spoke today] about the need for a good City Mission here in New Haven ...

The plan is to get a suitable building in the downtown district and have a real Rescue Mission, run by a man from Water Street, or some such place, and a few picked men from the University ... It would be great – just the thing to take a few sceptics ... and let them see the spirit of God really at work, regenerating men.[5]

One photo gives a glimpse of Borden's involvement with Yale Hope Mission. An early caption for this photo states that it was 'a friend's snapshot' of Borden 'in front of the Yale Hope Mission, which he helped to found and maintain while a student at Yale. He also left funds to provide for its future.'[6]

The caption conveys key information about Borden and Yale Hope Mission, but the photograph itself tells us still more: for it tells a story all on its own.

Another item we see in this snapshot of Borden is a more somber token: a black armband of mourning, worn around his upper left arm. From seeing this, we know that a year had not as yet elapsed since the death of Borden's father in April 1906. Armbands such as these were usually worn for a year. Given Borden's lack of winter

---

5. ibid., pp. 130-131.

6. Rev. Charles R. Erdman, D.D., *William Whiting Borden: An Ideal Missionary Volunteer* (New York: Funk & Wagnalls, 1913), p. 15.

attire, and the fact Borden didn't discuss creating the Yale Hope Mission for the first time until November 1st, 1906, we may surmise that this photo was taken in early spring 1907, probably near the end of March.[7] This would mean he was nineteen years old when the snapshot was taken.

Nineteen! and he was beginning the considerable challenge of financing and supervising the creation of a substantial inner-city rescue mission. All the while, his grades didn't suffer (academically, he was Phi Beta Kappa),

Borden outside Yale Hope Mission, the building he purchased to house an inner-city rescue mission for the destitute in New Haven, where Yale students served and volunteered (from the author's 1st British edition copy of *Borden of Yale*, 1926).

and he was active in sports, most notably rowing for his Class Crew, which won first place among the class crews at Yale in the fall of 1907. Borden rowed number four for his team.[8]

Two more things should be noted about the snapshot photo of Borden: the first is the sign for the mission just above its entryway.

7. See also page 482 of the February 13, 1907 issue of *The Yale Alumni Weekly*: 'John Borden was married on February 2 to Miss Ellen Waller, in the Fourth Presbyterian Church, Chicago, Ill. Edwin Corning, '06, was best man and W. F. Wallace, '03, A. E. Hamill, '05, George Low, '06, P. T. White, '06, A. B. Gregory, '06, and William Borden, '09, were ushers.' It is important to include this family event in the timeline of William Borden's life. In 1928, John and Ellen Borden's daughter (also named Ellen) married Adlai Stevenson, the Democratic Party nominee for President in 1952 and 1956. See 'Mrs Ellen Stevenson, Ex-Wife of Presidential Candidate, Dies,' in the July 29, 1972 issue of *The New York Times*, which states that Ellen Stevenson's father 'was John Borden, a millionaire oil man, an explorer, and an adventurer, and her grandfather was William B. Borden, who made a rich gold strike in Colorado.'

8. See Taylor, *Borden of Yale* (1926), 143n.

The word 'Yale' is centered on the sign, but underneath it, the words 'Hope Mission' are arched in such a way as to create the impression of an upward lift.

This was not unintentional. Visually, the sign was meant to tell all passers-by that here was a place that sought to lift people up. It conveyed the idea of welcome: for the words 'Hope Mission' were framed like arms open wide.

Last of all, Borden's travelling suitcase is set down on the steps beside him as he stopped for this photograph. With decorative stickers on its outside boards, it gives the impression of a young man who has places yet to go on his journey.

And that was very true.

Sometimes, statistics can do much to help bring a worthy endeavor to life. So far as Yale Hope Mission is concerned, a card from the mission titled 'One Year's Service to Needy Men' tells an important story.[9]

It's a chart, with one sentence of prose beneath it. 'Yale Hope Mission', it is stated there, 'aims to re-build human lives by the power of the Gospel.'

And just above this, the following chart is given—

Attendance at Gospel services 14,602

Meals that are meals 17,639

Clean, warm dormitory beds 8,592

Garments [provided] 610

Just one year, and thousands of lives helped for the better. The gospel was a message of hope for them. Borden's personal philanthropy and involvement lasted from 1907 till his departure for Egypt as a China Inland Missionary in late 1912.

---

9. This Yale Hope Mission Card is posted online at: https://www2.wheaton.edu/bgc/archives/treasure/tr99/rescuetalka.htm

If one conservatively places the number of those helped at 10,000 per year, some 50,000 people were helped through Yale Hope Mission during his lifetime.[10]

A remarkable thing altogether.

Here the story of one Yale student who knew Yale Hope Mission well should be told. His name was Kenney MacLeish, the brother of poet Archibald MacLeish. *The Yale Alumni Weekly* writes movingly of his 'interest in the work of Yale Hope Mission,'[11] still later, his bravery as a pilot during World War I. During valiant service, Lieutenant Kenney MacLeish was killed in action in 1918.

And what of William Borden himself?

An exterior view of Yale Hope Mission (from *The Interior* magazine, May 1913).

On January 10, 1908, he wrote his mother a letter saying that he'd given the gospel call at the close of a recent mission service – or the invitation to receive Christ as Savior. 'About eight men came forward,' Borden wrote, 'and I conducted things as best I could. I feel very hopeful about some [of the men,] and that we've got a most important work on our hands.'[12]

---

10. The statistics above ring true. In 1909, while William Borden was at Yale, 'about 12,000 men' heard the gospel preached at Yale Hope Mission; 846 'made an open confession of sin, by coming forward to prayer'; 3,848 were 'sheltered and fed,' and much clothing given to the needy, with employment found 'for a number who are today earning an honest living.' See Zwemer, *William Whiting Borden* (1913), p. 98.

11. See the January 31, 1919 issue of The *Yale Alumni Weekly*, p. 478.

12. See Taylor, *Borden of Yale* (1926), p. 141.

What this work entailed, day to day, was described in the May 1914 number of *The Yale Sheffield Monthly*. The building Borden had purchased and outfitted for Yale Hope Mission was called 'Hotel Martin,' named for one fondly remembered elderly man who was helped in the early days of the mission.

The Hotel Martin was a building with twenty-eight rooms. It directly adjoined the congregation room of the Mission, where nightly services were held. As stated, the prime object of the Yale Hope Mission was to 'provide food and lodging for the destitute men who come to the meetings ... a place where a man may stay until he can find employment, and where he will receive sufficient moral support to place him on his feet.'[13]

In the feature for the Yale Sheffield Monthly, we learn more of 'the manner in which the Hotel Martin received its name.'

Near to the first days of Yale Hope Mission—

> an old convert ... began coming to [the Mission, at 55] Court Street because he [sought] a place where he could hear religious services. [He] made a paltry living by mending umbrellas, and doing other small jobs. He was a very lovable old character, and the boys soon obtained a position for him on the [Yale] Campus. To them he was always known as 'Daddy Martin.' When he died, at ... eighty-seven, the Mission Hotel was named in his memory.[14]

Yale Hope Mission had a practical, vocational side to its offering of ministry services. In connection with the Hotel Martin was a well-outfitted workshop where 'upholstering, chair-caning, and general repairing' were done. And there was more, as *The Yale Sheffield Monthly* stated:

> work is provided for a number of men in the hotel itself, and, through the kind co-operation of some of the New Haven residents ... men are sent out to do odd jobs ... beating rugs,

---

13. See *The Yale Sheffield Monthly*, May 1914 (New Haven: Yale University Press, 1914), pp. 352-353.

14. ibid., pp. 352-353.

cleaning yards, sweeping stoops, and so forth ... People have sent furniture to be repaired, and chairs to be re-caned. As an illustration of the diligence and skill with which these men work after they have begun their reformation, two men have refinished the walls of the entire building ...[15]

As for 'Yale men,' who Borden and Magee hoped might benefit spiritually, one magazine account brings this side of the Yale Hope Mission story to life. And it is best to hear this story just as it was related originally: in a heartfelt and revealing letter from April 1916. 'One Yale man,' the article began:

wrote recently to the Superintendent [of the Yale Hope Mission]:

My dear Mr and Mrs William Ellis,

You have asked me to tell you what the mission has meant to me. Most gladly will I do it. Last fall, more from a matter of curiosity than anything else, I came to the Mission with Dr Robinson ... To this time I had absolutely no faith in God or Jesus Christ and ... very little faith in the Bible ... Sophomore year, I was a pure atheist ... There was so much selfishness and conceit in me ... I was unhappy most of the time.

The meeting at the Mission opened my eyes.

After attending several meetings, I saw that Jesus Christ could work miracles in men's lives. I began to get interested in the men, trying to help them get a new start, and firm hold on Christ.

This work at the Mission made me a Christian.

You may remember that after these few meetings, when I became convinced that what I needed more than anything else was Jesus Christ as my Savior, I consented to lead a meeting. I led several later on.

This work at the Mission has been the biggest joy of my college career. My only regret is that I did not have more time, [or] did not know of it earlier.

---

15. ibid., pp. 352-353.

More than anything else the Yale Hope Mission has determined my life work. I had [chosen a] college course in preparation for law. A few months ago I decided to go into the ministry; and now ... Y.M.C.A. work in foreign fields.

The only way I can thank you, and Mrs Ellis, and the Mission men, is by constantly remembering you in my prayers.[16]

The ministry William Borden funded and helped establish when he was nineteen became something remarkable in American collegiate life. We speak of service projects today. Yale Hope Mission blazed a trail for these types of endeavors. What's more, the Mission lived on past Borden's lifetime – for at least some forty years after it was founded.[17]

We learn of this from Borden's great friend, Kenneth Latourette,[18] who wrote to writer and researcher Bernard DeRemer in 1956:

[Monday,] October 8, 1956

Dear Mr DeRemer—

William Borden was one of my dearest friends, and our student days at Yale coincided.

I am glad to say that the Yale Hope Mission is continuing as a rescue mission. The history is briefly as follows.

The idea originated with my classmate, John G. Magee, who after his graduation from Yale College in 1906 remained for two

---

16. See *The Missionary Review of the World* magazine, April 1916, pp. 284-285.

17. K. S. Latourette to B. R. DeRemer, 8 October 1956, a letter housed in the Archives of Moody Bible Institute. NOTE: At the close of his letter Dr Latourette told Bernard DeRemer: 'In looking over your excellent article on William Borden, I found what seemed to be a mistake. I distinctly remember that William denied being related to the Borden milk people. His father's father was founder of the fortune, and made it through investments in Chicago real estate after the Great Fire of the 1870s.'

Three months later, DeRemer received double confirmation of this when Rev. W. Glyn Evans, a great friend of the Borden family, who had heard directly from Borden's elderly aunt (his mother's surviving sister, then still living) said 'William was **not** of the milk people. His father was a wealthy Chicago lawyer.' W. G. Evans to R. DeRemer, January 16, 1957, a letter housed in the Archives of Moody Bible Institute.

18. 'For many years,' said Latourette, 'I was on the Board of Yale Hope Mission [and] briefly its Chairman.' See *Beyond the Ranges* (1967), p. 84.

years as a graduate secretary of the Yale Y.M.C.A., usually known as Dwight Hall.

From a wealthy and socially prominent family in Pittsburgh, John Magee was at the same time a humble and sincere Christian, and later spent many years as a missionary in China.

While in Dwight Hall he had the conviction borne in on him that there should be a rescue mission in New Haven, where Yale students could see the Gospel at work in changing broken lives, and where they could share in the work. He had very little money of his own and approached William Borden, who at that time was heir to a part of his father's estate.

William gladly provided the money for the purchase of a building ...

I seem to remember that some [foreign] visitor at Yale said that what impressed him most was seeing [William,] this wealthy undergraduate, with his arm around a 'down-and-outer,' kneeling with him as [he] sought forgiveness and prayed the prayer of the publican: ['God be merciful to me, a sinner'] ...

Through the years, there has been an undergraduate committee that has fulfilled the dream of John Magee and William Borden of helping in the Mission by assisting in the services, and in other ways.

The Mission's chief service has been to alcoholics, and at the present time is cooperating with the state commission on alcoholism.

That does not mean that it is any less a rescue mission, or that its purpose has in any way changed. Nightly services are held every day in the week and efforts are made in a variety of ways, all of them subsidiary to the Gospel, for the rehabilitation of men, [from] what is commonly known as skid row ...
With every good wish,

Faithfully yours,

K. S. Latourette

There is no better way to close a chapter about Yale Hope Mission than this letter. Forty-three years after Borden's passing, his close friend Kenneth Latourette penned words to honor their friendship, telling the story of a pioneering collegiate ministry. For Yale Hope Mission *had* made history, which was conveyed in the title phrase of an article that ran in *The Continent* magazine for May 1913.

Those Yale Boys 'Started Something.'[19]

---

19. See *The Continent* magazine, May 8, 1913, (Chicago: McCormick Publishing Co., 1913), p. 635.

CHAPTER 6

Final Years at Yale

Elected to the presidency of Phi Beta Kappa, [Bill]
received the highest scholarship honour in Yale. There
was power written all over him. You either followed
him, or you let him alone ... I can vouch that he was the
strongest religious force in our class at Yale.[1]
– Maxwell Parry, 2nd Lieutenant, 147th Aero Squadron,
Killed in Action Over France, July 8, 1918

The secret of his life lies in his relation to Christ. He
came to a time of choice, and [wished] that Christ might
have the chief place in his life.

Ever after, there was an assurance about his every act that
comes only to those who give themselves unreservedly to
Christ Jesus. The center being right, the outreaching of his life
rang true ... Bill's life seemed to flow out with quiet power: into
the hearts and lives of many, wherever he went.[2]
– Charles Soutter Campbell

Thinking of Yale, and the final years of his time there, Borden
had written to Henry Weston Frost: 'my attachment for it is so
great.'[3] There were more than a few reasons why, and that is the
focus of this chapter.

---

1. See Taylor, *Borden of Yale* (1926), p. 149.

2. See Campbell, *William Borden* (1913), p. 29.

3. A letter from Borden to H. W. Frost, Sunday, January 17, 1909, housed at The
Billy Graham Center, Wheaton College.

One facet of his life at Yale during this time was a renewed and concentrated focus on academics following his first year. As Geraldine Taylor said:

> At the close of freshman year, Borden had discovered that his marks were not up to Phi Beta Kappa standard; and he decided to change his habits of study. Previously, he had gone on the method of studying up for each recitation, just before it came. Now he set himself to prepare a day ahead, and never retired for the night without … his preparation completed for the following day.
>
> 'It was a hard method to live up to,' commented his friend Campbell, 'and showed his strength of will. Think of what it meant on Saturday to get all Monday's work out of hand. For Bill never studied on Sunday.
>
> He would work till eleven or eleven-thirty at night, but not later.
>
> Then he could sleep quietly; and be ready for whatever calls upon his time might come. It meant much in his mental [preparedness]; and when it came to examinations.'[4]

As for where Borden lived on campus during his sophomore year, he chose a third floor room in the 'Hutchinson' on Crown Street.[5] He also resumed his keen determination to achieve a place on Yale's football team, but following an urgent request from his mother, he gave this goal up.[6]

The reason for it all was telling; and had much to do with the conditions of play chronicled in a recent *Washington Post* article tracing the history of collegiate football in America. During William Borden's time at Yale:

> Football … was more akin to rugby … Forward passes were not allowed, leading to short lateral tosses, large scrums of players

---

4. See Taylor, *Borden of Yale* (1926), p. 131.

5. See Zwemer, *William Whiting Borden* (1913), p. 85; and Campbell, *William Whiting Borden* (1913), p. 12.

6. See Campbell, *William Borden* (1913), p. 12.

[going] for the ball, and vicious hits ... The nation was aghast at the number of young men who died or were seriously injured playing the game [including] the November 1905 death of Union College halfback Harold Moore, who died of a cerebral hemorrhage after being kicked in the head while trying to tackle a New York University player.

[And one] cartoon in *The Cincinnati Commercial Tribune* showed the Grim Reaper atop a goal post.[7]

Yet the game Borden knew was still highly popular, if also the subject of controversy. As *The Smithsonian* magazine has noted:

By 1905, college football was all the rage, attracting tens of thousands of fans to games at a time when major-league baseball teams often attracted only 3,000 – and pro football was still more than a decade away.

But it was also an increasingly violent and deadly passion.

There were eighteen fatalities nationwide that year, including three college players (the rest were high-school athletes), and President Theodore Roosevelt, whose son was on the freshmen team at Harvard University, made it clear he wanted reforms, amid calls by some to abolish the college game.[8]

In time, reforms were made, with rules designed to curb the game's violence. But given the widely reported and lurid details above, it's little wonder Mary Borden asked her son to step away from this sport. He didn't wish to; but since his father had passed away only a few months earlier, he knew she'd no need of added worry, if he could do something to alleviate it.

Soon, another pressing matter occupied Borden's thoughts: the question of secret societies in college. For something within

---

7. Katie Zezima, 'How Teddy Roosevelt helped save football' an online article from *The Washington Post*, posted on May 29, 2014.

8. Jim Morrison, 'The Early History of Football's Forward Pass,' an article posted by Smithsonian.com on December 28, 2010.

him balked at the idea of secret, selective, or exclusionary groups.

There was another complication. His uncle H. A. Worcester had been one of the founders of the 'Wolf's Head' society, of which his elder brother John was also a recent member.[9] Should he forsake joining any such society, he would be flying in the face of prominent family tradition. Given that heritage, as Borden's friend Kenneth Latourette said, '[Bill] could have had anything here that he wanted.'[10] To say no to the many invitations that were surely forthcoming would give offense, since collegial regard was the intent of those who sought him out. Last of all, there was the specter of opprobrium to fall on him for 'spurning,' in many eyes, something that had become a rather hallowed Yale tradition.

Borden's friend Charlie Campbell had a near view of this, and remembered:

> How bitter the mental struggle was, any Yale man can picture …
>
> Bill occupied a position of real prominence, which … would have made him an early choice for a fraternity. His brother and uncle had both been fraternity and senior society men, so Bill had a [family tradition] which would naturally attract him to the fraternities. Further than this, his close friends in college, many of them earnest Christian men, were expecting to accept fraternity election should this be offered them.[11]

In short, Borden's decision to withhold any involvement in fraternities and societies would be little understood, and run the great risk of offending many. But this idea of secret and selective, or exclusionary groups – it all seemed so at odds with a Christian faith that for him was a commitment of the highest allegiance. He took the idea of an oath very seriously, and 'pledging' to a secret

---

9. See Taylor, *Borden of Yale* (1926), p. 125.

10. ibid., p. 125.

11. See Campbell, *William Borden* (1913), p. 13.

society was something he just couldn't bring himself to do. No one relished friendship and fellowship more than he did; but it was a step he wouldn't take.

How much this time of wrestling cost him was something his mother vividly remembered. 'The decision,' she wrote—

> not to join any secret society cost him many an anxious hour. This I know well, for I was present at the time. Of course, a Senior secret society at Yale is one of the big honors. [Dr] Henry Wright went over all this with William ...[12]

After much prayer, consultation, and reflection, Borden decided to say yes to something Dr Wright had asked him to consider: 'would [he] accept election to the Elihu Club ... a non-secret organization?' This he thought he could do.[13]

Though many did not understand Borden's resolve in all this, very likely his uncle and elder brother John most of all, something unforeseen and very welcome came of Borden's decision over time.

Some watching all this closely at Yale wondered if his decision 'not to go into a secret society would affect his influence at College.' One classmate stated that 'his influence would be absolutely ruined by such a step.'[14]

But Borden's mother heard from a very reputable source only 'a few months after, that far from hurting [William's] influence, it had made it stronger.'[15]

~ ~ ~

A part of Borden's time at Yale that brought unalloyed pleasure, and a deep sense of purpose, came with the welcome news that 'shortly before the time of the first fraternity elections,' he had been elected one of the four class deacons for the Class

---

12. See Zwemer, *William Whiting Borden* (1913), p. 82.

13. ibid., p. 82.

14. ibid., p. 82.

15. ibid., p. 82.

of 1909. It was something his friend Charlie Campbell long remembered.

Borden, at right, with his fellow Class Deacons at Yale (from the author's 1st British edition copy of *Borden of Yale*, 1926).

'Bill,' he said—

became increasingly earnest in the work of the [Y.M.C.A. and Dwight Hall]. All this time, there were regular studies, and daily times of [athletics]. Bill was not a one-sided man at all ...

Body, mind, and spirit came to their own in his well-rounded character.

Too often, the important claims of the spirit are ignored, and this always results in real narrowness. In spite of this, there are many who seem to be content to live their lives without developing qualities of heart and soul, which are, after all, the most important.[16]

In keeping with this, and in mid-October 1907, Borden told his mother about one special visitor to the Yale campus—

the Lord Bishop of London was with us today ...

16. See Campbell, *William Borden* (1913), pp. 14-15. Selection edited.

In the morning Woolsey Hall,[17] seating 2,800, was packed, and his sermon was fine, as many said – 'the best they'd heard at Yale,' and I agreed.

Well, you should have seen the crowd turn out in the evening, students, only ... voluntarily. Dwight Hall was packed to overflowing, there being 500 ...

[Many] had never been to a service before, fellows known as drunkards and fast [living] men. The secret of it all was that [Bishop Ingram] preached the Gospel in a remarkable way (to Yale men,) making it personal and practical.[18]

The Churchman magazine gave a detailed report on this important visit:

Oct. 13 [1907]. Bishop Ingram spoke to the undergraduates in Woolsey Hall. The attendance was said to establish a record for a religious gathering at Yale and, in deference to the visitor, for the first time probably since the Revolutionary War, a prayer was offered for the King of England.

The four essentials to a useful life at Yale, the bishop said, were [1] belief in God, [2] moral soundness, [3] Church spirit and [4] the passing along to others of the benefits of an education.

'Boys come up here,' he said, 'steady in ... faith, and accustomed to say their prayers. [Yet,] when they come to the university, their whole ideas become chaotic. They find men who don't believe in the old religion, nor in the old ideas of morality. I have found men who never did a badly wrong thing in their lives, who have had their character sapped by the influences of a university. [We need the best facets] of a university [to send] boys out [as] strong men for life' ...

[To close,] Bishop Ingram repeated ... counsels he had given at Harvard: that during vacations they should go down into the slums and work, as many of the young men from Oxford did.[19]

---

17. 'The Rt. Rev. Arthur Foley Wilmington Ingram, Lord Bishop of London, addressed the University service in Woolsey Hall, on Sunday, Oct. 13.' See page 90 of the November 1907 issue of *The Yale Sheffield Monthly* magazine.

18. See Zwemer, *William Whiting Borden* (1913), p. 89.

19. See *The Churchman* magazine, October 19, 1907, (New York: The Churchman Co., 1907), p. 580.

In this address, the Bishop of London took time to commend the very kind of work Borden and John Magee had begun with Yale Hope Mission. Little wonder, then, that Borden was thrilled to hear reflections that lent such a sense of confirmation for what he and John Magee had undertaken.

Meantime, Borden's circle of friends continued to grow, and deepen.

One Yale friendship that dates from this time was with Chengting T. Wang, later the Deputy Speaker of the Chinese National Assembly at Peking, and China's Ambassador to America. Many things about Borden stood out for C. T. Wang:[20]

> At Yale, we knew him as Bill, and he was much liked by his fellow students. When I was leaving the States for my homeland [in 1911], I had a long visit with him [about] mission work in general ... Bill was particularly interested in the Mohammedan [regions] of my people.
>
> I had two years' fellowship with Bill [at Yale], in which time I came to know him quite well. He was a man of great force of character ...
>
> *His intellectual equipment, coupled with his single-hearted purpose, would have certainly made profound impressions had he been permitted to carry on Christian work in China ...*
>
> That he wanted to strike out a new path in his mission work stamped Bill as a man of initiativeness, and originality. He used to tell me that he wanted to go where other missionaries had not been, [and] there was no missionary who had definitely prepared himself for work among the Mohammedans in China.[21]

---

20. C. T. Wang (1882–1961), Yale, Class of 1910, became a diplomat in the Republic of China. In January 1912, Wang was elected a member of the Provisional Legislature of the new Chinese Republic, and chosen its Deputy Speaker. He was China's Ambassador to America from 1936 to 1938. In February 1938, he hosted a party at the Chinese Embassy in Washington attended by his Yale classmate Henry Roe Cloud (the first self-identified Native American to graduate from Yale). This was a reunion of two friends who treasured William Borden's memory. See also the Yale University account of Wang and Roe Cloud's visit at: http://campuspress.yale.edu/mssa/party-diplomacy-the-ravi-d-goel-collection-on-henry-roe-cloud/

21. See Zwemer, *William Whiting Borden* (1913), p. 92-93. Italics added.

Borden was also a much-valued friend of Henry Roe Cloud, 'a member of the Winnebago Nation of Nebraska,' and a graduate of Yale, Class of 1910.[22]

After college, Roe Cloud was 'a prominent educator and national advocate for Native American people.'[23] Recalling Borden, he spoke with fond regard:

> William [wished to devote] his life to missionary work among the Mohammedan Chinese ... He was [a fellow] member of the Elihu Club, and a close friend of mine ... He consecrated his life, his wealth, and his all to God's service, [advising] me on many of the important steps I took at college.[24]

As for Borden's choice of a roommate and where to room on campus for his junior year, he took a room 'in White Hall on Berkley Oval, just off the old college campus.' Malcolm Burt 'Mac' Vilas of Cleveland was his roommate,[25] a friend 'of fine character, who had taken a positive Christian stand at the Lakeville Conference at the close of freshman year.'[26]

Their mutual friend Charlie Campbell had vivid memories of dormitory life as it was then. Next door to 'Bill and Mac,' Campbell said:

> I lived with Louis G. Audette ... and what times we did have! Every now and then we would [start] a big rough-house. We would nag at Bill until we had him roused, and then, *something*

---

22. See the essay, 'Henry Roe Cloud,' by the Yale Group for the Study of Native America at: https://ygsna.sites.yale.edu/henry-roe-cloud

23. See Yale's online biography at: https://nacc.yalecollege.yale.edu/student-groups/anaay/henry-roe-cloud-conference

24. See D. W. Messer, *Henry Roe Cloud* (Lanham: Hamilton Books, 2010), p. 89.

25. 'At the beginning of junior year [Bill] roomed ... in White Hall,' see Campbell, *William Borden* (1913), p. 15. 'When college opened for his senior year, Mrs Borden took a house in New Haven for the winter. Bill ... lived again on The Oval [Berkley Oval],' see Campbell, *William Borden* (1913), p. 17.

26. See Taylor, *Borden of Yale* (1926), p. 138. 'The suite occupied by Borden and Vilas, a study and two bedrooms, was on the fourth floor of White Hall (number 380) [looking out toward] Yale gymnasium and West Rock.'

would be doing! Around that room he would go like a tornado, crushing all opposition.

It was a sight to see him really roused. He was a fellow of unusual physical strength, and knew how to use it ...

We used to have many a tussle, but he was altogether too strong for the average man; and with his knowledge of wrestling, was more than a match for any of us. We would laugh at him because of his strength, and call him a 'brute.'

[In a far different vein,] activities in religious work [flourished] ...

There were the Bible groups – the mission study classes, the daily prayer groups, the Wednesday evening Bible classes, the Volunteer Band meetings—and the Yale Hope Mission—all of which occupied Bill's time.

[Yale Hope Mission] was specially absorbing for Bill ... I believe he took one night a week at the Mission, conducting the service [there].[27]

'One upon another,' Geraldine Taylor had written, 'even in junior year, responsibilities came crowding upon [Borden].' As she explained:

The Student Missionary Union of Colleges in the Connecticut Valley held its annual conference at New Haven that fall, and Borden was chairman at all the meetings. Months of preparation [were needed], and all the responsibility for speakers and arrangements had been on his shoulders.

Stephen W. Ryder, a classmate who helped [Borden], wrote:

As a stenographer and typewriter, I often took his dictation of letters to his friends. I specially remember quite an extensive correspondence which devolved upon him as chairman of the Connecticut Valley Student Missionary Conference. His apologies, his thoughtful explanations and general care to avoid misunderstandings, his desire to please, encourage, and inspire others often impressed me ... There was always frankness and sincerity in his letters.[28]

---

27. ibid., pp. 138-139. Italics added.

28. ibid., pp. 141-142.

Borden's friend John Magee, with whom he had worked to create Yale Hope Mission, also spoke highly of Borden's administrative gifts in relation to the Student Missionary Union of Colleges conference. He had true ability, as Magee saw it:

> *Bill was busy enough, with all he was doing in college, to take the time of any ordinary man.* But [it seemed he had] little difficulty running this Conference, [despite the] amount of work connected with it, of which I had had experience.
>
> It was held in New Haven that year (1908) and I remember hearing a number of people remark on Bill's ability as a presiding officer.
>
> He was a regular John R. Mott, and had everything at his fingers' ends, everybody knowing just what meetings were to be held, and where, through his [thoroughness and clarity]. All [letters] beforehand, tentative programmes, bills, etc., were [so] orderly … that he never had to waste time looking for anything.[29]

Borden's work for the Student Missionary Union of Colleges conference had been a considerable undertaking, but still more responsibilities came when he was elected to the Senior Council of his class at Yale. This entailed hours of work with college faculty, and many duties as a member of the Senior Class Book Committee.

As one of Borden's fellow class-deacons remembered:

> Bill was keenly interested in doing his full share of drudgery for the good of his class. I remember going into his room frequently when he was [tallying] class-statistics. He spent hours, collecting [the] votes for individual preferences. Often he would pause for a rest, and joke about some bright answer to a question.[30]

Borden's own standing, in a class of three hundred, when the Class Book for 1909 was published, ran as follows: third place

---

29. ibid., p. 142. Italics added.
30. ibid., p. 144.

in the vote for 'the hardest worker,' fourth among 'the most energetic,' ninth among 'the most to be admired,' and seventh in the vote for 'the one who had done most for Yale.'[31]

Beyond this, a sense of Borden in his true element comes in words Kenneth Latourette wrote. Vividly, he remembered Borden's deep, abiding commitment to missionary service. A naturalness in this regard impressed Latourette most:

> The outstanding thing in [my] memory of Bill is his missionary motive.
>
> He was so sane and unpretending about it ... yet it was so completely a part of his life. The memory of it, and his courage to carry the gospel to unreached fields is a constant rebuke and inspiration to me.
>
> He had the Pauline spirit, [and had no wish] 'to build on another man's foundation.' [Such resolve had] no small part, I am sure, in bringing *the largest [Mission] Volunteer Band in Yale's history* to the days of his college life.[32]

Latourette also recalled 'the secret of the power' that was woven in the fabric of Borden's Christian life. There was a vibrancy to his faith: no sham, no pretence. Just a young man who knew how to be a friend; and a friend who knew how to love God from the heart. 'How easy Bill was to pray with!' Latourette said:

> He was a jolly fellow, loved a rough-house, delighted to get hold of a man and crack his ribs! He could be jolly with the rest, and when the crowd was gone, it would be just as natural for him to say,
>
> 'Come [over,] and let us have prayer together.'
>
> There was no sense of [anything unusual in] it. I remember very vividly—how could one ever forget—those times of prayer, when just the two of us would kneel down and take to God some of the problems we were facing.

---

31. ibid., p. 144.
32. ibid., pp. 144-145. Italics added.

Bill was so simple in his prayer life, so natural, so trustful!
He was the easiest man to pray with I have ever known.[33]

Indeed there was a key practice to Borden's prayer life, much in keeping with Latourette's words about the ardent commitment to prayer that Borden displayed.

He had a 'card-system' for 'recording prayers and their answers' in relation to friends 'who were on his heart.' He also kept 'a loose-leaf note-book in which he listed subjects for prayer in groups, one for each day of the week.'[34]

Other friends thought of small habits and colorful things about Borden's time at Yale. One of them, E. F. Jefferson, said in a letter to a fellow-classmate:

No picture of Bill at New Haven would be complete, without the old slouch hat he used to wear so often. Remember it?

It was of brownish grey, pointed at the top, torn on the side, and with a large convenient hole used to hang it up by. One time, I set fire to Bill's hat. When he discovered the flame, he was suddenly active to rescue the treasure, and punish me for my presumption.[35]

Nor would Borden part with this battered old hat, so nearly brought to ruin. He kept it, and wore it, with an ardor Indiana Jones might have envied. This side of his college years was all the more welcome for its colorful, quirky nature. In so many ways, Borden was a young man beyond his years. People saw that.

But here, he was very much a young man – and a fun-loving collegian.

---

33. ibid., pp. 145-146.

34. ibid., pp. 145-146. In later life, Kenneth Latourette famously used a similar 'card system' for prayer requests and answers – a practice dating from the years of his friendship with Borden. See Latourette, *Beyond the Ranges* (1967), p. 34. See also the February 26, 2012 article in *The Yale Standard*, 'Uncle Ken,' archived online at: http://www.yalestandard.com/biographies/uncle-ken/

35. ibid., p. 146.

Few knew Borden better at Yale than his roommate during their junior and senior years, Malcolm Burt 'Mac' Vilas, a native of Cleveland. He recalled Borden's prowess athletically. For example, though he hadn't competed inter-scholastically, Borden was still an accomplished wrestler within competition on-campus at Yale.

'As to Bill's wrestling,' Vilas said in a letter to Charlie Campbell:

> you know what a bull he was, and how hard he wrestled and rough-housed. I remember in senior year one night, when Jeff was holding Lou and Frank at bay easily, how Bill just for fun rushed in, grabbed Jeff by the legs, and tossed him back on his couch, without much effort.
>
> You were there, I am sure.
>
> How thankful I am for those happy, happy days together, Charlie!
>
> Len Parks [also saw] Bill's physical prowess … They used to wrestle together [in competition], and Len was no slouch, but he couldn't throw Bill. He told me once that Bill was a 'regular bear,' and that though he didn't go in for fancy holds, etc., he was the hardest man to tackle in the whole gym.[36]

Sports of all kinds at Yale won Borden's loyalty. And Mac Vilas, who was a talented cross-country runner, remembered Borden's forceful presence at baseball games, or track meets against arch-rivals like Harvard:

> Bill attended practically all the games and meets, as I recall it.
>
> I remember well how he stood on Derby Avenue, between the bridge and the lower entrance to the track and baseball field on the day in November 1907 when we had the first cross-country run with Harvard. As we came up the little rise on Derby Avenue, before entering the gate, there was Bill – who had come down to meet us runners.

---

36. ibid., p. 148.

When he saw that I was in the lead, he let out a most encouraging yell!

Perhaps it was partly surprise, and I wouldn't blame him if it was.

You and all the other fellows may have been there, I don't [recall,] but Bill's enthusiasm for and interest in his roommate I can never forget.[37]

Mac Vilas also remembered that Borden was someone chosen many times for elective office at Yale. It was, he thought, a sign of his classmates' mutual regard—

I believe I am right in saying that Bill was elected to every class office for which he was nominated, and I well remember one stormy class-meeting, we could scarcely hear ourselves speak, when a word of suggestion from him brought order out of the chaos; and showed very clearly the quality of [others'] respect and admiration for him.[38]

As his time at Yale drew to a close, Borden had shown himself an admirable example of the 'student-athlete.' On the football field, in wrestling tournaments, throwing the shot and hammer in track, or as part of his class rowing crew, he'd shown skill and achievement, particularly when his class Club Crew won the inter-class championship in 1907. He played 'on the winning Philosophical and High Oration baseball team, and on the Phi Beta Kappa [baseball] team.'[39]

He'd acquitted himself well, and done much, in Yale athletics.

In academics, Borden joined the ranks of Phi Beta Kappa, and was asked to give the Phi Beta Kappa oration. This came from his election as President of Phi Beta Kappa for his class, while Harvey Hollister Bundy was elected Vice-President, and Charlie Campbell as Secretary. Borden learned of this signal honor on

---

37. ibid., p. 148.

38. ibid., p. 148.

39. See *The Yale Alumni Weekly*, April 25, 1913, (New Haven: Yale University Press, 1913), p. 816.

February 5, 1908, and his oration was an occasion.[40] As his friend Charlie Campbell said:

> The Phi Beta Kappa banquet is perhaps the finest of the yearly banquets given at Yale. Many celebrated men are invited from other colleges, and most of the best-known professors of the University, so that the dinner is quite an affair.
>
> I have a pleasant recollection of the dignified way in which Bill presided and made the opening address. It was a striking illustration of [his] maturity ...[41]

But there was yet another consideration, and Campbell was careful to draw attention to that as well. When Borden was elected President of Phi Beta Kappa for his senior year, Campbell said it was 'one of the many evidences that [Bill's] stand on the fraternity question had not hurt his influence or popularity.'[42]

Blazing a trail many had not at first understood, his consistent character and conduct had, over time, won his classmates' respect. And given the pain it had cost him to take this step, winning their respect must have meant a great deal to him.

∽ ∽ ∽

After final exams in 1909, as Charlie Campbell recalled, 'there was a gap of four or five days'[43] before commencement. Borden, with three classmates, decided on taking a fast train to Camden, Maine, and then sail from there to New Haven on the handsome Borden family sloop, the *Tsatsawassa*, arriving in style.[44]

Or so it was thought.

It was a fine plan. The four were filled with high spirits, and the thought of one last collegiate 'adventure' at sea: a time to unwind, and enjoy good fellowship.

---

40. See *The Yale Literary Magazine*, February 1908, (New Haven: Yale University Press, 1908), p. 233.

41. See Taylor, *Borden of Yale* (1926), p. 143.

42. See Campbell, *William Borden* (1913), p. 19.

43. See Zwemer, *William Whiting Borden* (1913), pp. 90-91.

44. See Campbell, *William Borden* (1913), p. 19.

Charlie Campbell wrote of this time in vivid detail:

Bill invited Billy Roberts, Mac Vilas, and [me] to come up to Camden and sail his boat, the *Tsatsawassa*, down to New Haven in time for commencement.[45] So off we packed to Camden, where we spent Sunday, speaking at the Young People's Service in the village church [there].

The *Tsatsawassa* is a knock-about sloop, about fifty feet overall, with a cabin where four can sleep quite comfortably and room forward for more. She is a very sea-worthy boat, capable of good-speed, but not a racer. Bill seemed to belong to the boat, and [to] wax a past-master at handling her.

The only chance of making New Haven in time for commencement was to sail night and day. Accordingly, we divided the night into two watches.

Bill and I slept until two in the morning, while Captain [Arey] and Mac ran the boat. From two on, Bill and I were in charge, and the others slept. It was a great experience to be hauled out of bed in the dead of night and go on deck for the early morning hours, seeing the day-break ...

On this cruise we sailed fairly close to the Maine coast, until well on our way to Boston. Here, we struck out boldly across to Cape Cod.

We were having bad luck with the winds, making only slow progress against a head wind. We mapped out our course, as best we could by dead reckoning, having no experienced navigator with us.

When Bill and I came up on watch at two a.m., we found out that we had made a mistake in our reckoning, which would have resulted in our missing Cape Cod by a good many miles. This would have meant that we would have been running many miles out to sea. We changed course so as to rectify this ...

---

45. During World War II, William Payne Roberts (1888–1971) was interred in a detention camp under Japanese guards – a camp located outside Shanghai, and featured in the film, *Empire of the Sun*. See Augustine Roberts, *Finding The Treasure* (Collegeville: Liturgical Press, 2011), p. 6. Roberts graduated from Yale in 1909, and later became a missionary to China as the Rt. Rev. W. P. Roberts, under the auspices of American Church Mission.

When Bill and I came on deck next morning, the boat was skirting along close to the Cape Cod shore, and now we began to pass many boats, as we were in the regular channel. It was interesting to see the big boats loom up out of the early morning mist and pass swiftly by. [When] the sun had risen on the last day [we realized] there was no chance to make New Haven, even under the most favorable circumstances. So we put into Hyannisport and took the first train back to Providence, and then on to New Haven.[46]

True enough, as the old saying has it, the best-laid plans often go awry.

Still, there had been days at sea, and good company, for these young men so soon to bid farewell to Yale – that was something worth doing. Charlie Campbell's pen had captured it all, in wonderful detail.

---

46. See Zwemer, *William Whiting Borden* (1913), pp. 90-91.

CHAPTER 7

Interlude: Gatherings and Friends

... an open hand, and heart, and life –
through which God can give what He longs to.[1]
– S. D. Gordon

You have life before you. Once only, you can live it.[2]
– Henry Drummond

Sometimes the weight of great renown in later years may take away, though unintentionally, a true sense of what someone was like in their younger years, or in the time before renown came to them. We tend to see them only through the lens of a certain fame, or celebrity – as though either one was inevitable.

But we can never know, in real time, that such things *will* be.

Before William Borden became 'Borden of Yale,' he was a promising collegian and graduate student: forming friendships, learning about life, and discovering what it meant to live a life of faith. Throughout that journey, there was always a mixture of uncertainties and fine moments, common enough to us all.

---

1. S. D. Gordon, *Quiet Talks on Prayer* (New York: Revell, 1904), p. 14. Borden knew S. D. Gordon. See Taylor, *Borden of Yale* (1926), pp. 121-122: 'July 3, 1906. Whom do you suppose we had with us Sunday? S. D. Gordon! [After breakfast,] we met with Mr Gordon. At 10 a.m. he gave us a talk on Power. It was wonderful ... In the afternoon, down by the brook, he spoke on John 7. 37-39 in his quiet way.'

2. See Henry Drummond, *The Greatest Thing in the World* (London: Hodder & Stoughton, 1890), p. 9.

But as he made his way in life, William Borden was rich in the gift of friends. Others who knew him felt the same. And their stories paint a picture of Borden as a person who drank deeply and vibrantly of life.

So here we may take some time, apart from a more structured look at his life, and see him as an active collegian who reveled in good company, and was thought to be good company. Amid sporting events and pastimes, fellowship proved a tonic for him. It was a great blessing, and he cherished the gift of friends.

To see Borden in this way is to have a fuller appreciation of who he was. For high among his 'achievements,' there were ways he knew how to be a friend.

Sporting events brought many such moments for Borden.

As his friend Charlie Campbell recalled: 'Bill was a keen follower of athletic games at college and afterwards. I can see him now, arranging where he would meet me at some football game or baseball game. He would become most interested in a good game and excited. He told his mother once—

'Mother, I thought my heart would stop beating.'[3]

～～～

And during his years at Princeton Seminary, Borden made a special effort to invite Charlie Campbell to many sporting events. Here Campbell remembered—

'I visited Bill several times ... and he me at Essex Fells [New Jersey]. We always got in a game of tennis if possible ... Sometimes he would telephone over that he had an extra ticket or two to some game, and would ask [friends] over.'[4]

Another chum recalled: 'I can see [Bill] now as he entered so whole-heartedly into the excitement of the football games at Princeton; he was as enthusiastic as any, and as eager as any to have Yale win.'[5]

---

3. See Zwemer, *William Whiting Borden* (1913), p. 111. Selection edited.

4. ibid., p. 111.

5. ibid., p. 110.

Borden's ardor for the 'Yale football eleven' was always razor keen. During his freshman year in New Haven, he'd played alongside many skilled players. He was deeply grateful for his course of graduate studies at Princeton; but when it came to athletics, he would always be 'a Yale man,' first and last.

Another setting Borden's friends fondly remembered was one they visited in his company after the close of fall semester at Yale, 1908.

Charlie Campbell's memories of this time were especially vivid—

In our Christmas vacation (junior year) Bill went with Mrs Borden and [his younger sister] Joyce to The Lake Placid Club in the Adirondacks. It was a beautiful winter, with several feet of snow on the ground in the mountains.

Bill and his mother, with their [vaunted] hospitality, decided to have a house-party. So invitations came to Isabel Corbiere, Mary Abbe, and three of my sisters, with Mac Vilas, Bill Roberts, Lou Audette, and myself. All but Mac Vilas were able to accept; and we arrived on New Year's Eve.

How crisp the mountain air was as we drove up in sleighs from the station, and started in for a glorious party! We cast off all thought of work and settled down to [tobogganing, tramping, and indoor games].

Bill was in the thick of it.

We would all dress up in our warmest old clothes, and go out to the toboggan course. The snow was soft, and all kinds of stunts were possible.

We spent a good deal of time trying to go down the hill standing on the toboggans. Four or five of us would get on one toboggan, standing up, and would then launch out. There always came the time when one would lose balance and upset the rest, and away we would go, head-first into the snow ...

Bill was right in his element.

Over on the road, coasting on the bob-sled was possible, and near the Club was good skating. One day, [I recall,] we all ploughed off in the deep snow, and climbed a little mountain nearby.

> Every night we would turn up tired … and ready for the biggest
> kind of dinner, and the soundest sort of sleep. Bill simply reveled
> in good fellowship and sport … It did one good to be with him …[6]

Sporting contests and Christmas at Lake Placid held many special moments, but of all the places Borden knew and loved, his family's summer home in Camden, Maine, was his favorite setting for fellowship and hospitality.

Many years before William F. Buckley, Jr became famous as a Yale alumnus deeply devoted to sailing;[7] readers of *Borden of Yale* knew how devoted Borden was to summers in Camden, and days at sea aboard the 'friendship sloop' *Tsatsawassa*.

To recover these moments and memories of his life is to find something rare and fine about Borden's love of the sea. It was a true part of his family's heritage. His elder brother John later became famous as a maritime explorer, and his younger sister Joyce circumnavigated the world in the yacht *Northern Light*. Their names were justly celebrated; but they knew what a skilled sailor their brother William was.

Verse by John Masefield, from 1902, captures Borden's love of the sea—

> *And all I ask is a tall ship, and a star to steer her by,*
> *And the wheel's kick, and the wind's song, and the*
> *white sail's shaking;*
> *And a grey mist on the sea's face, and a*
> *grey dawn breaking.*[8]

---

6. See Taylor, *Borden of Yale* (1926), pp. 139-140. See also Campbell, *William Borden* (1913), p. 17. Italics added.

7. In 1951, 25 years after *Borden of Yale* was published, Buckley's book *God and Man at Yale* was published. In six months it sold 35,000 copies and became *a cause célèbre*. See page 92 of J. B. Judis, *William F. Buckley Jr* (New York: Simon & Schuster, 1988). Dr Thomas Kidd states that *Borden of Yale*, '09 'became one of the most widely printed missionary accounts of the twentieth century, with approximately 12 American, Canadian, and British editions … and a Chinese translation in 1960.' See page 66 of *American Christians and Islam* (Princeton: Princeton University Press, 2009).

8. John Masefield, *Salt-water Ballads* (London: Elkin Matthews, 1913), p. 55. This poem was written in 1902.

Geraldine Taylor has given one of the best descriptions we have of Borden as a skilled and devoted mariner. He 'loved the sea,' she wrote, 'and was at home on it, and in it. Most of his vacations during [his] student years were spent at Camden, Maine, where he almost lived on the white-sailed *Tsatsawassa*.'[9]

Another among Borden's close friends, Inglis Frost (the medical doctor son of Henry Weston Frost), vividly recalled such times at sea.

'There were few things,' he said:

> that Bill liked better than to don his canvas jeans and jumper, and sit behind the tiller of his yacht in a spanking good breeze. Many a pleasant sail I have had with Bill, and many a time we have been together in sloppy weather.
>
> One well-remembered summer we took a cruise down the Nova Scotia shore, and there is no time like a cruise for getting to know one another. Bill was our skipper, and an ideal one, but he didn't stop at being in charge. There were few meals we ate that he hadn't cooked. Life on the boat was full of joy from beginning to end, with Bill to keep things going.
>
> One morning we were becalmed in the middle of the Bay of Fundy. It was a hot sultry day, and we had been talking about sharks. Suddenly Bill said:
>
> 'Sharks or no sharks, here goes!'
>
> And he was overboard in a moment, swimming round the yacht.
>
> One learned in those days more of the secret of Bill's life, that his strength lay in his prayer-life. No matter what the weather might be, he would always hand over his trick at the wheel, and go below for his times of quiet. I remember him distinctly one very rough day—with the boat standing on her beam-end—coming below and climbing up on his berth, and losing himself in his God.[10]

---

9. See Taylor, *Borden of Yale* (1926), p. 156.

10. ibid., pp. 156-157. Inglis Folger Frost (1886–1983) was the son of Henry Weston Frost and Abbie Gridley Ellinwood Frost, who married on September 12, 1883.

Inglis Frost's mother, Abbie, also had memories of visits with the Bordens in Camden; and what William Borden, in particular, was like at sea. On occasion, she would chaperone a house-party for mixed company on the *Tsatsawassa*.

'The time I came to know him best,' she said:

> was on the cruise we had in August 1911 … seven days of good thorough testing in close quarters …
>
> [William] was captain and steersman, steward and cook for a party of ten hungry people, and well he did it. It was something more than the salt sea air that made his coffee and tea, and corned-beef hash and pancakes, so popular.
>
> Between times, he was ready for any game.
>
> Stretched out in the cockpit, at dominoes, his hearty laugh rang out with any success that was achieved.
>
> On Sunday, we went to morning service ashore. And in the evening, as we finished our meal and had a sing—with perfect naturalness and simplicity—he led in a brief prayer service. It was always a pleasure to me to have him conduct prayers … conveying the feeling that God was near and real.[11]

Much as Charlie Campbell saw of his friend Borden at Yale, he felt Camden was perhaps the setting where some of his friend's best qualities were seen:

> Three weeks of one summer, and the larger part of another, I was [with the Bordens at Camden]. That time … opened my eyes to Bill's real self …
>
> At Yale, I had learned that he was a rare man to work with; our weeks together in his summer home showed me he was a rare man [there also].
>
> At college I knew, as did all his friends, the strength and intensity of the serious purpose of [faith in] his life … Every-day comradeship at Camden taught me more of his [qualities], and his enjoyment of outdoor life …

---

11. ibid., pp. 157-158.

There was no mistaking the fact that Bill liked to sail, that he liked to swim, play tennis and golf. His laugh was always the heartiest, his enthusiasm the most contagious, and his delight at doing well the most evident.[12]

One sail to Bar Harbor, Maine, was a time that gave Campbell a rich store of memories. His friend Borden's hardihood, and spontaneous nature, were much in evidence. And laughter was a welcome companion as well:

> I remember one evening anchoring off Bar Harbor about seven o'clock. By the time all was ship-shape, the sun had set, and the riding lights were shining from all the boats in the harbor. Before getting supper, Bill suggested that we have a swim. The air was chilly, and the black water ripping by with the outgoing tide looked colder than I had ever seen it.
>
> But overboard we went, swam a few strokes, took another dive, and were out again and dressing. The splendid reaction put us in the best of spirits as we prepared supper. I can see Bill now—hustling round that cabin—whistling, singing, just full of the joy of living.
>
> It was that same time, I think, that we sat on deck, talking of another trip when we had put into Bar Harbor, after sailing the entire preceding night. We had anchored at about the same spot, [then] turned in for a little sleep.
>
> Before long, we had wakened to find the boat dragging her anchor and almost upon the rocks. I can feel Bill's hearty slap upon my back, and hear his laughter still, as we recalled how we had had to hustle to get out of danger.[13]

In keeping with Borden's penchant for impromptu feats when at sea was one occasion Campbell remembered when they sighted whales nearby. Before he quite knew what was happening, a close and rather worrying encounter took place.

It was a moment not to be forgotten, as Campbell recalled:

---

12. ibid., p. 158. Selection edited.
13. ibid., pp. 159-160.

One day off the Massachusetts coast, we had been watching a school of whales blowing at some little distance. A few moments later, one of them came lazily to the surface, not a hundred feet from our fifty-foot yacht.

In some alarm one of the party called to Bill, who was at the wheel, to keep the boat off. His response was to edge in a little nearer, with – *'Oh, let's have a good look!'*[14]

Then too, as Campbell remembered, there was the occasion when Borden decided all at once to take part in a race that he hadn't registered to enter.

'One day,' Campbell said:

we sailed over to Eagle Island, to take part in some races that were being run there. The wind was very light, and we came to the starting-line just after our race had begun. There was no time to report to the judges, and no time to put the tender ashore. Bill managed everything. We just hauled the tender up on deck, and went after the boats that had already started.

All through the race, Bill was captain – giving his orders, and making every point to get the most out of his boat. We were heeled far over most of the time, as a good wind had sprung up.

It all resulted in our crossing the winning line, well in the lead. We were not allowed the victory, because we had not reported before-hand; but the winning was just as real all the same.[15]

~ ~ ~

No view of Borden's life at Camden would be complete without reference to memories that his great friend Captain Arey had among his store of recollections.

One of Borden's best qualities, the good captain said, had much to do with his thoughtfulness and consideration of others.

In words rich with the tang of the sea, Arey said:

if the boat wasn't fixed up quite as it ought to be, perhaps if ladies came aboard and the brass wasn't cleaned, I'd tell [Mr Borden]

---

14. ibid., p. 160.
15. ibid., pp. 160-161.

about it, and he'd smile and say it was all right. He never spoke a cross word to me all the time I was with him.

He lent me two books by [S. D.] Gordon, *Talks on Prayer* and *Talks on Power*. [And] we had a Young Peoples' Meeting in the Baptist Church here ...

He would sometimes lead our prayer-meeting. If I had the job, I'd get him to do it for me. Others did too, for they liked to hear him.

He could always hold the audience. Sometimes the young people are a little noisy at their meeting; but they was still when he spoke.

Sometimes he'd tell us he was going to be a missionary, [and] seemed to think he was mapped out for it ...

One summer here, he and Mr T. held open-air [gospel] meetings.

They'd begin right in front of the hotel, about 7.30, and get the crowds sort of interested. They had a little organ and would sing. William could sing quite well. He had a strong voice. Then they'd go into the Opera House, which they'd rented ... Sometimes it was crowded full. The last two evenings they'd have after-meetin's, and many stayed [to talk more about faith] ...[16]

∽ ∽ ∽

These stories convey things Borden loved about Camden: dusk and sunrise over the ocean, the brisk wind and cool temperatures that came across the water – and days at sea, under the sails of the *Tsatsawassa*.

To enjoy all these things, in the company of friends, was a blessing that never diminished for him. Each day in Camden was a gift.

∽ ∽ ∽

D. L. Moody's Northfield, a famous center for summer conference gatherings, was another setting for cherished times of camaraderie Borden knew as a collegian.

'[He] loved fellowship,' Samuel Zwemer observed, and 'to use college slang, was "a great mixer."' So in 1908 and 1909, Borden

---

16. ibid., pp. 162-163.

went to Northfield, camped in tents with the friends from Yale, and 'helped wait at the tables.'[17]

To this, Charlie Campbell added:

'[Bill] taught a Bible class, and worked hard [to encourage] the interest of missions. He also took part in the ball games, and other sports which are a great feature of the afternoons at Northfield.'[18]

College banners were set amid dozens of tents pitched around the campus. There were evening campfires, keen competition in athletic events—college rivalries much in evidence—and more contemplative times, when friendships were deepened; and thoughts about a choice of calling in life were considered.

And Charlie Campbell also picked up on something else: Borden's habit of waiting on tables during mealtimes at Northfield, saying:

> [Bill] never did this when he knew there was a [college man of modest means] needing the job to help meet expenses, but when the coast was clear, on would go the waiter's apron, and he would do the waiter's work, and would get nothing to eat until the crowd had left the dining room.
>
> He never told me why he did this. It may have been partly to keep friends company (who had to serve as waiters for monetary reasons); but I always felt it went deeper than that ... Bill was trying to be 'among us as Him who served.'[19]

Northfield and its environs were hallowed for Borden.

First, the birth of the Student Volunteer Movement had taken place in 1886 during a conference led by D. L. Moody (at the nearby Mount Hermon School).

Second, Borden felt a profound debt to D. L. Moody's Christian example in his own life, expressing regret he hadn't 'the opportunity of seeing and hearing Mr Moody in his

---

17. See Zwemer, *William Whiting Borden* (1913), p. 91.

18. See Campbell, *William Borden* (1913), pp. 16-17.

19. See Zwemer, *William Whiting Borden* (1913), p. 91.

lifetime,' yet saying 'it was through his work, and the precious Gospel he preached ... the influence of the Moody Church, and [Moody] Bible Institute, that while going to schools in the East he had been kept in the faith.'[20]

Among Northfield's high hills and vistas, Borden knew what it was to walk to the crest of Round Top, the hill D. L. Moody loved, to see the westering sun fall beneath the mountaintops of the Pioneer Valley. He knew what it was to lift his voice in song in that place: one of many young people, from around the world, who found that stirring hymns brought things of eternity near, and a deep desire to know and walk with God.

Northfield was a place where many missionaries-to-be heard the call of God upon their lives. It was like a voice on the wind. They knew whence it came.

It was a call William Borden heard – in the company of many friends.

And so the reasons for a chapter like this. To show who William Borden was among his friends, and how life ran strongly within him.

For it is worth knowing the character of someone who could win friends as he once won them. His faith, and many qualities, were for the making of friends.

They knew that and cherished it.

And even though the years of their friendship with him were too few – their memories remained strong and vivid: moments they kept with them all their lives.

Someone like that is worth knowing; and remembering.

---

20. See *The Christian Workers Magazine*, March 1910, (Chicago: Moody Bible Institute, 1910), p. 582.

CHAPTER 8

Princeton and the President's House

[At] Princeton Theological Seminary, [William Borden's] intellectual
and spiritual life, and many other admirable qualities, endeared him
alike to professors and students … [He] was [also] elected [a Trustee]
of the Moody Bible Institute … a Director of the National Bible
Institute … and a member of the North American Council of the China
Inland Mission. During his three years' stay in Princeton, his mother
transferred her residence from Chicago; and made her home first in
the Cleveland Mansion, and later at 'Edgehill.' The students of the
seminary treasure the memory of the wide hospitality extended in this
home: to them and to Christian workers from many parts of the world.[1]
– Dr Charles R. Erdman (May 1913)

Asked in 1909 to become University Secretary of the Y.M.C.A.
at Yale, Borden chose Princeton Seminary instead, saying:
'I must take time for thought and study …'[2]
– Geraldine Taylor (1926)

---

1. See *The Princeton Seminary Bulletin*, May 1913 (Princeton: Princeton Seminary
Bulletin, 1913), pp. 8-9. This tribute strongly appears to have been written by Dr C. R.
Erdman, since the sentence on page 9, 'It is probable that in the history of the Christian
Church no man of his years has ever provided so largely for the evangelization of the
world,' is almost the precise wording of a sentence Erdman wrote with attribution about
Borden in the August 1913 issue of *The Missionary Review of the World*: 'William Borden,
in addition to other abiding influences of his life and service, has bequeathed for the
evangelizing of the world a larger sum than any man of equal years in the entire history
of the Christian Church.'

2. See Taylor, *Borden of Yale* (1926), p. 174. Citation paraphrased.

For Borden, the Camden summer of 1909 was partly spent in preparation for fall entrance to Princeton Theological Seminary. His friend Charlie Campbell had a near view of the opportune moments, taken for study:

> [Bill] was brushing up his Greek, the summer of our graduation from Yale, with a view to the entrance examination at Princeton. Out in the yacht [*Tsatsawassa,*] he would often go below, and plug away at Greek.
>
> He did a great deal of studying aboard [this] boat during the years I knew him; and was a past-master at making the odd moments count.[3]

Princeton Theological Seminary as it was in Borden's years there (from the author's 1st British edition copy of *Borden of Yale*, 1926).

Borden had much to look forward to at Princeton Seminary. It was a school founded, as its catalogue said, 'to form men for the gospel ministry who shall truly believe, and cordially love, and therefore endeavor to propagate and defend [the gospel], in its genuineness, simplicity and fullness ...'[4]

3. ibid., p. 160.

4. See *Princeton Theological Seminary Catalogue 1910–1911*, page 28.

That he'd decided on Princeton Seminary had come about through a telling gift of friendship: the wisdom and guiding counsel of Dr Henry Weston Frost, the Director in North America for China Inland Mission.

As Geraldine Taylor observed: '[Borden] owed not a little in the deeper things of the spiritual life to his friendship with Dr Frost, whose love ... was almost that of a father for a son. William had long consulted him in matters of importance.'[5]

For his part, Dr Frost remembered:

The first time William ... spoke to me about offering himself to the China Inland Mission ... he was in his sophomore year at Yale. He had already come to feel that his work should be in China, and desired ... to reach that land. But I felt he was then too young ... and I advised him to postpone considering the matter. At the end of his university course he again consulted me about going to China. Once more I advised him to defer the decision, and urged him to prepare himself further by taking the seminary course at Princeton. This he did, with credit to himself and the Seminary.[6]

Another indicator of how close Borden was to Henry Weston Frost rests in a Christmas gift that Frost sent to Borden in December 1910.[7] Seated at his desk at 1020 Lake Shore Drive, Chicago, Borden took up his fountain pen and wrote:

[Thursday,] December 29, 1910

Dear Mr Frost,

Thank you very much for the volume of your poems.[8]
    I shall be pleased to read them, and am sure I will enjoy them. I gave [my sister] Joyce the other copy ...

---

5. See Taylor, *Borden of Yale* (1926), p. 180.

6. ibid., p. 180.

7. See the letter from Borden to Frost, dated December 22, 1910, where Borden refers to packages that look 'like presents.'

8. See Henry Weston Frost, *Pilgrim Songs: Verses for Christians* (New York: Gospel Publishing House, 1910).

I left Princeton Monday, and Mother and Joyce followed Wednesday, arriving this morning. I have been with the [Henry] Crowells at their home in Winnetka – 'Castle Content,' as they call it.[9]

I think that's a beautiful name for a Christian home ...

I enclose a check for the [China Inland] Mission for $200.[10]

I wish you all a Happy & Blessed New Year.

Very sincerely yours,
William W. Borden[11]

Henry Parsons Crowell and Susan Coleman Crowell were an older Christian couple of great hospitality, with an abiding commitment to philanthropy. Borden knew Henry Crowell through his service as a Trustee of Moody Bible Institute. Crowell was Chairman of that Board.

As for the volume of poems Henry Weston Frost sent, *Pilgrim Songs,* it was rich in devout, fine hues of hymn-like verse. One of these poems read—

Jerusalem, my heavenly home,
To thee I lift mine eyes,
To thy fair fields of living green,
To thy blue, cloudless skies.
To thy sweet flowers, which ever bloom
Beside the murm'ring streams,
To thy cool shades, 'neath spreading trees,
Where sleep the sun's soft beams.[12]

Other places in Frost's book held reverence, and lines of quiet adoration:

---

9. 'Henry Parsons Crowell (1855–1943).' In 1927 Crowell created the Henry Parsons Crowell and Susan Coleman Crowell Trust. As for 'Castle Content,' the founding family of 'Quaker Oats' built a Newport-style house close to Lake Michigan, in 1898.

10. $200 in Borden's time would be worth $5,000 today.

11. A letter from Borden to H. W. Frost, Thursday, December 29, 1910, housed at The Billy Graham Center, Wheaton College.

12. See Frost, *Pilgrim Songs* (London: Morgan & Scott, Ltd., 1911), p. 80.

Life of life, and light of light,
Full of wisdom and of might,
Ruler o'er created things,
Lord of lords and King of kings,
Perfect in Thyself and ways,
Worthy of eternal praise.[13]

Still other lines from *Pilgrim Songs* cast images of the sea. Surely, they spoke to Borden as a mariner who followed the Lord of all deep places on the earth: the One to trust in all seas, in every time and place:

My Pilot will be there;
His hand will hold the helm …
Till I shall reach the realm
Where lies my haven fair.[14]

It is telling and important to know that Borden read Henry Weston Frost's collection of poetry, still more to hear how he valued this text. We know so little of the books that he read – though some have been quoted in epigraphs on other pages of this book: volumes by Henry Drummond, S. D. Gordon, Robert E. Speer, J. H. McConkey, and J. Hudson Taylor. Their books were part of Borden's library.

Among them all, this is the sole book of sacred verse that we know he read.[15] It was a treasured book, and brought spiritual blessing for Christmas 1910—

Do you hear the angels singing …
… voices ringing, through the sky,
Oh, the fulness of their song …[16]

---

13. ibid., p. 238.

14. ibid., p. 85.

15. Borden read Byron's verse at Yale, and doubtless other famous poets. See Taylor, *Borden of Yale* (1926), p. 115.

16. See Frost, *Pilgrim Songs* (1911), p. 156.

Novelist F. Scott Fitzgerald, who began studies at Princeton within a year of William Borden's time there, penned a famous passage showing what the university campus was like in those storied, halcyon days before World War I.

Fitzgerald's prose brings this setting to life:

> Around Princeton, shielding her, is a ring of silence – certified milk dairies, great estates packed with peacocks and deer parks, pleasant farms and woodlands ... The busy East has already dropped away when the branch line train rattles familiarly from the junction. Two tall spires and then suddenly all around you spreads out the loveliest riot of Gothic architecture in America, battlement linked on to battlement, hall to hall, arch-broken, vine-covered: luxuriant and lovely over two square miles of green grass.[17]

As for the courses Borden took during his three years of study at Princeton, its 1910–1911 catalogue listed the roster of courses all three-year seminarians were required to take. It makes for a fascinating read. The teachers Borden knew were scholars who provided what many then considered the finest seminary education in America. He would enroll in some of the best classes available for pastoral training.

Among them were the following courses:

In Year One of his time at Princeton Seminary, Borden had a class on theism with Dr F. L. Patton, president of the seminary. He learned Hebrew from Dr R. D. Wilson, and J. Gresham Machen taught a class on the 'Exegesis of Paul's Epistles.' Borden studied theology with B. B. Warfield and C. W. Hodge, took a class with Dr William Brenton Greene entitled 'A General Introduction to Apologetics,' and also studied the English Bible with Dr Charles R. Erdman.[18]

---

17. F. S. Fitzgerald, *Afternoon of An Author* (New York: Scribner's, 1957), pp. 71-72; and see *Ten Years of Princeton* (Princeton: Princeton Univ., 1929), p. 38.

18. See the *1910–1911 Catalogue of Princeton Theological Seminary*, p. 42. On page 59, Borden is in the 'Advanced Hebrew Section of the Junior Class.'

For Year Two, Borden continued studies with Dr Greene in a class called the 'Evidences of Christianity,' and Dr Geerhardus Vos for 'Biblical Theology of the Old Testament.' Drs Warfield and Hodge were his instructors for 'Anthropology and Christology,' and Dr C. R. Erdman was his teacher for three classes: 'English Bible,' 'Ecclesiastical Theology,' and 'City Visitation' (a class on urban ministry).[19]

Year Three for Borden brought something like a capstone course with Dr Greene, 'Christian Ethics & Christian Sociology.' Drs Warfield and Hodge were his instructors for 'Soteriology & Eschatology,' and Dr Geerhardus Vos for the course titled 'Biblical Theology of the New Testament.' Rounding out the list were classes on 'Pastoral Theology' and the 'English Bible' with Dr C. R. Erdman.[20]

All in all, it was a remarkable course of study, and Borden acquitted himself with academic distinction. As C. R. Erdman said, with a mentor's pride: '[William] graduated with honor from Yale and from Princeton; and was counted one of the best-equipped men that has ever started for the foreign field.'[21]

Dr Erdman wrote at greater length of the impressions Borden left with him as a seminarian. 'Fidelity to Christ,' Erdman remembered, 'made his friendship precious.'[22] But there was yet more to say. 'No student,' Erdman stated:

---

19. See the *1910–1911 Catalogue of Princeton Theological Seminary*, pp. 42-43. And on page 17, Borden is listed as rooming in '21 B H' at Princeton Theological Seminary. Princeton Seminary Archivist Kenneth Henke states that 'BH stands for Brown Hall. It was the only major building constructed in Princeton during the Civil War years; and was completed in 1865. It is located on College Road.' Email correspondence from Kenneth Henke to the author, Tuesday, 19 February 2019.

20. ibid., page 43.

21. 'William Whiting Borden,' by Dr C. R. Erdman, in *The North American Student*, June 1913, (New York: Council of North American Student Movements, 1913), p. 166. And on page 165 Erdman said: 'Newspaper men have continually designated [William Borden] as "the millionaire missionary." His great wealth was, however, the least striking thing about him. What did impress even the most casual acquaintance was the power of his body and mind, and charm of his personality, and the evident beauty of his character. To his [closer] friends were revealed a peculiar steadfastness of purpose, strength of faith, and devotion to Christ.'

22. See page 14 of the May 1913 issue of *The Princeton Seminary Bulletin*.

exerted a greater personal influence over me than did William Borden ... due both to the fact of our [close] friendship, and to his [uniquely] strong and impressive personality. His judgment was so [sound] and so mature that I always forgot there was such a difference in our ages. His complete consecration and devotion to Christ were a revelation to me, and his confidence in prayer a continual inspiration.

He had doubtless inherited unusual gifts [intellectually], but these were developed by the most careful and persistent discipline, requiring great determination and fixity of purpose ... [Yet] the strain of unremitting application [to study] was relieved by a keen sense of humour, [and] delight in the society of relatives and friends. His friendship was one of the [most rewarding] with which I have been blessed.[23]

Borden left lasting memories among his fellow students at Princeton also. One of them, A. B. Fowler, recalled: '[Bill] had the ability, wholly unconscious to himself probably, of impressing men on first acquaintance with the power that was in his life.'[24] At the same time, Borden's friend from Yale, Charlie Campbell, saw first hand what his life at Princeton was like, academically and otherwise:

Bill took the full first-year course and several extra-curriculum courses – among these being Arabic. He felt that he would be better prepared for his work in China [among Moslems], if he knew the language of the Koran ... He was careful [at the same time] not to neglect his morning and evening devotions. Though his classroom work was along religious lines, he never substituted it for the personal devotion and prayer that is absolutely essential to the Christian.

---

23. See Taylor, *Borden of Yale* (1926), pp. 178-179.

24. See *The Princeton Seminary Bulletin*, May 1913 (Princeton: Princeton Seminary Bulletin, 1913), p. 11. And on page 12, Fowler said: 'I always felt when dealing with him, whether he was studying or whether he was playing tennis, or whether he was out for a bicycle ride with one of the boys – whatever he was doing, he was doing all to the glory of God ...'

It was his custom to read a chapter from the New Testament in the morning, and two chapters from the Old Testament in the evening. He did so because *in this way he would be able to read through the Bible once each year.* And what is more, he seems to have stuck faithfully to this program.[25]

Borden himself was indebted to a friendship that was especially important during his years at Princeton Seminary. As Geraldine Taylor said:

[Borden] owed not a little in the deeper things of the spiritual life to his friendship with Dr Frost, whose love for him was almost that of a father for a son. William had long consulted him in matters of importance, and especially as to his [work] with [China Inland] Mission.[26]

And if Henry Weston Frost was a mentor and example for Borden, others at Princeton saw those same qualities in Borden himself. James McCammon, later a missionary in China, spoke to this side of Borden's influence:

[Bill's] thoroughness, especially in his studies, was evident to us all. He kept up his work from day to day; so that he was not 'rushed' as many of us were when examinations came round. So well did he have his knowledge in hand that long before the three hours' period for an exam was over, he would have finished his paper and handed it in ...

It was my habit to look in on a classmate in Alexander Hall daily, and there, two or three afternoons in the week, I was sure to find Bill Borden and his friend, [A. B.] Fowler, doing extra-curriculum work on Arabic.[27]

I discovered ... they had formed the project of making an *'Arabic Concordance of the Bible,'* and had ... begun work upon

---

25. See Campbell, *William Borden* (1913), pp. 20, 22. Italics added.

26. See Taylor, *Borden of Yale* (1926), p. 180.

27. A. B. Fowler recalled: 'Another outstanding characteristic was his zeal in study ... when we were working on Arabic [and] in looking up words he was much more careful than I ... He conquered the studies which were before him.' See *The Princeton Seminary Bulletin,* May 1913, p. 11.

it. I had known of their studiousness before, but this more than astonished me ...

[One] conviction that dominated his life was that the Bible, from first to last, is the inspired Word of God. To him it was the Book of books. He had not only an intellectual grasp of its teachings, such as one may get in a theological seminary; but [a true] spiritual understanding of it, which only comes through prayerful and devotional study, in humble dependence on the Spirit of God ...

The secret of William Borden's life, as it seems to [me,] was his belief in the sufficiency and abiding presence of the Lord Jesus Christ. For this was more than a belief: it was with him an experimental reality.[28]

Here, words from Borden himself serve as a fitting close for a chapter on his early years at Princeton. His studies were a gift and privilege: deepening his love for the first things of faith, and how those tenets can guide one's journey in life.

So he wrote of the book that held them:

I am beginning to see what a wonderful storehouse of good things the Bible is ...[29]

---

28. See Taylor, *Borden of Yale* (1926), pp. 183-184. In keeping with McCammon's reflections are some from Borden's Princeton Seminary Professor, C. R. Erdman, who wrote: '[William] held a firm and intelligent belief in all the great doctrines of the Christian faith, and his supreme desire was to have the Gospel preached in all the world.' See also 'William Whiting Borden,' by Dr C. R. Erdman, in *The North American Student*, June 1913, p. 166.

29. ibid., p. 69.

CHAPTER 9

The Edinburgh Conference

During his first summer vacation from [Princeton]
Seminary, Borden went to Europe ... representing the
China Inland Mission at the Ecumenical Missionary
Conference in Edinburgh (1910), where he was the
youngest of two thousand delegates.[1]
– Geraldine Taylor (1926)

Men and women ... who had heard His command: 'Go ye into
all the world and preach the gospel,' determined to obey that
call, and to get others to do likewise ...[2]
– William Borden, on 'The Origin of
the Student Volunteer Movement' (1913)

In the summer of 1910, the Edinburgh World Missionary Conference was held in the Assembly Hall of the United Free Church
of Scotland, Edinburgh.[3]

William Borden was the youngest of all delegates to attend
this landmark gathering, and deeply honored to have been given
such a privilege.

---

1. See Taylor, *Borden of Yale* (1926), p. 181.

2. W. W. Borden, 'The Origin of the Student Volunteer Movement,' *Christian
Workers Magazine,* March 1913, p. 456.

3. See W. H. T. Gairdner, *'Edinburgh 1910' An Account ... of the World Missionary
Conference* (London: Oliphant, Anderson & Ferrier, 1910). This conference of Protestant
missionaries took place in Edinburgh, Scotland, from Tuesday, June 14 to Thursday, June
23, 1910.

Writing to Henry Weston Frost on June 22, one day before the close of the Conference, Borden described the last stage of his pleasant journey there, traveling 'from Plymouth to Edinburgh, through some of the Cathedral towns.'[4]

As Borden's steam engine train made its way across the British countryside, images of small villages in the near distance alternated with glimpses of fields and hedgerows, or the sight of Edwardian-era stations in urban centers. All the while, his thoughts ran to anticipation of what this conference would be like: for it promised to be a once-in-a-generation event, and he would have the chance to hear missionary speakers he'd read about and admired for years – pioneers whose ranks he hoped to join in the near future, once his time at Princeton Seminary had concluded.

Among the 'bright spots and strong notes' of the conference, Borden told Frost of addresses given by the Bishop of Durham, H. C. G. Moule, and H. W. Webb-Peploe, Prebendary of St Paul's Cathedral.[5] Webb-Peploe had been a great friend of D. L. Moody – a speaker at the Northfield Summer Conferences during Moody's lifetime, and in the years after. Thus Borden knew Webb-Peploe's writings.

Remarkably, a photograph of Borden from the Edinburgh Conference has survived.[6] It shows him seated beside his mother (who'd traveled with him), on the balcony just behind the Conference moderator's chair and lectern. Borden is shown listening intently; taking notes of the proceedings.

And Borden's note-taking bore important fruit. For his Princeton Seminary classmate James McCammon, later a missionary to China,

---

4. A letter from Borden to H. W. Frost, Wednesday, June 22, 1910, housed at The Billy Graham Center, Wheaton College.

5. ibid.

6. Among the many copies of this photo now in existence, one is housed in the archives of Columbia University, and posted online at: https://blogs.cul.columbia.edu/burke/2013/03/28/world-missionary-conference-records-the-sequel/

Borden (seated behind the balcony column) at the Edinburgh World Missionary Conference, in Assembly Hall, New College, University of Edinburgh (see *Echoes from Edinburgh 1910*, by W. H. T. Gairdner).

said Borden returned to the seminary full of inspiration from all that he'd seen and heard in Edinburgh:

[Bill] was one of the most faithful attendants we had at the Y.M.C.A. and Student Volunteer meetings in the Seminary. He took his turn in leading such meetings, and his messages were [full] of a devotional and missionary character, [showing] thorough preparation of mind and heart.

One term, he [led us] through the Reports of the World's Missionary Conference, which he had attended in Edinburgh, giving them in the form of a resume week by week. Those talks I shall never forget.

[Bill's] mastery of the facts was astonishing. He gave us in clear, condensed statements, from carefully prepared notes, a synopsis of each of these Reports, bringing out the spiritual bearing of the facts dealt with. It was a remarkable evidence of his knowledge [and commitment to] foreign missions.[7]

---

7. See Taylor, *Borden of Yale* (1926), pp. 183-184.

141

Still later Borden wrote about the kind of missionary spirit that inspired the Edinburgh Conference, even as it inspired his missionary commitment, saying:

'The ultimate aim of foreign missions is to remain what it has been, namely, the establishment of a self-supporting, self-governing and self-propagating church in each of the countries where this condition does not exist … It is not a prophecy of what will occur, but rather the statement is a rallying cry of what might and should be done to help to bring it to pass.' Everyone, he said: 'should be given the chance to become Christians.'[8]

During the Edinburgh Conference several stirring, majestic hymns were sung in worship. How fine a thing it must have been to hear two thousand voices lifted in song, singing anthems like 'O God Our Help In Ages Past,' 'When I Survey The Wondrous Cross,' 'Crown Him With Many Crowns,' 'All People That On Earth Do Dwell,' and 'The King Of Love My Shepherd Is,' a hymn which declared—

> The King of love my shepherd is,
> whose goodness faileth never.
> I nothing lack if I am his,
> and He is mine forever.
>
> Where streams of living water flow,
> my ransomed soul He leadeth;
> and where the verdant pastures grow,
> with food celestial feedeth.[9]

During the days of the Edinburgh Conference, which lasted from Tuesday, June 14 to Thursday, June 23 1910, another meeting also took place, organized by Annie Van Sommer: a gathering 'of representative workers from Mohammedan lands at the house where she was staying.'[10]

---

8. W. W. Borden, 'The Watchword of the Student Volunteer Movement,' *Christian Workers Magazine*, April 1913, p. 504.

9. See Philip Schaff, *Christ in Song*, v. 2 (New York: Randolph & Co., 1895), p. 307.

10. See Taylor, *Borden of Yale* (1926), p. 181.

Dr Samuel Zwemer chaired the meeting, and two missionary statesmen from Cairo, Egypt were there also: W. H. T. Gairdner, and Dr William St Clair Tisdall. To facilitate introductions, Dr Zwemer asked each person present to rise and 'give his or her name and field.' Borden listened with interest, and when his turn came, he stood, and 'without hesitation' stated that 'his prospective field [would be] the Mohammedans of North-West China.'[11]

It was a public and very prominent declaration of Borden's missionary call. For him, the Edinburgh World Missionary Conference had been more than just a watershed event to attend on behalf of China Inland Mission.

It gave him the chance to tell people he'd long respected and admired that he wished to join their company; and serve the people of China.

As one telling phrase has it: the man and his mission had met.

~ ~ ~

In his brief memoir, Borden's close friend Charlie Campbell recounted what the remainder of Borden's time in Europe was like.

Once the Edinburgh Conference closed, Campbell wrote:

[Bill] went to Norway to visit with some friends. From Norway, [he] proceeded to Germany, and spent a month there studying the language. He had taken a year's work in German at Yale; and felt he could pick up a good deal of the spoken language, if he could live in Germany for a short time.

So he spent a month, living with a German family, and he certainly made remarkable progress. A Yale classmate, whom Bill met in Switzerland just after his stay in Germany, found him carrying on a good conversation with those with whom he had occasion to talk in German. His mastery of the language was far from complete; but still he had a speaking knowledge of it that many a tourist would have envied.

---

11. ibid., p. 181.

This was characteristic. [He] was gifted with the ability of seeing a thing, believing it was good, and then going ahead and doing it. Once started, he rarely stopped before he finished what he had set out to accomplish.[12]

Borden also, as Campbell remembered, 'spent several days in Lucerne:'

> where he gave himself up to the enjoyment of the sights and sports of the place. It was at times such as this that the social qualities of Bill were seen to advantage. He had a fertile imagination, a fund of ideas, and an enthusiasm that was contagious. On Sunday he attended the morning and afternoon services of the little [Scottish] mission church; and for anyone who knew Bill's habits of giving, it was easy to tell where the twenty-franc piece came from as it lay in the plate each service, equaling perhaps the entire remaining collection.
>
> In the matter of giving, Bill always followed the injunction, 'Let not thy left hand know what thy right hand doeth.' He insisted that not even his initials should be put with a gift when a list of benefactions was printed. He always asked that a gift of his should not be made public.
>
> It almost seemed to irritate him when he was found out. His best friends never knew even a small percentage of the gifts he was making. Many surprising incidents could be told, if all who have been helped by him could be induced to tell their stories.
>
> Bill's checkbook would show how little he spent for himself and how much he was constantly giving to others. With it all, he gave wisely; and conducted his financial affairs in a business-like fashion.[13]

Borden's time in Norway, mentioned above, was especially important as well. For this visit was with Robert P. Wilder, who was at that time working for the Student Volunteer Movement 'among students in England, and on the Continent.'[14]

---

12. See Campbell, *William Borden* (1913), pp. 22-23.

13. ibid., pp. 23-24.

14. See Taylor, *Borden of Yale* (1926), p. 181.

Borden looked forward to this visit on a personal level, but this visit was also important symbolically. Wilder was a pioneer of the Student Volunteer Movement, and Borden was a student volunteer among the generation of young people seeking to follow Wilder's example. Borden deeply admired him, and their friendship was much like that of a mentor and protégé.

On June 22, 1910, Borden wrote to Henry Weston Frost: 'Mr Wilder has invited me to go to Norway with him, and I have accepted. I am looking forward to it greatly, from many standpoints.'[15]

Not quite one month later, on Monday, July 18, Borden wrote to Henry Weston Frost again, with news of his visit with the Wilder family:

[Mr Wilder and I] travelled together from Edinburgh to Veldre, where he lives, and had a very nice trip, though it was a bit rolly [aboard ship] in the North Sea.

Norway was beautiful, but I enjoyed most being in his delightful home and getting to know him and his family. Mrs Wilder is very nice, and so are the children. We had prayers in Norwegian in the morning, and English in the evening – which I thought very nice, though I needed an interpreter myself for the Norwegian.

I was in his home just a week, and then we travelled together to the West Coast and did a little sight-seeing together. We had some good talks and seasons of prayer together, and were drawn close to one another. I am certainly glad that I have made such a friend, whom I can work with in such perfect sympathy.[16]

For his part, Robert Wilder said of this memorable visit with Borden:

[William] took a real interest in our home-life and all our doings. He helped the children learn to ride their bicycles, running by each of them in turn. Mrs Wilder specially remembers how,

---

15. A letter from Borden to H. W. Frost, Wednesday, June 22, 1910, housed at The Billy Graham Center at Wheaton College.

16. A letter from Borden to H. W. Frost, Monday, July 18, 1910, housed at The Billy Graham Center, Wheaton College.

when a box of aerated water had come by train, and she was thinking of sending to the station for it, we saw to our surprise [that William was] coming up the steep hill with the box on his shoulder ...

He and I had long talks over God's Word and work, frequently pausing to pray about the matter we were discussing.

He seemed never out of sight of the Mercy Seat.[17]

After Borden's visit in Norway with the Wilder family, we learn from the pen of Geraldine Taylor that 'a week in the Engadine,' in south-eastern Switzerland, gave Borden 'the conquest of the Piz

Pallu, and the Piz Julier as glorious memories; and a few days at Lucerne' brought delightful days with Charlie Campbell and his bride Mary,[18] who were 'there on their wedding journey.'[19]

Borden and a guide, mountain climbing in Switzerland during his last summer there (from *The Missionary Review of the World* magazine, page 567, August 1913).

As Charlie Campbell remembered:

[Bill] joined us in Lucerne. There were also a young Irishman and his bride in the same [lodge], and for several days we five had a great time! We went to the Glacier Garten, went rowing on

---

17. See Taylor, *Borden of Yale* (1926), p. 182.

18. Campbell married Mary Lathrop Abbe on June 15, 1910. See *Annals of Iowa*, v. 32 (1955), pp. 559-560.

19. See Taylor, *Borden of Yale* (1926), p. 182.

the lake, and swimming in it, and altogether acted like a bunch of kids.

Our afternoon teas were a wonderful mixture of assorted cakes, and unlimited cups of tea.[20]

In September 1910, when it was time to return to the United States, Borden sailed home aboard the *S.S. Minneapolis* of the Atlantic Transport Line. During this voyage, he copied a poem out on a sheet of *S.S. Minneapolis* stationary. It was titled, in his handwriting, 'A Morning Prayer, Frank W. Gunsaulus.' He placed it 'among his favorite poems kept ... in a special envelope.'[21] The poem read:

> *Guard me for yet another day,*
> *For life is new with morning's ray;*
> *And foes are strange, untrod the way:*
> *Guard me through this, an unknown day.*
>
> *Gird me for yet another day,*
> *Though guarded, I must fight and pray:*
> *Teach me to draw my sword or stay:*
> *O gird, while guarding me today.*
>
> *Guide me for yet another day;*
> *Guarded and girded, yet I stray,*
> *Find paths for me, and I obey:*
> *Guard, gird, and guide me – one more day.*
>
> *Guard, gird, and guide me every day,*
> *So when all things of time decay,*
> *In morn of heaven, by grace, I may*
> *Enter Thy perfectness of day.*[22]

---

20. ibid., p. 182.

21. See Zwemer, *William Borden* (1913), p. 196.

22. See Campbell, *William Borden* (1913), p. 24. Here, Borden quotes from a printing of this poem by Dr Frank Wakely Gunsaulus (1856–1921), Pastor of Central Church, Chicago. See page 11 of the July 27, 1911 issue of *The Advance* magazine, a 'Congregational Weekly' published in Chicago.

Nor was poetry the only pursuit which Borden followed on his voyage home. During his days at sea, he was 'deep in Arabic, with a view to the advanced course he was taking' in that language, and Aramaic.

'I spent most of my time in London buying books,' he wrote to his friend Charlie Campbell, 'and am taking home a small library of theological and Oriental literature.'[23] Days aboard the *S.S. Minneapolis* were devoted to study, interspersed with fine walks on the promenade deck, to take in the crisp sea air. There were surely sunset walks too, till the night sky brought stars a sailor knew and welcomed. The Pleiades, Orion, and that sentinel of evening: Polaris, the North Star.

How they must have shone, out over the sable depths of the sea.

---

23. See Taylor, *Borden of Yale* (1926), p. 183.

CHAPTER 10

The Seminary's Centenary Year

A Christian is not merely one who trusts in Christ
for salvation, but one who strives earnestly to
please Him in all things, great and small.[1]
– William Borden (circa 1912)

Commencement exercises were especially memorable the year
[William] Borden graduated from Princeton, as they coincided
with the Centennial celebrations of the Seminary...

'President Patton was at his best,' Borden remembered,
'and preached a tremendous sermon on "The faith once
for all delivered to the saints."'[2]
– Borden of Yale (1926)

After his three years at Princeton Seminary, a friend told William
Borden:

'I have recently been reading that little book of Hudson
Taylor's which you so kindly gave us at one of those bright spots
in our Seminary course, not quite a year ago.'[3] Borden's friend was

---

1. See Zwemer, *William Whiting Borden* (1913), p. 118, who says Borden wrote these
words in 'What Does It Mean To Be A Christian?' for *The Bible To-Day* magazine while
at Princeton. Borden became part of the National Bible Society in 1910, and 1912 a likely
date for this article.

2. See Taylor, *Borden of Yale* (1926), p. 206. Selection edited.

3. See Zwemer, *William Whiting Borden* (1913), p. 109. Borden's friend refers to J.
Hudson Taylor's book, *A Retrospect* (London: Morgan & Scott, 1905). This book is 128
pages long.

referring to J. Hudson Taylor's book, *A Retrospect*, published in London by Morgan & Scott in 1905. Its title page held the verse:

Thou shall remember all the way which the Lord
thy God led thee (Deut. 8, verse 2)

This vignette opens an eloquent window on Borden's days at Seminary: for Geraldine Taylor, later to be Borden's biographer, was the daughter-in-law of missionary pioneer Hudson Taylor. Indeed Geraldine Taylor and her husband Howard actually met William Borden: a story that he told briefly and memorably in a letter from the very year he graduated from Princeton, 1912:

'I am very glad,' Borden told Henry Weston Frost, 'to say that I had some most pleasant visits with C.I.M. friends while in England … [And we] had some very nice half hours with Dr and Mrs Taylor, then at Keswick.'[4]

And if memories of the Taylor family, or the pages of Hudson Taylor's book, made one facet of Borden's years at Princeton Theological Seminary special, there were many other moments that friends and family remembered also.

Charlie Campbell was one of them. 'Life at Princeton,' he recalled, 'was brightened by the happy home influences that surrounded [Bill]. The Borden home was hospitably open to all. Students, missionaries and prominent lay workers were frequent visitors.'[5] It was all rather like a salon for friends of faith.[6]

Kenneth Henke, Curator of Special Collections and Archivist at Princeton Theological Seminary, has shed further light on this side of Borden's life:

---

4. Borden to H. W. Frost, Sunday, Sept. 1, 1912, a letter housed at The Billy Graham Center, Wheaton College.

5. See Campbell, *William Borden* (1913), p. 22.

6. See P. B. Fitzwater, 'William Whiting Borden,' in *The Missionary Visitor* magazine, June 1913, p. 196. 'It was [my] privilege to be with [William] Borden in Princeton Theological Seminary last year [1912]; also invited to share the courtesy and hospitality of the Borden home.' P. B. Fitzwater (1871–1957) spent a year in graduate studies at Princeton, joining the faculty of Moody Bible Institute in spring 1913. See Otho Winger, *History of the Church of the Brethren in Indiana* (Elgin: Brethren Publishing House, 1917), p. 288.

'During his studies at the seminary William Borden's mother transferred her residence to Princeton, staying first at [Westland,] the former home of President Grover Cleveland on Library Place, and later at Edgehill (now Tennent Hall at [the] seminary, but then a private residence).'[7]

'Westland,' the former home of President Grover Cleveland, where the Borden family lived during his years at Princeton Seminary (from the author's photo collection, postcard circa 1912).

Francis Shunk Downs, another of Borden's Princeton friends, tells us more: 'I remember so well when [Bill] entered Princeton Seminary. He was so solid, so sincere, yet withal so human and full of fun – He would have some of us [over] for dinner in the Cleveland home which his mother had leased, and a most gracious and thoughtful host he would be.'[8]

Dr William Brenton Greene, Stuart Professor of Apologetics and Christian Ethics at Princeton Theological Seminary, remembered this of his student:

---

7. Email correspondence with Kenneth Henke, Curator of Special Collections and Archivist at Princeton Theological Seminary, Wed., Jan. 10, 2018.

8. See *The Princeton Theological Review*, July 1927, p. 518.

[William] had the rare good fortune to have his family here living in the town, and much of his time he himself lived with them ... His home was made in a very true sense your home. The beautiful hospitality of his mother rendered this possible. It was a great privilege ... for us all.

But I am sure that what must have impressed most who were in that home was his dutifulness toward his mother; the way in which he fulfilled all his duties in the family – a lesson which young men just coming into their manhood and [family] rights need, perhaps, more than others to learn. It was my privilege on one occasion to have a most striking example of this.

A reception had been given by his mother when they were living in the Cleveland Mansion. I had the pleasure of being present. I shall never forget [seeing William] as he stood [so kind and thoughtful] that night by his mother.

What would I not give to have the skill of an artist to reproduce the picture [in] my mind's eye.[9]

Even as Westland, the former home of President Grover Cleveland, was the setting for well-remembered moments of Borden's years at Princeton Seminary, his involvement with the National Bible Institute, in the heart of New York City, was another. For as his friend Charlie Campbell recalled, 'in the fall [of 1910, Bill] was made one of the directors of the National Bible Institute of New York City.'[10]

This took place on the eve of Borden's twenty-second birthday, and how it came about was a fascinating story. It all began in the late 1800s, and was tied to the Y.M.C.A. At this time D.O. Shelton, a young man who had very promising career prospects, chose instead to follow a call to work with the Y.M.C.A., and serve as a Christian leader in various Bible conferences.

During these years, from the 1890s on into the 1900s, Shelton came to the conclusion 'that something new and different in the

---

9. See *The Princeton Seminary Bulletin*, May 1913, p. 10.

10. See Campbell, *William Borden* (1913), p. 21.

way of approach was needed if the multitudes who never darken a church door were to hear the gospel.' It was an era when statistics had shown that 'more than half the people in the United States [were] outside the membership of any church.'[11]

Knowing this, Shelton and a set of friends from the business community in New York City decided to begin an outreach initiative for the crowds that would gather each day for the lunch hour at Madison Square Garden.

Those early days, as Geraldine Taylor described them, began with:

> a June day in 1907 ... the first meeting was held at the busy hour of noon. A low platform, under a tree in Madison Square Garden was [the setting], with a little organ and a group of singers to lead familiar hymns. The speakers were businessmen; the language was that of the newspaper rather than the theological hall. But the results were amazing. It was no unusual thing to see 300 men listening with riveted attention through the daily half-hour, and very soon other noon meetings had to be [started,] and a School for Lay Evangelists, to meet the need of training for such work.[12]

Within a few weeks, the results of this outreach initiative had proven far-reaching and transformative. As Shelton wrote at the time:

> The people hear the gospel gladly. In Madison Square Garden, more men have assembled daily to hear the message than gather on Sundays for any Protestant church service in Greater New York ...
>
> Working-men from nearby buildings, clerks from offices, boot-blacks sitting on their kits, street cleaners, messenger boys, police officers, contractors, well-to-do business men, drunkards, the unemployed and discouraged, editors and professional people, all listening with the same interest ...

---

11. See Taylor, *Borden of Yale* (1926), p. 188. One survey from 1906, citing Census Bureau data, states only 41 per cent of Americans held 'membership in religious organizations.' See the online survey data given on page four of the PDF posted at: https://www-tc.pbs.org/fmc/book/pdf/ch6.pdf

12. ibid., p. 189.

We never take up a collection. The one object is to reach [people;] from the beginning, we have had crowds of them. The work thus far has resulted in many transformations of character ... We believe that we are carrying out Christ's idea in going to the people, and not waiting for them to come to us.[13]

From the first, on learning of its mission, Borden felt a keen interest in the work the National Bible Institute had undertaken. Further acquaintance with this outreach initiative only increased his sense of its value.[14]

By the summer of 1910, after the burgeoning mission of the National Bible Institute began its third year, Borden's ardent interest led to active involvement and support. Shelton told the story of how this all unfolded.

In the summer of 1910, Shelton recalled, as Borden was leaving for Europe to attend the Edinburgh Missions Conference, and walked the deck of the steamer docked at the pier in New York City, the two had a far-reaching conversation that grew out of a recent meeting, and things Borden had learned about the work of the National Bible Institute. As Shelton spoke, Borden listened intently.

After a few moments, as Shelton paused for a reply, Borden said quietly:

'I want to help you in the work you are doing, and will send you a hundred dollars a month for the next year. If you will come to my cabin, I will write the first cheque now.'[15]

'We went down [to his stateroom],' Shelton said, 'and he wrote the cheque, and gave it to me. When I reached home, I found it was for two hundred dollars. "He is going abroad," I thought, "and has made it for two months this time." But exactly one month later came another cheque for two hundred dollars, and again the following month, two hundred.'

---

13. ibid., pp. 189-190.

14. ibid., p. 190.

15. ibid., p. 187.

'He is giving it all in six months,' was my conclusion.

'But when he returned at the end of the summer, he continued to send two hundred dollars a month through the entire year. I was learning to know Will Borden, one of [whose characteristics] was always to do better than he promised – more, and not less, than he led you to expect.'[16]

This shipboard visit, in June 1910, led directly to Borden's being invited by Shelton to become one of the directors of the National Bible Institute.[17]

'It was a call he could not refuse,' Geraldine Taylor wrote in her biography:

[However,] the position was no sinecure. It involved frequent journeys to New York to attend [the National Bible Institute] Board Meetings, and the problems of the work called for much thought and prayer. A large part of [Borden's] vacation in the summer of 1911 was spent in the heat and hurry of New York, taking a full share in meetings and other activities.

Shelton later remembered this good season vividly, saying:

I find in my diary under the date of May 8, 1911, the following:

'[Will Borden] came up from Princeton today to co-operate for a few weeks in the work of the National Bible Institute. A noble, generous, Christ-like young man – a rare gift of God to the work under his care ...'

[And so,] we placed a desk for him in my own office, and he continually manifested an eager desire to enter into the work; in every possible way.

Though he was only twenty-three, responsibility for our four [city] gospel halls was delegated to him [the McAuley Cremorne Mission on West 29th street, the Living Waters Mission on lower 3rd avenue, the Beacon Light Mission on upper 3rd avenue, and the Manhattan Gospel Hall on Manhattan street].

---

16. ibid., p. 188. This meant Borden gave $200 for eight months during 1910, or $1,600 (i.e. $40,000 today).

17. ibid., p. 190.

He kept in close touch with the [four] superintendents, counselling with them in [all necessary] details. He investigated men who were being considered for positions of trust. He gave much thought and prayer to drafting the *Principles and Practice* of the National Bible Institute, and prepared a document [of] great value in [NBI's] development …

It is a joy [also] to recall his first [talk] at our Madison Square meeting in the open air. His address was brief, but remarkably vigorous and direct. He stood there as a witness to the saving power of Jesus Christ. As he spoke, I rejoiced that the large company of listeners [could hear his] fervent testimony. [It] made the occasion memorable.

As a member of the [NBI] Board of Directors [Will Borden] was a valued counsellor. He turned the white light of Scripture on every matter that came up for consideration. His presence, in any meeting, was a moral and spiritual tonic. All his work began, continued, and ended in prayer.

Again and again, at our office, he would suggest before taking up the consideration of any important matter that we should unite in waiting upon God. Prayer was to him the first means to be used … He prayed as one confident that his heavenly Father would hear and answer.[18]

Borden's 'eager desire to enter into the work' of the National Bible Institute, as D. O. Shelton had described it, led to a remarkable series of events in summer 1911. *The New York Observer* recounted them in its May 23, 1912 issue:

… the outdoor work [of gospel gatherings grew in New York City,] until over seventy meetings a week were held during the summer of 1911. Printing House Square, Union Square, Madison Square, Herald Square, Longacre Square, Greeley Square, Sixth Avenue (at Twenty-Seventh Street), Third Avenue, in Harlem, various points on the Bowery, and Battery Park – all [were] used as centers for this campaign.

---

18. ibid., pp. 190-191.

> Exhaustive and properly conducted inquiries [later revealed]
> that more than seventy-five percent of those who attended
> [weren't] members of any church ... *Over one hundred and fifty
> thousand men were reached ...*[19]

Over seventy meetings a week, attended by more than one
hundred and fifty thousand people – nothing like this had ever
taken place before in New York's great metropolis. Borden was
at the heart of it all, during his Princeton Seminary vacation
days, 'and in the midst of summer heat,' immersing himself in
this ground-breaking work, and learning to preach in the city's
famous thoroughfares.[20]

A photo of William Borden preaching at Printing House Square, New York City
(from *The New York Observer* magazine, 23 May 1912).

Moreover, Shelton's statement that Borden 'gave much thought
and prayer to drafting the *Principles and Practice* of the National
Bible Institute, and prepared a document of exceedingly great

---

19. From pages 661-662 of the 23 May 1912 issue of *The New York Observer* magazine.

20. See page 50 of the May 1913 issue of *China's Millions* magazine.

value in [NBI's] development' is a telling statement to consider in further detail. Essentially, it meant that Borden had been, in a very real sense, one of the National Bible Institute's founders.

He was certainly a key benefactor; and was also (despite the many demands on his time as a graduate student at Princeton Seminary) one of the National Bible Institute's most important administrative leaders.

Borden had yet to finish his studies at Princeton, but had already emerged as a co-founder, leader and benefactor of a nationally prominent ministry.[21]

Many gifts rested in this young man of twenty-three.

And there was yet one more facet to Borden's involvement with NBI.

For during his last year at Princeton Theological Seminary, Borden prepared 'a course of lectures ... to deliver to the students of the National Bible Institute.'[22]

This was a serious undertaking, and one that garnered prominent notice in the New York City press. As Geraldine Taylor described this series of lectures:

> The Epistle to the Galatians was [Borden's] subject, and the long list of books he consulted shows how thorough was his preparation. *Luther's Commentary* he enjoyed especially, but it was only one of several [he used].
>
> How he [made] time, in the midst of his 3rd year in Seminary to complete and deliver these seven lectures [was] a mystery. Week by week his class in the Marble Collegiate Church numbered from sixty to a hundred [students].[23]

---

21. The National Bible Institute school was a Venetian-Gothic building at 340 West 55th St., between Eighth Ave and Ninth Ave in Manhattan, built in 1925. See: https://www.revolvy.com/page/National-Bible-Institute-School-and-Dormitory-%28New-York-City%29

22. See Taylor, *Borden of Yale* (1926), p 194. See also *The New York Observer*, Oct. 26, 1911, p. 529. 'William W. Borden will conduct a course in the epistle to the Galatians,' see *The New York Observer*, Sept. 28, 1911, p. 409.

23. See page 7 of the Monday, January 15, 1912 edition of *The Brooklyn Daily Eagle* newspaper.

For many readers, this mention of the Marble Collegiate Church will prompt a flicker of recognition. For this church was the very setting where, beginning in 1932, Dr Norman Vincent Peale would serve for fifty-two years as Senior Minister. Dr Peale is best-remembered as the author of *The Power of Positive Thinking*, which sold over twenty million copies.[24]

Returning to Borden and his lecture series on Galatians for 1912, his friend and National Bible Institute co-founder, D. O. Shelton, paid this tribute, saying: '[Will's] handling of this difficult Epistle showed that he had completely mastered his material. His outlines were clear and comprehensive, and he made the book a living message to [those who heard him].'[25]

Fine press notice of Borden's course on Galatians began in *The Brooklyn Eagle* newspaper, which stated on Monday, January 15, 1912:

> The National Bible Institute's School for Christian Workers announces a course on the Epistle to the Galatians to start … Thursday night, [January 18,] and [taught] by William W. Borden of Princeton Theological Seminary. The sessions [will be] held in the chapel of the Marble Collegiate Church.[26]

Further coverage of Borden's course ran in *The New York Observer*, which described why New Yorkers might wish to be a part of this lecture series—

> The [National Bible Institute] winter program includes … an interdenominational evening school, [with] sessions every Thursday evening in the Marble Collegiate Church, Fifth-Avenue and Twenty-Ninth-Street.
>
> Many prominent Christian workers [will] conduct courses … among them the Rev. Dr C. I. Scofield, Edgar Whitaker Work,

---

24. See 'Marble Collegiate Church: History,' an article posted online at: http://www.marblechurch.org/welcome/history/

25. See Taylor, *Borden of Yale* (1926), p. 194.

26. See the January 15, 1912 edition of *The Brooklyn Daily Eagle,* p. 7.

the Rev. C. X. Hutchinson, [D. O.] Shelton, William W. Borden, [H. R.] Monro and Joseph A. Richards.[27]

The New York Observer's mention of C. I. Scofield pointed to the noteworthy company Borden was part of as a lecturer at the National Bible Institute. Scofield was General Editor of the famous Oxford University Press *Scofield Reference Bible* – only recently published, in January 1909. In print today, the *Scofield Reference Bible* sold over one million copies by the end of the Great Depression, and in excess of two million copies by the close of World War II.[28]

Other lecturers for NBI's winter program were prominent also.

In 1917, Edgar Whitaker Work became the author of a very fine text called *The Bible in English Literature*. It was published by F. H. Revell, the famous publisher of D. L. Moody's books. Tracing how the Bible shaped literature and culture, E. W. Work spoke of 'its permanent worth for human thinking and living.' And, as he noted: the Bible has 'entered into the very mold of English literature.'[29]

Fittingly, he cited Nicholas Murray Butler, President of Columbia University, who had written that 'without the Bible, it is impossible to understand the literature of the English language, from Chaucer to Browning.'[30]

H. R. Monro, Vice-President of the Niagara Lithograph Company (the printer for *National Geographic*),[31] and Treasurer of the National Bible Institute, was a friend Borden knew well. A gifted businessman—he was an eloquent speaker and writer—and a familiar figure at Christian conferences. His articles were

---

27. See *The New York Observer* magazine, October 26, 1911, (New York: S. E. Morse and R. C. Morse, 1911), p. 529.

28. See R. T. Mangum and M. S. Sweetnam, *The Scofield Bible* (Colorado Springs: Paternoster, 2009), pp. 1 and 169.

29. See E. W. Work, *The Bible in English Literature* (New York: Revell, 1917), p. 17.

30. ibid., p. 17.

31. The Niagara Lithograph Co. printed for many famous publishers: National Geographic, Simon & Schuster, HarperCollins, and Random House.

published in prominent periodicals. His oft-stated intent, as a communicator, was to speak with 'a clear eye, a warm hand [of friendship], and a loving heart.'[32]

For Borden to be featured among such scholars and lecturers at the Marble Collegiate Church was a sign of his rising prominence nationwide.

He was a gifted and learned young speaker, among accomplished peers.

∾ ∾ ∾

Even as Borden was actively involved with the early years and work of the National Bible Institute while at Princeton Seminary, he'd also been an integral part of the leadership of another prominent school: Moody Bible Institute.[33]

On September 16, 1909, when he was twenty-one and beginning his studies at Princeton Seminary, Borden was elected a Trustee of Moody Bible Institute, joining leaders and educators like H. P. Crowell and Dr James Martin Gray.

Crowell was a noted benefactor and leader, while Dr Gray's distinguished career as an educator began in the 1890s, when he worked with Dr A. J. Gordon to found the Boston Missionary Training School, the forerunner of Gordon College.

Gray cherished Borden's friendship, young as he was, and spoke of Borden's 'wise counsels, and many a stirring address to the student-body' at Moody Bible Institute. Gray also praised Borden's keen interest in MBI's 'curriculum, its method of work, and its plans for development.' Last of all, Borden was a faithful source of 'generous gifts' to the school D. L. Moody founded.[34]

---

32. See Hugh R. Munro, 'The Layman's Call to Evangelism,' in *Men and Missions* magazine, Dec. 1914, pp. 113-116. This article was an eloquent plea for Christians to take part in what is now called 'marketplace ministry,' going 'where people are' in places like New York City.

33. 'While still pursuing his seminary course, [Borden] was elected [a Trustee] of the Moody Bible Institute of Chicago, a Director of the National Bible Institute [and] a Member of the North American Council of the China Inland Mission.' See *The Princeton Seminary Bulletin*, May 1913, p. 9.

34. Dr James Martin Gray, quoted in *The Missionary Visitor*, June 1913, p. 197.

Nor was this the full extent of Borden's legacy at Moody Bible Institute.

Dr Gray treasured the scholarship Borden brought to bear on drafting a new 'statement setting forth the doctrinal standards' of Moody Bible Institute. He served with distinction on the committee 'appointed for that purpose.' During this time, Borden submitted his best thoughts for this Statement of Faith by letter, and ever after, Dr Gray kept it among his choice possessions. 'This letter is much valued by me,' he was later to tell biographer Geraldine Taylor.[35]

By the time of Borden's graduation from Princeton Seminary, he'd served on Moody Bible Institute's Board of Trustees for nearly three years. Trips to Chicago for MBI board meetings became a regular occurrence during his seminary years, and they gave him a chance to meaningfully guide the growth of an institute of increasing national influence and stature.

Young as he was, William Borden had become a genuine educational leader.

∽ ∽ ∽

Charlie Campbell saw first-hand how Borden took up these responsibilities and duties during his Princeton Seminary years. It was a compelling story:

> [One could] see that the calls on [Bill's] time would be many. Few men of his age could so well have handled the duties that pressed upon him. [Yet] his singleness of purpose helped him, and gave such direction to his life that no one, even among his nearest friends, saw anything but a quiet, consistent, unhurried doing of each task that came. [And] the unusual feature of his relationship to all such organizations was that he was never satisfied with merely giving generous financial aid ... Almost every month, he went to New Haven to look over the work of the Yale Hope Mission. New York, New Haven and Chicago trips succeeded one another, and still, he never seemed to neglect his [class

---

35. See Taylor, *Borden of Yale* (1926), p. 202.

studies,] though he carried a much heavier schedule than the average man. More than this, he stood very high in scholarship [at Princeton Seminary].[36]

Commencement at Princeton Seminary in 1912 was particularly meaningful for Borden, and others who attended. 'From all over the world came congratulatory messages [for the seminary's centenary year.] Many distinguished visitors were there for the occasion and the Borden home was full of guests.'

As to Borden himself, he remembered: 'President Patton was at his best, and preached a tremendous sermon on "The faith once for all delivered to the saints."'[37]

～ ～ ～

What was it that Borden so admired in President Patton's discourse?

Given his heartfelt commendation of this 'tremendous sermon,' it is worth taking some time to consider the key points Patton spoke about.

For to be sure, they were also things Borden valued and cherished.

Dr Patton's sermon bestowed moments of eloquence, insight, and wisdom – keepsakes for Borden, his fellow graduates in the Centenary Class of 1912, and all those in attendance. It was a call to remember; and remain faithful.

He began with a dash of humor: 'Princeton Theological Seminary opened its doors a hundred years ago,' he mused, 'one professor, and three students: a ratio of instructors to pupils which ought to satisfy the most exacting demands of modern pedagogy!'[38]

Next, Patton stated, many of Princeton Seminary's ablest professors 'brought with them the ripe results of a long experience in the pastorate.'

---

36. Charles Campbell, quoted in Taylor, *Borden of Yale* (1926), pp. 175-176.
37. See Taylor, *Borden of Yale* (1926), p. 206.
38. See *The Princeton Seminary Bulletin*, May 1912, p. 14.

This, he observed, 'is a matter for which we should be profoundly grateful. There should always be in the Seminary—as there are today, and never in larger proportion than today—a number of men who, when they speak to students in regard to the work upon which they are about to enter, can speak out of an affluent ministerial experience.'[39]

Patton also praised the theological character of the Seminary: 'Princeton's boast,' he stated, 'if she have reason to boast at all, is her unswerving fidelity to the theology of the Reformation. *Semper eadem* is a motto that would well befit her.'[40]

Then, alluding to 'this very progressive age,' Patton painted an interrogatory scene for those who listened to him:

'Do you mean to tell us,' Patton imagined some objector saying:

> that you still adhere to that old theology of the Reformers, which men in these days have so generally abandoned? [Patton then replied:]
>
> I am not aware, to begin with, that it is so generally abandoned. But if it were, that would not prove it to be untrue. It would only prove that it is not fashionable.
>
> Professor [William] James [of Harvard] remarks somewhere, in one of his later books, that 'souls are not fashionable.'
>
> Some of us, nevertheless, go on believing in 'souls,' hoping that by and by there will be a reaction, and that some of our philosophical friends will reconsider their hasty attitude toward the spiritual side of our nature. This is the way we [at Princeton Seminary] feel toward the old theology.
>
> *It may come into fashion again.*[41]

Dr Patton was nothing if not adept at rhetorical flourish; and showed this with a continuation of his imagined dialogue. He posed a second question, saying: 'Has not modern philosophy

---

39. ibid., p. 15.
40. ibid., p. 18. *Semper eadem,* in Latin, means 'always the same.'
41. ibid., p. 18. Italics added.

made it difficult, if not impossible, to maintain the positions of the old theology?' someone might ask. In answer, Patton replied:

'I am not aware of that state of things. I know that certain forms of philosophical opinion are incompatible with [orthodox] Christianity. But I do not know of any <u>necessity</u> for adopting those forms of philosophical opinion.'[42]

This was to say that streams of modern thought do not, merely because they are modern, unsettle any commitment to historic Christian belief.

Novelty does not imply unassailable cogency.

Moving next to defend 'the theology of the Reformation,' Patton said that:

> All problems of ethics, all questions of duty, all phases of individual and social morality are … legitimately within the sphere of the Calvinistic theology. All the moral sciences, and all the speculations of philosophers in regard to human conduct, must come under the view of Him who looks upon conduct as related to a supreme norm of Right, and an ideal conception of the Good.[43]

Beyond this, Dr Patton voiced deep concern over those who relegated Jesus to the place of an ancient teacher from Palestine, or the 'historic Jesus.'

To do so, Patton said, was to strip Christ of 'the insignia of Divine royalty,' and instead, pin upon Him 'the gaudy decorations of a minimizing theology.'

Here, perhaps, was the heart of Dr Patton's Centenary Sermon. 'My friends,' he said:

> I want you to understand it, I want you to know that if this view be true, these minimizing utterances be correct, we are absolutely no better off today than they were in the days of Thales, Pythagoras, and Democritus.

---

42. ibid., p. 18.
43. ibid., p. 19.

We have had Platonists, we have had Stoics, and idealists and materialists, and we have had agnostics in abundance throughout the centuries – and today [champions of minimizing theology] are no better off than were those old philosophers of Greece. It is a sad position.[44]

Last, Dr Patton offered a passage in his sermon rich in nautical allusion and imagery. Such things were close to Borden's heart as a mariner, and he must have listened closely to them. 'This proud ship of Christianity,' Dr Patton began:

we have freighted her with all our hopes, and we have embarked in her the fortunes of our souls. She has plowed the ocean this well nigh two thousand years; she has weathered the storms of persecution; she has sailed through the fogs of superstition; she has encountered the collisions of philosophy; she has been swept from stem to stern by great waves of scepticism, but in spite of it all, we have paced the decks with a sense of unwavering security; we have felt sure no wind could harm her.[45]

And yet …

Patton asked all those who listened to consider the 'unhappy moment' when some, by their own admission, saw orthodox Christianity striking 'the iceberg of historical criticism.' Were they then ready to consign her 'to a fathomless grave?'

Since many thought-leaders, Patton said, perceived orthodox Christianity as a tempest-beaten ship, listing or foundering, it was a time for deep concern.

'Do you realize the situation?' he asked:

Do you hear with calm complacency and unconcern the order that is given to leave the proud ship of Christianity, and lower the boats of [a lesser] philosophy? Are you ready to sit in your little dory of philosophy and, under an unlighted sky, look out over

---

44. ibid., p. 22.
45. ibid., p. 22.

the waste of black water, and hope that somehow, or some way, or some when, you will drift to some shore of happy destiny? Is that your position?[46]

The theology of the Reformation, Dr Patton advised, is the hope that truly sustains: in all times and places. He closed with these thoughts, for William Borden, and all the graduates of the Seminary Class of 1912—

> But be strong. Know well the strength of the cause which you have espoused, and be unwavering in your loyalty to it ... Remember, that no small part of your duty is to see to it that you earnestly contend for the faith once delivered unto the saints.[47]

And as for William Borden himself, Samuel Zwemer stated—

'He was high among the foremost men of his class [at Princeton] and won not only the love but the high esteem of his professors.'[48]

Dr William Brenton Greene, Stuart Professor of Apologetics and Christian Ethics during Borden's time at Princeton Seminary, was one of the gifted scholars who felt gratitude for having such a fine student in his class. Placing his memories of Borden side by side, we learn that Dr Greene said the following—

> He seemed to feel that God had sent him here [to Princeton] ...
>
> He valued scholarship [for all] its help to him in [learning] to preach to those who were far off 'the unsearchable riches of Christ' ...
>
> [His] mental power [was] great; [and his] scholarship ... distinguished ... He had such a rugged conviction of the truth of Christianity, arising out of his own deep experience of its power ...
>
> [Then too, his] influence [was] great on the other students ... He was a living force, and a mighty force for all that was orderly and right.

---

46. ibid., p. 22.

47. ibid., p. 23. Italics added.

48. See Zwemer, *William Whiting Borden* (1913), p. 114.

> It was [special] to come into the classroom, and see him
> sitting in one of the forward seats …[49]

Distinguished academics are often known for professorial reserve.
Borden's character and achievements at Princeton Seminary were
such that Dr Greene set aside any such reserve to offer warm
commendation.

That was telling, and memorable. Borden's legacy at Princeton
Seminary was that of a gifted intellect, guided by faith.

Once commencement was over, and after such a full, taxing final
semester at Princeton Seminary, Borden was 'eager for a few weeks
in Switzerland among the [mountains and] glaciers' he loved.[50]
He certainly had earned a rest, and a genuine reward, for all that
he'd accomplished during his time at Princeton.

So he booked passage on a steamship bound for Europe, and
prepared for a trip of several weeks' duration on the continent.

Just before he embarked, however, worrying news came: his great
friend and National Bible Institute co-founder D. O. Shelton was
on the verge of a nervous breakdown. Deeply concerned, Borden
rushed over to the NBI offices, and learned that Shelton's physician
had given strict orders that Shelton was to step away from all official
duties for a long period of complete rest. He would be away for
months, if not longer, and there was no one to take his place.

Borden did not hesitate in deciding what was to be done:
'Looks as though I might have to change my plans a bit, and help,'
was his journal entry for that day.[51]

'Quietly then,' as Geraldine Taylor wrote—

> his passage was given up, and the trip postponed. He was
> sufficiently familiar with the National Bible Institute to step in
> effectively, and before long was fully in charge …

---

49. See *The Princeton Seminary Bulletin*, May 1913, p. 10.
50. See Taylor, *Borden of Yale* (1926), p. 195.
51. ibid., pp. 195-196.

He was responsible not only for the office-work. There were the daily open-air meetings; the oversight of the students in their classes and practical training; the charge of four Rescue Missions and of a monthly magazine, [*The Bible To-Day,*] as well as the financial care of all this work.

It was a serious undertaking, the more so as Borden had decided before entering upon it that he must not be his own Providence in the matter of [monetary] supplies. Mr Shelton was not himself in a position to finance the work, and when sufficient means were not forthcoming, he and his helpers had no resource but prayer.

To strengthen them in their attitude of looking to the Lord in faith had long been Borden's desire. He believed that the promises of God were absolutely true and dependable. Here then was an opportunity for proving the reality of his own faith as well as strengthening that of his fellow-workers.

He would continue to give just as he had been giving; but would not permit himself to escape difficulties by the easy method of drawing upon his own banking account.[52]

This led to a remarkable thing, as Shelton's wife Matilda wrote—

There followed a time of severe testing along financial lines for [Borden]. Days passed without a dollar coming in, and mission superintendents and others needing their salaries! Some time before, [he] had faced the question of making up known deficiencies in the various Christian enterprises in which he was interested; and as his gifts were always thoughtfully and prayerfully given, he had decided against it.

Yet here was a temptation! How much easier [it would have been to] put his hand in his pocket, and make up this lack than to spend hours in prayer alone and with friends, awaiting God's gracious answer. But the answers came – and with them such a sense of the reality and nearness of the living God as days and hours of ease could never have afforded.[53]

---

52. ibid., p. 196.
53. ibid., p. 197.

Amid this challenging work, supervising the National Bible Institute in Shelton's absence, Borden had still another concern to look to.

He was asked by his family to help with a medical need. In the midst of the hottest summer in New York for many years, a time when 'the heat of the city was over-powering,' Borden was asked to help care 'for an invalid uncle.'[54]

He quickly complied in saying yes to this request. So he traveled frequently to Long Beach, where his relatives lived, 'to be a cheer to his aunt, and to wheel the patient up and down the boardwalk in a chair, [thence] returning to the city by an early train in the morning.'[55]

His caring nature was never more manifest than in these days: when he gave so unstintingly to his family, and the National Bible Institute.

After Princeton Seminary, Borden undertook a literary venture. It pointed to the kind of book he might well have written in time: a book of spiritual reflections.

'The Price of Power' was an essay-length article he crafted at Long Beach for the magazine of which D. O. Shelton was editor, *The Bible To-Day*. It was 'the out-growth of a thought that had long been in his mind.'[56]

And why so? A saying oft-quoted by D. L. Moody had stirred him greatly:

> *The world has yet to see what God can do*
> *with a fully consecrated man.*

This, said Geraldine Taylor, was Borden's 'highest ambition.'[57]

---

54. ibid., p. 197.

55. ibid., p. 197.

56. ibid., p. 198.

57. ibid., p. 198.

So it was that Borden, in the summer of 1912, took up a fountain pen at his desk in the family lodgings at Long Beach, and wrote what was the most revealing article published during his lifetime. His thoughts were stirred by the phrase so closely associated with Moody: and it was a point of departure also for moments from his own journey of faith. He spoke of things he saw at the heart of that journey. Seated perhaps by a window overlooking the sea, he set his best thoughts in prose.

He began with an arresting word: 'Power to be effective workers for Christ in this needy world is a thing which many Christians long for.'[58] But how to go about it? To pursue wisdom, in framing an answer, would be Borden's guiding purpose.

He began with an allusion to two transformational figures from Christian history, Moody and Charles Finney. They were exemplars for him.

'The average Christian layman or minister,' he said, 'who thinks on these things at all, looks back at men like Moody and Finney and longs for a portion of their spirit to fall on him.' Or perhaps, Borden mused, such a layman or minister 'thinks of some great saint, living or dead, who seemed to have great power in a less spectacular, but nonetheless real way.'[59]

What was the one trait that such Christ-followers had in common?

For Borden, the gift of 'power in witnessing for Christ' was bestowed by the Holy Spirit on people whose lives were marked by a deep and abiding resolve to seek and obey God in all things.[60] He phrased it this way in his article:

'The nature of the obedience which is required,' is obedience that 'involves unconditional surrender and also complete consecration [i.e. dedication to God].'[61]

---

58. See *The Bible To-Day* magazine, summer 1913, (New York: The National Bible Institute, 1913), p. 132.

59. ibid., p. 132.

60. ibid., p. 132.

61. ibid., p. 132.

To explain this, Borden looked to the apostle Peter's 'Pentecostal Sermon,' during which he had declared: 'Each of you must repent of your sins and turn to God, and be baptized in the name of Jesus Christ for the forgiveness of your sins. Then you will receive the gift of the Holy Spirit' (Acts 2:38).[62]

'You may think,' Borden observed, 'this is going back to the first principles of faith in Christ.' Borden agreed; but there was a reason why he did this.

Repentance and baptism, he stated, 'apply also in the sphere of the higher spiritual life. If we are to obey God fully,' Borden explained, 'we must come to Him penitently, confessing our sins and putting them away.' Here he paused a moment. 'It may not be a welcome thought,' he said, 'but I believe it is true … [For] where sin reigns, Christ cannot reign; and in just so far as His jurisdiction is thus limited, do we lessen His ability to use us.'[63]

Then, Borden asked his readers to look to Christ Himself, saying: 'Even so must we, if we would be His disciples, say no to self.'[64]

And in prose reminiscent of C. S. Lewis, Borden continued:

'Follow Me' means that we take Him and enthrone Him as Master and Lord of our lives, putting ourselves under the orders of the Captain of our salvation … This is but natural and right in view of what He has done for us; and when we consider His wisdom and love, what reason for hesitating and holding back can there possibly be? And yet how the human heart rebels against this step, and contests every inch of ground.[65]

This was a reasoned and eloquent plea – acknowledging challenges, yet seeing the better part of wisdom. Here Borden showed himself a gifted, insightful teacher.

---

62. Acts 2:38, New Living Translation.

63. See *The Bible To-Day*, summer 1913, p. 132.

64. ibid., pp. 132-133.

65. ibid., p. 132. C. S. Lewis once wrote of 'the observed frontier situation, in which everything looks as if Nature were not resisting an alien invader but rebelling against a lawful sovereign.' See C. S. Lewis, *Miracles* (New York: Simon & Schuster, 1996), p. 46.

His reflections held things worth hearing; and his was a promising pen.

Next Borden spoke directly to his peer group, collegians and seminarians, for inasmuch as he was speaking of experiences on a road he had traveled, he wished to commend wisdom he found on the way. He wished to befriend fellow travelers.

'For young people,' he stated, 'the greatest stumbling block seems to be the question of life work.' Borden understood this, but urged readers to consider things from an important, but perhaps overlooked perspective.

If we, he asked, 'fix our eyes upon our loving Lord, whose plan for our life is the very best possible … ought [it] to be hard to consecrate ourselves fully?'[66]

Then came some of the most compelling lines from his pen:

> Have you ever fully consecrated yourself to Christ? Are you willing to say what He wants you to say, to do what He wants you to do, to go where He would send you, and be what He would have you be? In short, have you made Christ supreme in your life in things small and great? If you haven't, and want power truly to serve Him, consecrate yourself now.[67]

Here, once more, Borden adverted to Christ's example, saying: 'He did His Father's will always, in all things. And this, He Himself tells us, was really the secret of God's abiding with Him.'[68]

In John 8:29, Christ had explained this sterling truth: 'And He that sent Me is with Me; He has not left me alone; for I always do the things that are pleasing to Him.'[69]

---

66. ibid., p. 133.

67. ibid., p. 133.

68. ibid., p. 133.

69. A slight paraphrase of the King James Version of this verse that Borden originally cited.

Building on this foundation, Borden said: 'Daily, Always, that must be the rule – and when it is the rule, [or standard], the flow of power will be continuous.'[70]

~ ~ ~

Yet how does this power show itself? For Borden, it centered on love in the lives of followers of Christ. Exploring this theme, Borden penned one of the most stirring passages in his article:

> God is love; but we would never have known it, had He not created us, and revealed Himself to us. So we, as we may have true love in our hearts, let us seek to express it in some appropriate word or deed.
>
> Even a cup of cold water given in His name is pleasing to the Father. Surely this is enough to point out the way in which we should seek to make Him supreme in every nook and corner of our lives.[71]

And then, the close of Borden's article offered lines filled with hope—

> If these conditions are met, God will make good His promise. In the moment we do our part, He does His. We need not all expect to be Moodys or Finneys, nevertheless the promise is sure …
>
> 'If any man thirst, let him come unto Me, and drink,' as Scripture hath said, 'and within him shall flow rivers of living water.'[72]

Scripture held true riches of teaching about discipleship, as Borden observed in a companion reflection to his article. We may seek and find those riches.

'If we are to follow His way,' Borden observed, 'we must be guided by the directions which He has given us in His Word.'[73]

All these reflections lent a store of wisdom for the journey of faith.

---

70. See *The Bible To-Day*, summer 1913, p. 133.

71. ibid., p. 141.

72. ibid., p. 141.

73. See W. W. Borden, *Gospel Addresses* (Chicago: The Bible Institute Colportage Association, 1914), p. 40.

In the family study in Long Beach, at a desk by the sea, Borden had written words of abiding life and purpose. And they still speak, across the years.

If 'The Price of Power' was a literary task, just after Princeton, Borden had another experience, several months before then, of a wholly different nature. And it yielded, as he said: 'the first sermon or talk I have ever written out fully.'[74]

It took place far from the ivy-covered walls of academe, for Borden's sermon was spoken before a throng of 'some two hundred men in New Haven County Jail on January 21, 1912.'[75]

We know little of the circumstances which led to this event, but it seems it likely came about through the agency of friends from Yale Hope Mission, many of whom, including Louis Bernhardt, had either spent time in prison, or knew people incarcerated there.

All through his time at Princeton Theological Seminary, Borden returned to New Haven and Yale Hope Mission periodically to see how things were faring. He was active in its leadership, and of course, he was still a primary benefactor. It would have been natural for him, on hearing about an upcoming prison ministry visit, to wish to be part of it, and to be willing to speak if he'd been asked to do so.

In this unlikely setting, several worthy moments in prose came. And because Borden published few things in his lifetime, it's the more important to look at these reflections, and what they say of his faith – in various turns of phrase.

Some of these reflections were straightforward declarations, as when he told the inmates how hope becomes a living reality. 'We live in an age of grace,' he said, 'when salvation is freely offered to all men who will believe on Jesus.'[76]

---

74. ibid., p. 7.

75. ibid., p. 7.

76. ibid., p. 15.

Another phrase in simple prose, looked back to Christmas, just passed, with tidings like a carol: 'He came first to this earth,' Borden said, 'a lowly babe; born in a stable, and laid in a manger.'[77] Here Christ was the one to make all things new.

Nor was the theme of resurrection far from Borden's thoughts, as when he said that Christ 'arose from the grave and ascended into heaven, from whence He will come again … in glory, with all His mighty angels with Him.'[78]

And there could be blessèd assurance as well, for all who listened.

Borden told the prisoners at New Haven: 'surely He is one in whom to have perfect trust and confidence.'[79] Then he spoke one seven-word phrase which held a whole world of meaning: 'Cast yourself upon the mercy of God.'[80]

Salvation was like a harbor beacon in a storm-tossed sea, and in light of the mercy he'd just spoken of, Borden told the inmates: 'There is but one thing to do: put your case absolutely in Jesus' hands: let Him plead for you, and agree to do as He directs.'[81]

Borden was speaking to prisoners; but words like these held resonance for all settings and places. His thoughts gave timeless images of transforming grace.

And this was true as Borden spoke of Christ's goodness to all who believe:

'He is in heaven on the throne of His father, ever living to make intercession for us: the prints of the nails in His hands and feet … bear eloquent testimony to the price that was paid – to secure the priceless gift of salvation for us.'[82]

---

77. ibid., p. 16.
78. ibid., p. 16.
79. ibid., p. 14.
80. ibid., p. 12.
81. ibid., p. 13.
82. ibid., p. 15. Selection edited.

With words like this, things of heaven drew near in the New Haven jail. ∾ ∾ ∾

Young as he was, during his last year at Princeton Theological Seminary, and just after, Borden had become a genuine leader. He was a Trustee of Moody Bible Institute (appointed in 1909),[83] and had served for two years on the National Bible Institute's Board of Directors. Both were nationally prominent institutions.

He'd assumed these roles, even as he was completing his own education.

Nor had his seminary studies been neglected, for in the words of his former professors, he had achieved excellent marks for scholarship, even as he assisted with important family duties – helping to host guests at the Cleveland mansion, or caring for his invalid uncle at Long Beach for several weeks.

As Borden looked ahead to his ordination in autumn 1912, and the start of his tour of American colleges as a Traveling Secretary for the Student Volunteer Movement, others knew he was a gifted and dedicated leader.[84]

They had seen great things in him; and expected great things from him. ∾ ∾ ∾

Still, not everything in Borden's life centered on important responsibilities. It is important to recall that he was still a young twenty-something, and grateful for occasions like his first 'triennial reunion' at Yale, or the 'third anniversary' of his graduation in 1909: a time of hilarity, hi-jinks, and glad reunions with friends.

Borden was only able to get away from his pressing duties at the National Bible Institute for a little more than two days,

---

83. *The Herald of Gospel Liberty,* Sept. 23, 1909, p. 28, states Borden became a Trustee of Moody Bible Institute on Wed., Sept. 22, 1909. He was 21.

84. Borden's close friend Kenneth Latourette was a Traveling Secretary for SVM in 1909. See K. S. Latourette, *Beyond the Ranges* (Grand Rapids, Michigan: Wm. B. Eerdmans Co., 1967), p. 37. And here, Latourette's SVM service may well have influenced Borden.

but he made the most of his time in New Haven. And there is a bittersweet quality to it all: for this would prove to be the only such reunion he was ever able to attend at Yale.

That fact alone makes it important to describe what this glad occasion was like, and what it meant to Borden. It's a window on a too-little-seen facet of his life: a rare and special time for friends and fellowship.

Borden's triennial class reunion took place over four days: Saturday, June 15 until Tuesday, June 18. As Geraldine Taylor, writing of this time, said:

> A great occasion was on hand, the first reunion of his class at Yale, and [Borden] managed to get away for the weekend.
>
> But the triennial banquet, the climax of the proceedings, did not come until Monday [June 17], and there was a Board meeting of the National Bible Institute that day that he felt he should attend.
>
> Great was the consternation of his classmates when it appeared that he was leaving before the banquet. Many old friends were there, among them his roommate [during his junior and senior years], Mac Vilas.
>
> 'Indeed, you won't go to New York,' they exclaimed with insistence. 'We won't let you go!'
>
> 'But we might as well have talked to the Rock of Gibraltar,' Vilas said.
>
> [Still,] Borden managed to return the following day, and that he entered fully into the spirit of the occasion may be seen in his Journal—
>
> *'Attended to a few things at the office and left for New Haven, getting there just in time for the picture and the parade to the field for the game, which Yale won from Harvard, 9-6.*
>
> *Our class wore farmers' costumes. It was a great jollification!'*[85]

To learn more about this festive occasion, the pages of the July 5, 1912 issue of the *Yale Alumni Weekly* hold a trove of details.[86]

---

85. See Taylor, *Borden of Yale* (1926), pp. 201-202. Selection edited.

86. See *The Yale Alumni Weekly*, v. 21, July 5, 1912, (New Haven: Yale University Press, 1912), p. 1031.

As for the wearing of farmers' costumes, one of Borden's classmates and a good friend, Maxwell Parry, came dressed as former president Theodore Roosevelt, and marched around the stadium at Yale under a wide brimmed hat blazoned with the initials 'T.R.' In tandem with Parry, or rather 'T.R.,' was a classmate touting a large white placard on which an inscrutable phrase had been written in bold script:

Ask Teddy who loves the farmer[87]

Other vivid, whimsical details from this boisterous conclave appeared in the *Yale Alumni Weekly* also, including this rehearsal of reunion happenings:

> By Saturday night nearly a hundred fellows had registered in the rustic 'Hutel Lobby' at 1081 Chapel Street, the day was quiet, except for [boisterous] greetings here and there. Not until Monday morning, when nearly two hundred farmers poured out from the '09 headquarters into Chapel Street, did things really begin to happen. We all strolled down to A1 Osborn, where Harold Stokes tried to control the gathered steam of three years and a rainy day.
>
> He arose. We cheered; and threw up our straw hats.
>
> 'Gentlemen—' said he. We roared, pounded the seats and stamped. After three years here we all were again in old Osborn, alive, happy, a hundred and more old friends ... together.[88]

Borden reveled as much as any of his classmates did in such a setting. He was grateful for the gift of friends, and his classmates at Yale felt much the same about him. To see them together in this way, for one last time, was special.

---

87. ibid., p. 1030.

88. ibid., p. 1031.

Interlude: A Sojourn at Shelving Rock

Anyone who knew [Bill] at all could not but be influenced by his ideals and ambitions; and to us who counted ourselves friends of his, they were much more.[1]
– Elsa Frost (1913)

One of the most vivid memories I have of [Bill] is as he sat before our open fire at camp one Sunday evening. We were all there singing hymns, and the only light was that of the fire, which shone full on his face. How earnest it was, and [how] he sang the hymns he loved! 'O Love That Will Not Let Me Go' and 'In The Secret Of His Presence' were among his favorites. But it was not the firelight only, that brought that light to his face.[2]
– Rosalie Day (Bryn Mawr, Class of 1912)

Most memories of William Borden, by an expanse of water, center on times at sea on board the family sloop *Tsatsawassa* – under full sail off the coastal waters of Camden, Maine. But there are recollections of Borden tied to inland waters; and in particular to Lake George, in the Adirondack Region of New York State.

---

1. See Taylor, *Borden of Yale* (1926), p. 169. Selection edited. Elsa Frost was the wife of Dr Inglis Frost, son of H. W. Frost, Dir. of China Inland Mission, North America.

2. ibid., p. 169.

As Geraldine Taylor has recounted in her biography:

A group of later recollections, running on into Princeton years, come from the family of [William's] College friend, Sherwood Day. The Days were fortunate in having a camp of their own, [at Shelving Rock,] tucked away on the low shoulder of a mountain overlooking Lake George. William loved the spot, close to that [fine] expanse of water ...[3]

Sherwood Sunderland Day, Yale, Class of 1911, was born in Catskill, New York, in April 1887, the son of Orrin and Rosalie Sunderland Day. While at Yale, he was active in religious work, serving as a Bible class leader, a mission study group leader, a class deacon and president of Dwight Hall, the Y.M.C.A. group at Yale. He was also secretary of the University Football Association. Day's ardent hope was to one day go into foreign mission work.[4]

Given their mutual interests, Day and Borden likely met as soon as Day came to Yale in the fall of 1907. By that time, Borden was already well known as a leader of campus religious activities at Dwight Hall, and the two new friends would have had a mutual friend and mentor in Dr Henry Wright, the young scholar who had done so much to help Dwight Hall become a center of spiritual life at Yale.

When Borden arrived at Shelving Rock, he took to rustic camping with the Day family as though he'd been a guest with them all his life.

For one thing, there was no standing on ceremony during his time in the Adirondacks with the Day family. He pitched in, and helped with many tasks.

As one of the gathering recalled of Borden's visit:

From the room in which I write I can see where a limb has been cut off a tree, high up from the ground. [Bill] cut it off. Someone had

---

3. ibid., p. 156. Orrin Day, Sherwood Day's great-grandfather, was a 'founder of the American Bible Society in 1815.' See F. A. Gallt, *Greene County* (Catskill: no pub. listed, 1915), p. 280.

4. See *History of the Class of 1911, Yale College,* v. 1 (New Haven: Yale University Press, 1911), p. 106.

expressed a wish [when he was with us] that the dead limb might go, because it looked like an ugly clenched-fist, and he set out to do it.

The ladder was not long enough, and he had to prop it up – it was on a steep hillside, and almost dangerous to do so. He had to hang on with his right arm, and saw with his left, in an almost impossible position.

I can see him doing it now, sawing and resting and sawing again; but sticking at it until the limb fell.[5]

This gift for ready friendship had shown itself even before Borden arrived at Shelving Rock: in an act of thoughtful regard that one guest recalled vividly:

A kindness [Bill] did in a New York station is one of the things I have recalled repeatedly. We were going out to take a train, when I noticed that he had dropped behind, and turning, I saw him helping a very poor immigrant woman who was struggling along with many bundles, and a baby in her arms.

[And] how well I remember, at camp, how he used to stand near the kitchen door, and watch for a chance to be of use. We often said that the table was never cleared so quickly as when Bill did it.[6]

Beyond this, one text that speaks of Borden's friendship with the Day family isn't really a text at all. Rather, it's a photograph that holds a story all its own.

Out on Lake George, Borden is one of a foursome seated on what looks like an early Gar Wood-style wooden motorboat. Rosalie Day is at the wheel, while her brother Sherwood is seated just across from Borden, who is busy taking a few quick notes about something that's come to mind – perhaps for a letter to his family in Camden. Looking on, just to Borden's left, is another pretty young woman named Harriet, a Day family friend, who is watching Borden write.[7]

---

5. See Taylor, *Borden of Yale* (1926), p. 167. This person's identity is unclear.

6. ibid., p. 168. This person's identity is unclear.

7. Careful genealogical study shows this 'Harriet' wasn't a Day family relative, but she may be Harriet Maria Root (1885–1975), Wellesley College, Class of 1907. She, and the entire Day family, were listed as members (in 1921) of *Christ's Presbyterian*

It might seem a very pedestrian photo, a circa 1910 snapshot, and not much worth noticing. But really, just the opposite is true.

For all the fine stories about Borden and his friends that we know, there are few photos actually showing him with friends – likely a result of them all too often having such a good time that

no one thought to take a photo. But here, during a summer visit to Lake George, is a photo showing Borden in an unguarded moment, jotting down notes for a letter, only to quickly pick up the thread of animated conversation with his friends.

There was a cool breeze out on the lake that day, for all are dressed in sweaters, save Borden, who was wearing a dapper bow tie and sports jacket: a smart-casual look for on-the-water boating. A breeze

Photos of the *Tsatsawassa* and fresh-water boating with the Day family at Shelving Rock, Lake George, in New York State (from the author's 1st British edition copy of *Borden of Yale*, 1926).

was up when this photo was taken, for Borden's hair is wind-blown – a detail worth noting, for it's one of the very few photos that show him so informally. It speaks of youthful moments, and life.

That Harriet, the visiting Day family friend, was seated next to Borden is also important to note: for there is a second photo showing them together, and it points to a fast friendship, and perhaps something more, as Mrs Day wrote later.

Church and Congregation, Catskill, N.Y. Photos of Harriet Root and the Harriet whom William Borden knew bear a striking resemblance. Harriet Root never married, and she served many humanitarian causes (on 'missions of mercy'). She was named a Life Board Member of the Salvation Army in 1963.

That one summer, she remembered, 'Harriet was with us:'

[I] remember how she dubbed [William] 'the Parson,' but you cannot know the amused little smile with which he responded to her fun. The two frolicked together so much that I remember Sherwood's saying:

'I wish the College fellows could see this side of Bill!'

We knew that he went in for athletics and out-door life, but until then, it seemed as if even [these activities] were *serious* undertakings. But with Harriet, the playful side was brought out ...[8]

In a word, Borden and Harriet were flirting with one another; and greatly enjoying each other's company. The photo of Borden and Harriet captures his smile at her as she bent to look over the contents of a picnic basket. They are standing by a mountain stream in the sunlight, and, since Mrs Day was likely the person once more taking the photo, she may have thought that here was a budding romance.

Borden with his friend Harriet, during a summer visit with the Day family at Lake George, New York State (from the author's 1st British edition copy of *Borden of Yale*, 1926).

In the end, however, it's a wistful thought – for we learn nothing more of Harriet in any surviving papers. Yet it's a gift to see this much of a glimpse into a time when Borden was a young man in summer: enjoying the good company of a pretty and charming friend. His early passing meant he never had the chance to marry; but it is hard not to think that if he had, he

---

8. See Taylor, *Borden of Yale* (1926), p. 166.

would have married someone like Harriet, a sweet, fun-loving young lady who brought such a ready smile to him.

Other memories of Borden's visit to Shelving Rock and Lake George survive. They show what Borden was like in a circle of company, or showing kindness and regard in the conversational 'round-robin' so commonplace in evening hours.

As a devout family, the Days often talked about matters of faith. But their guests weren't always Christians. Indeed, on one evening, some guests voiced ardent skepticism about the historical reliability of Genesis.

Rosalie Day, Sherwood Day's sister, long remembered the way Borden spoke when asked what his thoughts on the matter were—

> I have learned much, too, from the way Bill stood for truth. We always noticed that the more earnest he became, the lower, not the louder, he spoke. When others, in argument, would raise their voices, he would grow more quiet and speak more low, with the result that everyone listened ...
>
> [Then,] one of our pro-suffrage guests denied much belief in Genesis ...
>
> I don't remember that up to that point Bill had said much; but somehow, the first thing I knew, he was talking along, and the other guests were listening.
>
> We all listened. Much that he said was beyond us. We did not know enough to follow it fully. But the impression was made that there is such a thing as a deep scholarly conviction as to the authority and inspiration of the book, and that the speaker was no unthinking conservative; but an intelligent believer in the Bible.
>
> I do not know that he convinced the friends in question. They did not talk long. But he did what I felt at the time was perhaps more needed: [he] showed that we could hold to the old views in these matters, after thinking. Real certainty, and security in the truth, is unruffled when [questioned].
>
> [Bill] was so sure, as on that occasion, of what he believed— [and of] Him whom he believed—that he did not get excited,

and loudly insist on his opinions. *He could wait to say what he knew.*[9]

Rosalie Day had also seen the quiet way Borden kept to what people in their era, as now, called 'devotional life.' While at Shelving Rock, she recalled:

> [Bill] was up early for his Morning Watch as regularly as, I am sure, he must have been at the Seminary. I can see his Testament coming out of his pocket now! As surely as he carried that Testament, he carried his [faith]. You felt he would never be one to want a vacation from religious duties. They were not 'duties' to him. It was just natural to him to take that morning hour for fellowship with God; and he bore its imprint all through the day.[10]

At this time, Rosalie Day was a student at Bryn Mawr, and would graduate from that prestigious, academically challenging school in 1913.[11]

She long remembered how Borden had offered to help her 'prep' for some upcoming course work in German. Summertime though it was, he thought to allay her worry about this fall semester work, and as she wrote:

> what a help [Bill] was in some German I had to do for an [upcoming] examination at Bryn Mawr! The days at camp were pretty well filled with picnics, canoeing, swimming, etc., and it was not easy to make time for study. He was anxious that I should finish that German reading. If a thing had to be done, it was his way to do it; and then put it from his mind.
>
> When there were a few minutes before it was time to start on a picnic or other outing he would say: 'Can't we get some of that German done now?' I do not know how I should ever have

---

9. ibid., p. 166. At this time, near Lake George, in places of Greene Country like Catskill, women's suffrage activities took place, with ties to the 'National American Woman Suffrage Association.' Such clubs and meetings were often held. See *Dear Old Greene County* (Catskill: no pub listed., 1915), pp. 174-175. Italics added.

10. ibid., pp. 166-167.

11. See *Bryn Mawr College Calendar, 1920*, p. 66.

'tackled' it without this encouragement. His help during the few days he was there gave me, so to speak, 'a running start,' and I was able to finish it in the required time …

But with all his seriousness there was [much] playfulness and love of fun. [Bill] had an inexhaustible store of tricks, which kept us entertained many an evening. I remember specially a spelling-game called 'Ghost,' which he enjoyed immensely.[12]

A chapter centered on recollections of a summer visit to Lake George might seem like a digression from the more important moments in Borden's life.

But it isn't. Indeed, nothing could be further from the truth.

For if we would see Borden as he really was, we need to see him as his good friends saw him. He was someone 'made for friendship,' as an old and very apropos phrase has it. And he lived so many moments of his life in days of friendship.

His days at Shelving Rock, so well remembered, bring this home.

---

12. See Taylor, *Borden of Yale* (1926), pp. 168-169. 'Ghost' is a word game in which each player adds a letter to a word fragment, while trying not to actually spell a word. If they accidentally spell a real word, they lose a round of the game, and are assigned one letter from the word 'Ghost.' The first to acquire all letters of the word 'Ghost' loses.

CHAPTER 12

To Serve the Sovereign of Heaven

[I] went out to Chicago [at] the end of September, and was
ordained at The Moody Church. The service was very nice
indeed ... Dr Gray very kindly preached the sermon, and
Dr Stone delivered the [pastoral] charge ...[1]
– William Borden, to Walter Collins Erdman,
aboard the *R.M.S. Mauretania*, Sunday, December 22, 1912

Before the pulpit from which [D. L.] Moody preached for many years,
William Whiting Borden, a Chicago millionaire just through with
university and seminary, was recently ordained a minister.[2]
– The Continent magazine (October 1912)

I charge you, be a man of apprehension ... keep faith, keep wisdom ...[3]
– Dr John Timothy Stone (September 1912)

'I knew William Whiting Borden from his boyhood, [seeing]
the preparation this beloved brother had for [Christian]
service, and the ardent desire of his soul to enter upon it ...[4]
– Dr James Martin Gray (June 1913)

---

1. See Zwemer, *William Whiting Borden* (1913), p. 130.

2. See *The Continent* magazine, October 10, 1912, p. 1419.

3. See the feature article on Borden's ordination on page 3 of the Sunday, September
22, 1912 edition of *The Chicago Tribune*.

4. Dr James Martin Gray, quoted in *The Missionary Visitor* magazine, June
1913, p. 197.

Near the time of William Borden's ordination,[5] he sat for a photo portrait in the famous studio of J. R. Matzene, a gifted European artist and émigré. Matzene's reputation was well deserved, for this photo of Borden achieved the rare feat of capturing both likeness and character.

'Strong, bold, and thoughtful,'[6] is the phrase Dr Os Guinness, the great-nephew of Borden's biographer, Geraldine Guinness Taylor, has used to describe it.

The kindness so many recalled in Borden was also present, and a more subtle something as well: the photo seemed to reveal friendship, and honesty of purpose. It was a feat of artistry that Matzene's studio could yield an image with these shades of character within an hour's sitting, or little more, as Borden's schedule was so often very crowded. But we may be grateful this one hour's appointment was taken.

Increasingly, it's now understood that photos are a 'text' all in themselves. And if Edmund S. Morgan once said that we who are living can never, regrettably, hear the tone of Benjamin Franklin's voice, the Matzene photo of William Borden does allow us to see things clearly written in his character. Some photos hold a magic all their own, an artistry that is revelatory. This handsome portrait does.

And yet ...

Notwithstanding the symbolism and meaning of Borden's September 1912 ordination in the church D. L. Moody founded, just five days before it, Borden was still trying to arrange several elements of his plans for that day. In such a context, he wrote to Henry Weston Frost. It's a letter showing a very human side of his life and personality, lending a you-are-there quality to this time—

---

5. Newspapers throughout America ran feature articles on the ordination of William Borden as a 'millionaire missionary' to be. Thus, a page 1 feature on Borden's ordination ran in the September 21, 1912 edition of *The Washington Post,* titled 'Missionary Has $5,000,000.'

6. Dr Os Guinness, email correspondence with the author, Saturday, 7 July 2018.

60 East 55th St., New York,

[Monday,] September 16, 1912

Dear Mr Frost,

Thank you for your telegram and letter. *I'm afraid I've been guilty again of letting things go too long, and then having to do them in a hurry.*

September 21st is the only date available apparently, if I am to be ordained before entering on my fall term's work, so I am afraid I'll have to hold to it. I realize your position, and want you to have a good rest and Mrs Frost too. I have also asked Dr Erdman (W. J.),[7] and while I have not heard definitely, [I] am quite sure he can come, so please feel free to decline.

I had wanted you to deliver the [pastoral] charge on account of your intimate knowledge with things missionary.

You would have to leave Friday at the latest, and not get back 'till Tuesday, and as it would probably mean other work at [Moody] Church and the Institute, I don't feel like urging you at all.

There are others besides old Dr Erdman that I could fall back on.

I've been hoping to see Ing and Elsa,[8] but haven't succeeded as yet, maybe I will tonight.

Very sincerely yours,

William W. Borden[9]

In asking 'old Dr Erdman' to be part of his ordination, Borden voiced an express wish to align himself with the church where

---

7. Dr William J. Erdman (1834–1923), consulting editor for *The Scofield Reference Bible* (Oxford Univ. Press, 1909), a good friend of D. L. Moody, the father of Princeton Seminary Professor C. R. Erdman, and one-time Pastor of The Moody Church (1876–78).

8. Inglis & Elsa Frost, the son and daughter-in-law of H. W. Frost. Inglis Folger Frost (1886–1983) was one year older than William Borden.

9. A letter from Borden to H. W. Frost, Monday, Sept. 16, 1912, housed at The Billy Graham Center, Wheaton College. Italics added.

he'd come to faith, the church D. L. Moody founded. For Dr William J. Erdman had worked very closely with Moody.

And these 'pre-ordination details,' as it were, had coverage in a somewhat unlikely setting: a full column on page 1 of *The Chicago Examiner,* William Randolph Hearst's midwestern newspaper.[10] It was a curious provenance, but very prominent coverage; and a story that quoted Borden directly. Describing this young candidate for the pastorate, the article began—

[William Borden], who is twenty-four years old, handsome, tall and athletic, and a college graduate, will be ordained as a clergyman tonight ...

Inland China will be his field of missionary endeavor ... His ordination [will take place] at the Moody Church, West Chicago and LaSalle avenues ...

Born and raised in an environment of wealth and fashion, [Borden,] while an undergraduate at Yale founded Yale Hope Mission for homeless men. He gave $20,000 to this work, for the purchase and outfitting of a building. He was assisted by a former convict, Louis Bernhardt. The mission is still in existence ... Choosing a religious life, Mr Borden [declined] a professional career ... [In his teens], he said, he 'received a call from God to become a missionary.'

After his graduation from Yale in 1909, he entered Princeton Seminary. He completed a three years' course ... Following his ordination tonight, it was his purpose to journey [overseas immediately,] to begin his missionary work ...

[But] at the urgent request of the Student Volunteer Movement, which has branches in all the large colleges and universities, he [decided] to postpone his trip. Instead, he will spend this Fall and Winter in visiting the larger places of academic learning,

---

10. William Randolph Hearst, famous as the publisher of *The Examiner* in San Francisco and *The New York Journal.* Hearst entered the Chicago market in 1900 by founding *The Chicago American,* an evening paper. In 1902, he started a morning edition, *The Chicago Examiner.*

addressing the students on 'the claims of the [mission field] to know the gospel of Christ.'[11]

Borden also told *The Chicago Examiner* about the context of his 'call to preach the gospel [in] other lands,' with a word for consideration to the sons of other well-to-do families—

> 'I wish,' he said, that 'other young men of wealthy parents could visit foreign fields and see for themselves, as I did, the need for missionary work there ... I believe that more of them would become preachers of the gospel of Christ.' [He then continued:]
>
> 'The rewards of missionary effort are incalculably greater than any rewards that can follow social achievements. I never had any craving to enter society. I prefer the missionary field.'[12]

Borden then touched on a consideration some might not have anticipated: training beyond learning the language of a foreign land.

In London, he explained, he planned to 'take a short course in medicine as a safeguard against pestilences and other diseases' in foreign countries. And given the length of this course, he said he probably would not reach China for two years.

Next, *The Chicago Examiner* gave details of Borden's forthcoming ordination—

> Tonight ... Rev. John Timothy Stone, pastor of the Fourth Presbyterian Church, will deliver the charge, and the Rev. James M. Gray, Dean of the Moody Bible Institute, will preach the ordination sermon.
>
> Mr Borden for several years has been a Trustee of Moody Bible Institute. He also [serves as] a Director of the National Bible Institute of New York City, closely identified in religious work with such well-known men as Robert E. Speer, John R. Mott, [D. O.] Shelton, and Hugh Munro.[13]

---

11. See 'Young Borden ... Tells of Call to Become Missionary,' in the Sept. 21, 1912 edition of *The Chicago Examiner*, p. 1.

12. ibid., p. 1.

13. ibid., p. 1.

The *Chicago Examiner's* coverage was extensive and noteworthy; but it wasn't the only prominent newspaper to cover Borden's ordination. *The New York Times* ran a page one story about the event: an article centered on the contrast between a life of missionary service, and Borden's background of family wealth and privilege.

In so doing, the *Times* pointed to the singular nature of Borden's choice in life. It was striking to think that someone with his background would choose a life of missionary endeavor, when so many more conventional choices lay open to him. Borden hadn't sought publicity; but it came nonetheless, because what he'd chosen to do was so unheard of. The 'why' of it all captured the interest of the *Times,* and by implication, the interest of many readers throughout America.

So with the heading, 'Special to the Times,' the brief article entitled 'W. W. Borden to Preach' appeared, with the subtitle: 'Wealthy Yale Graduate ... Will Be A Missionary in China.' Its dateline stated—

CHICAGO, Illinois. Sept. 20th.

W. W. Borden, a graduate of Yale and Princeton ... will be ordained as a minister of the gospel at the Moody Church tomorrow, and will serve as a missionary in China. [He] is the son of [William] Borden, who died several years ago, leaving an estate of $5,000,000. One million, perhaps a little more, was left to the son who now becomes a preacher. Young Borden ... resides on Lake Shore Drive, the most exclusive residence section of the city. While in college, [he had] devoted much of his time to Christian work ...[14]

This *New York Times* article had run next to one about George W. Vanderbilt and the Biltmore Estate. Borden's 'story,' so to speak, was of a very different nature; but juxtaposed with the Vanderbilt

---

14. See page 1 of the Saturday, September 21, 1912 edition of *The New York Times.*

article, it cast his calling to missionary service in sharp relief. Here was news out of the common road.

So, on the evening of September 21, 1912, gas lamps illumined the corner of Chicago Avenue and LaSalle Street. Invited guests for Borden's ordination alighted from carriages, horse-drawn trolleys, and cars before the three-arch entryway of the Moody Church. Guests new to this setting would have seen the impressive red brick exterior, with its marble-edged lintels, and the round, turreted tower of the church, as the great bell in its steeple tolled 'come to service.'

Entering the church sanctuary, guests would have seen its great pipe organ, and overhead the large circular Tiffany-style stained glass ceiling, built to let ambient light hallow and color daylight hours. There were also crafted chandeliers, balconies around the perimeter of the sanctuary, and handsome wooden seating on the center floor. These were individual chairs which could be moved about at need to allow for more creative audience seating, be it small groups or large crowds.[15]

On this occasion, aside from all invited friends and Borden family members, students from nearby Moody Bible Institute were in attendance, since Borden was a Trustee of MBI, with three years' service. One MBI student was a young man named Louis Talbot, of whom more will be said below.

On the walls, to the right and left of the great dais where the pipe organ and pulpit were, visitors to the Moody Church could see two great banners that were set like regal scrolls. Both proclaimed: 'Christ Rose For Our Justification.'

This then, was the storied setting for William Borden's ordination.

---

15. Chicago Avenue Church could hold up to 10,000 people; and was dedicated in June 1876.

Many details of this special service were given in a long story that ran on page three of *The Chicago Tribune*.

'With several hundred people looking on,' the *Tribune* reported:

> William Whiting Borden [was ordained] at The Moody Church …
>
> The [pastoral] charge to the young missionary … was delivered by the Rev. John Timothy Stone, Pastor of the Fourth Presbyterian Church, which the Borden family attends …
>
> E. Y. Woolley, Assistant Pastor of The Moody Church [began the service, saying Borden] had been elected worthy of ordination. He introduced the Rev. Charles Inglis of London, [a good friend of D. L. Moody] who read a brief passage from Paul's Epistle to Timothy, and [Dr] James Gray, who preached a sermon on 'the right manner of man' needed for missionary work. Then Dr Stone spoke:
>
> 'I charge you, be strong,' he said, 'strong with a strength that the world may not at first recognize … I charge you, be a man of apprehension. See ahead a better Chicago, a better New York, a better London. See ahead better things for the suffering in China, in India, in Africa. Keep the spirit of a clean life, keep faith, keep wisdom, keep power.'[16]

Following this, E. Y. Woolley stepped forward to the pulpit once more, and told the guests in attendance: 'Mr Borden has been with us but little; but he has done much. If we all were as useful present, as he has been [useful when] absent, what would we not do! His life is an inspiration.'[17]

The *Tribune* then described a more solemn part of the service saying:

> Silently, the score of deacons and elders of The Moody Church walked to the platform and surrounded young Borden, as he knelt by the pulpit …

---

16. See 'Borden Ordained for Chinese Post,' an article in the Sunday, Sept. 22, 1912 edition of *The Chicago Tribune*, p. 3.

17. ibid., p. 3.

With the assistant pastor, [E. Y. Woolley,] leading in prayer, they bowed their heads and joined in a booming chorus of 'Amens' at the close. The choir started [singing] Isaac Watts' old hymn, ['When I Survey the Wondrous Cross']. The closing verse ran:

> Were the whole realm of nature mine,
> That were a present far too small.
> Love so amazing, so divine,
> Demands my soul, my life, my all.

'And some of those who came out of curiosity,' the *Tribune* said, 'guessed why [William Borden] had been willing to [forego] the worldly pleasures a fortune brings, and go to China.'[18]

~ ~ ~

As stated just above, a Moody Bible Institute student named Louis Talbot attended Borden's ordination service.

Many years later, he was Dr Louis T. Talbot, President of Biola University,[19] and he spoke of Borden's ordination in one of his radio broadcasts, which went out over the airways across America.

'I had the privilege,' Talbot said—

of meeting one of the finest young men that I ever saw: [William] Borden, and his biography is [called] *Borden of Yale* ...

I was present at his ordination service, held in Moody Church.

Soon after that, he [prepared for service in] China, going out under China Inland Mission. On the way to the field, he [studied] for a time at Egypt. There he contracted a disease, [and] passed into the presence of the Lord.

I shall never forget the day Dr James Gray made the announcement to all of us students. The newspapers, including the *Chicago Tribune,* had the story on the front page, with a sketch of the life of William Borden.

---

18. ibid., p. 3. Citation edited for clarity.

19. L. T. Talbot (1889–1976) was twice President of Biola University, from 1932–1935, and again from 1938–1952.

> When many people read the news, they said, 'Oh, what a sacrifice!'
>
> But in my heart I said,
>
> 'Oh, what a privilege; to lay down one's life in the Lord's service.'[20]

Herein lies a moving truth: Borden had no way of knowing how the story of his life would influence the life and faith of Louis Talbot; but his story *did* influence the young student whom he'd met so briefly on that autumn day in 1912.

This prompts a further guiding thought.

'There are no small moments,' it has been said. And in the case of Borden's brief kindness to Louis Talbot, it might have seemed a very small moment indeed.

But it wasn't. For the rest of his long life, till 1976, Louis Talbot remembered William Borden. And in sharing what he said of Borden in his radio broadcast, the ripple effect of a brief meeting and its importance went wide – far beyond anything Talbot or Borden himself might then have imagined.

In being faithful to his call to missionary endeavor, and seeking ordination, Borden had set events in motion that brought a blessing unlooked for.

But then, he might well have said, that is the way of things with God.

~ ~ ~

As it happened, Henry Weston Frost was unable to attend and take part in Borden's ordination. Both sincerely wished it was otherwise, but Borden wrote a letter to Frost a little over a week after The Moody Church service, pointing to the good things he would remember about his time of ordination, even though Frost hadn't been able to be there. Borden's letter read, in part—

---

20. See Carol Talbot, *For This I Was Born: The Captivating Story of Louis T. Talbot* (Chicago Moody Press, 1977), p. 33.

> Hamilton College, Clinton, N.Y.
>
> [Tuesday,] October 1, 1912
>
> Dear Mr Frost ...
>
> Please don't worry about [not attending] the ordination. I'm sure you did the right thing, [taking time for the rest you so greatly needed].
>
> I am glad I was ordained at The Moody Church ...
>
> The interest of those earnest people, and the assurance of their prayers, is worth a great deal ...[21]

This letter shows that in Borden's mind, things had come full circle for him. He had attended The Moody Church as a boy, and he voiced his first profession of faith there. Now, one month from his twenty-fifth birthday, he was ordained there. He'd long regarded The Moody Church as a place of sacred hope, and he had deep respect for D. L. Moody. To be associated with this church, through his ordination, was a great gift. He cherished that thought.

Moving beyond Borden's thoughts about his ordination, a revealing article by Herbert H. Smith appeared soon after that event in *Men and Missions* magazine.

It was titled 'Millionaire Borden's Decision,' and pondered the wider significance of his life to date; with the example and lessons it held for readers.

Smith's article was as fine a summary of these things as any published at this time, and much worth reading. 'Before the pulpit from which Dwight L. Moody preached for many years,' Smith stated—

> William Whiting Borden, a Chicago millionaire [who is] just through with university and seminary, was recently ordained a minister ...
>
> There comes to every earnest young man ... the question of what he shall do with his life ... When such a [one], a leader among

---

21. A letter from Borden to H. W. Frost, Tuesday, Oct. 1, 1912, housed at The Billy Graham Center, Wheaton College.

his [peers, with] a fortune which reaches [a] million dollars, decides to leave friends and home [to] tell the Mohammedan Chinese of the peace through Christ, the decision is of more than usual interest. Young Borden decided before he entered Yale that he would be a foreign missionary, [saying it was] after a trip through foreign mission stations in 1904-05 that he [began to think] of mission work ...

Mr Borden is twenty-four years old, and [his] wealth will enable him to make extensive investments [in the] means of helping [others].

But more than the [investment] in China is the influence of his decision on the thousands ... who [will] hear of it. The Chicago newspapers [have] printed column articles on the front pages; and papers all over the country [have told] the story of 'the millionaire missionary.'

[And] Mr Borden, through [giving] several months to Student Volunteer work, will increase greatly the results of his decision [among college students].

More than one, [it's thought,] will recall the example of the Chicago man who freely gave up the luxury available to large wealth, to embrace the difficult task of making his life count for something.[22]

'Making life count for something': it's the kind of phrase so many young people have voiced down the years. Herbert Smith's article pointed to the way Borden had looked to this ideal, as it was shaped by his journey of faith.

Now his life would be one of missionary endeavor, moved by compassion for the people of China. Borden believed Christian faith brought his life meaning and hope. He wished to bring that hope to China's millions.

---

22. See *Men and Missions* magazine, Dec. 1912, pp. 25-26; and *The Continent* magazine, Oct. 10, 1912, p. 1419.

CHAPTER 13

Interlude: Channels of Philanthropy

... seek in the life of Christ for ...
those principles which should guide our lives.[1]
– R. E. Speer (1902)

The life of Trust [is shown in someone]
who constantly keeps open these two doors
of Faith and Love ...[2]
– J. H. McConkey (1897)

The life of William Borden, said his friend H. R. Munro, was
'a benediction' for those who knew him, 'a summons also, to a
closer following of the Saviour.'[3]
– Borden of Yale (1926)

This chapter, set between Borden's ordination, and the start of
his autumn 1912 tour of colleges and universities for the Student
Volunteer Movement, traces the many philanthropies he supported

---

1. Robert E. Speer, *Principles of Jesus* (New York: F. H. Revell, 1902), p. 11.

2. J. H. McConkey, *The Three-Fold Secret of the Holy Spirit* (Harrisburg: Kelker, 1897), p. 121. See also Taylor, *Borden of Yale* (1926), p. 216. She writes that Borden's copy was 'marked in the way he had with all his best-loved books, one sentence standing out as meaning much to him. *"The supreme human condition of the fulness of the Spirit is a life wholly surrendered to God to do His will."'*

3. See Taylor, *Borden of Yale* (1926), p. 272. Munro was Vice-President of the Niagara Lithograph Co.

during his college and seminary years. They open a window on his faith, and are a deeply revealing part of his character.

One part of Borden's philanthropy, or 'love for others,' in translation from the Greek, showed itself in generous gifts of time.

For two winters, within the years 1909–1912, Borden taught Sunday School in a 'small African Methodist Church' near Princeton. This would have been the Mt Pisgah African Methodist Episcopal Church, sited on Witherspoon Street, a modest two-storey church that is now part of Princeton's Historic District.[4]

Mt Pisgah AME Church was built in 1860 for a congregation founded in 1832, by Samson Peters, a clergyman from Trenton, New Jersey. This makes Mt Pisgah the oldest African American congregation in Princeton.[5]

It is unclear how Borden initially decided to volunteer as a teacher in this 'small African Methodist Church,' as Geraldine Taylor described it, but it would not have been out of character for him to have seen the church and its congregants when he rode his bicycle around Princeton, something his seminary professor, Dr William Brenton Greene, often saw him doing.[6]

Such times lend themselves readily to getting to know a neighborhood. And given Borden's urban ministry work at the Yale Hope Mission, it is easy to imagine how he would have been drawn to a congregation like Mt Pisgah; and once he'd found friends there, have volunteered to teach.

---

4. Email correspondence between the author and Kenneth Henke, Curator of Special Collections and Archivist at Princeton Theological Seminary, who stated on Tuesday, 21 August 2018: 'I have no independent source information about where William Borden taught Sunday School while he was in Princeton, but I have no reason to challenge Mrs Taylor's statement, particularly as a memorial service seems to have been held at Mt Pisgah. The material she presents is always well-informed. It was not unusual for our students to volunteer to teach Sunday School at the two African-American churches in Princeton—Witherspoon Presbyterian and Mt Pisgah AME.'

5. 'Mt Pisgah AME Church,' by the New Jersey Historical Commission, at: https://www.princetonnj.gov/properties/mt-pisgah-ame-church

6. W. B. Greene, in *The Bible To-Day* magazine, June 1913, p. 133. Here, Dr Greene recalled often seeing Borden 'from my study window, dashing down Library Place on his bicycle to the early morning recitation.'

There was also a direct connection between Mt Pisgah and Princeton Seminary. Rev. Henry Hammond Pinckney 'entered the Seminary at Princeton in 1899 as a partial student,' and remained two years. While attending the Seminary, 'he was pastor of the A.M.E. church of Princeton.'[7]

Seminaries often post ministry opportunities, so students can get practical, 'hands-on' experience as they pursue their studies. These opportunities are, in their way, a kind of internship. So perhaps Borden simply saw a notice relating to Sunday School at Mt Pisgah, one more likely to have been posted given recent ties to the seminary through Rev. Pinckney, who had been there as recently as 1901. When Borden started his studies in fall 1909, it was only eight years after Pinckney completed his studies at Princeton Seminary. It's a likely scenario.

Sadly, however, the name of the pastor at Mt Pisgah during Borden's time at Princeton is unknown, but his recollections of Borden are not. Perhaps wishing to remain anonymous, a common trait of modesty in the early 1900s, he forwarded his recollections of Borden to Geraldine Taylor.

He described a young student of 'deep consecration and unassuming, Christ-like life.' The children of Mt Pisgah had taken to him right away, and so did other church members. Yet they'd no idea of Borden's wealth, for he never mentioned it. To them, he was just 'William,' a student from the seminary. He shared kindness, lessons from his wide knowledge of Scripture, and rallied the children with his good sense of fun. He saw their smiles, laughed with them, and felt gratitude for the ways they took the Bible's teachings to heart.

'We asked him to teach,' the pastor told Geraldine Taylor, and Borden had done so in ways that made him a fondly remembered friend.[8]

---

7. See *The Necrological Report ... of Princeton Theological Seminary* (1921), p. 139.

8. See Taylor, *Borden of Yale* (1926), pp. 270-271.

Another window on Borden's philanthropy appears not in something he did, but rather in something he did not do.

We learn of this from Borden's Princeton Seminary friend, C. F. Vale, later an Army Medical Corps physician during World War I.[9] As Vale remembered—

> One Sunday evening [Bill] asked me to walk home with him to dinner [at Westland]. This was during our [time] at Princeton.
>
> As we were walking along Stockton Street, a big touring car passed us, and I said, rather thoughtlessly—
>
> 'Why don't you get a car, Bill? You would never miss the money.'
>
> He turned on me, with his quiet smile, and said [metaphorically]—
>
> 'Get thee behind me, Satan. I settled that long ago. I cannot afford it – when the price of a car will build a hospital in China.'
>
> He let me know something of the real spirit of stewardship, [Vale stated] his money was as completely devoted to Christ as he himself was.[10]

There was, as it happened, a back-story to Vale's recollection. It comes from biographer Samuel Zwemer, who said that 'Borden was never an ascetic; he loved life, [as well as] good clothes, a comfortable hotel, and a carefully prepared menu. But he had no extravagant habits; and lived [by design] economically.'[11]

---

9. 'Claire Fremont Vale (1887–1966) studied at Princeton Seminary from 1909–1911; but he later enrolled in the medical school of the University of Pennsylvania, graduating in 1916. He served in the Army Medical Corps from April 1918 until August 1919, then took up a surgical residency in the Receiving Hospital in Detroit.' Information provided through email correspondence with the author from Kenneth Henke, Curator of Special Collections and Archivist at Princeton Theological Seminary, on Tuesday, 21 August 2018.

10. See Zwemer, *William Whiting Borden* (1913), p. 212. See also Mrs E. C. Cronk, in *The Missionary Review of the World*, May 1918, p. 368: 'No part of the training of that faithful-unto-death young missionary, William Whiting Borden, was worth more than the actual missionary work he did, when he put the automobile he might have had during his college days into funds for the Yale Hope Mission and knelt there, night after night, with his arm around some "down-and-out" trying to lead him to Christ.'

11. See Zwemer, *William Whiting Borden* (1913), p. 210.

Zwemer then quoted Borden's mother Mary, who recalled: 'All the time we were at Princeton, I think [William] was longing to get away into simpler living.'[12]

She went on to say that—

> I think [William] felt it was inconsistent for him as a Christian to have [an automobile]. Two years later, when I considered getting one myself, he thought he might share it with me. We [had] practically decided to get it together.
>
> [But later,] when he left ... for a short trip ... he telegraphed back:
>
> 'If you do it, you will have to do it alone.'
>
> I believe nothing would have given him keener pleasure than to have had a car. But he never said a word to me about this, or any other self-denial ... I think William's real reason [was his unease with] the luxury seen in the lives of many Christians ... He did not feel justified in using his money for this purpose.[13]

If this sounds rather strict, it really wasn't. The standard price for a good, but not extravagant touring car in Borden's time was $5,000. In today's currency, that would be a purchase cost of $125,000 – a not inconsiderable sum.

This said, Borden's keen interest in 'automobiling,' or 'motoring,' went back to his round the world tour of 1904-1905. On his first visit to Cairo, in 1905, Borden told his father he was 'tired of sight-seeing, and [would be] glad to do as his father suggested, and take lessons in automobiling when he got to Paris, as well as lessons in French.'

Diary entries during his summer 1905 stay in Paris are full of descriptions of how much he enjoyed this new mode of transportation. Eagerly, he took lessons for several days at a time—

---

12. ibid., p. 210.
13. ibid., p. 211.

Friday, June 23 [1905:]

Lesson in the big machine. [A] fellow on [a] motorcycle ran into us as we crossed the streets. Didn't hurt himself or his machine much, but lots of trouble. They formed a combination, [accusing us,] and we were 'it,' being foreigners. Paid one hundred francs. Not my fault at all.

[Monday,] June 26:

Lesson. Small machine broke down in St Cloud's for various reasons. In afternoon we drove down to Jardin des Plantes.

[Tuesday,] June 27: Young machine. [It] went pretty good, [and the car] chain only came off two or three times.

[Wednesday,] June 28: Short lesson. Went to St Dennis in the afternoon, [taking only] five minutes in the big machine.[14]

'After these lessons,' said Samuel Zwemer, Borden 'became an expert driver … and one of the things he would keenly have enjoyed would have been to possess a motor-car of his own. But he never bought one, feeling that the money could be better used for other purposes.'[15]

Borden's great concern, as a good steward of his resources, was that they had been given him in trust. He hoped to wisely meet that responsibility.

∾ ∾ ∾

Still another friend, Arthur T. Upson, Superintendent of The Nile Mission Press, saw a very different side of Borden's devotion to personal philanthropy—

'As to his secret beneficence,' [said] Mr Upson, 'not only was he most generous in his gifts, but none knew what he gave: save his Father above.

Several times during February [1913] alone did he open the door of my private office and march past the 'ENGAGED' placard (the only visitor who dared to do this) saying, 'Sorry to disturb

---

14. ibid., pp. 210-211.

15. ibid., p. 211.

you just now, but I want you to lighten my pocketbook; it's too heavy. I've just bought something to help you.'[16]

Borden also posted gifts of money to his great friend Robert P. Wilder, the pioneering founder of the Student Volunteer Movement. In a letter Borden wrote on August 24, 1910, from England, he told Wilder—

> What I wish especially to write about ... is my helping you in your work.
>
> I feel that you should be in a position to make the most of any and all opportunities you may have to further the preaching of sound doctrine. So I am sending you £80 to be used at your discretion for trips across the North Sea, books for yourself or others, publication of leaflets, etc., etc.
>
> [I] hope you will accept this gift; and do me the favor of letting me know of any special opportunity you may have in the future which may require additional financial help.[17]

Here, Borden had forwarded a substantial gift. £80 in 1910 would be worth just under £9,000 today, or an amount equal to about $11,500 in U.S. currency.

Generous as this was, it was only a portion of Borden's yearly giving. When writing his book, Samuel Zwemer discovered that Borden's financial gifts found—

> a channel among all denominations, and for all kinds of work in many lands. For four years, he [gave] a large sum [yearly] for a Daily Vacation Bible School in The Moody Church. He supported, or helped [to] support, missions in Chicago, New Haven, [and] New York ... He paid the annual budgets for traveling secretaries of various student [organizations, providing] missionaries and busy Christian workers with stenographic help; and in a hundred other ways 'got rid of some of this money,' as he once phrased it ...

---

16. ibid., p. 209.

17. ibid., p. 208.

He kept two accounts with his [financial] agent in Chicago, [A. P. Spink]. One of them was his private account, with which he did not 'bother much;' the other account was the real one ...[18]

Using Borden's gift to R. P. Wilder as a guide for the charities above, it is easy to see how Borden's giving to them would have run easily into tens of thousands of dollars a year in today's purchasing power.

His stewardship was wide-ranging and great-hearted.

Beyond this, there were financial responsibilities Borden felt obligated to in his various leadership capacities: as with his place as a Director of the National Bible Institute. Early in 1912, as Geraldine Taylor told the story:

> The National Bible Institute was passing through a time of no little trial. In spite of the Directors' efforts to keep clear of debt, a deficit of five thousand dollars had accumulated. There was much prayer about it, and an earnest desire to learn by past experience.
>
> But how was the deficit to be wiped out?
>
> A meeting of the Board was called, for it looked as though there would have to be serious retrenchment. Borden had come up from Princeton. His financial contributions to the work were considerable, and no one was looking to him to do more.
>
> The morning had passed in earnest conference and prayer. 'I must make the 2:04 train,' Borden said at length, 'and shall have to run for it.'
>
> He was writing on a slip of paper as he spoke, and pushing it across the table to the Treasurer, [H. R.] Munro, he made for the door.
>
> It was a cheque for five thousand two hundred dollars ...
>
> Without a word, [Borden] had taken up the entire indebtedness. It was not only the gift, but the way in which it

---

18. ibid., p. 205.

was done that was so like him. [No one knew] he was writing a cheque: and before they realized it, he was gone.[19]

Borden's NBI gift would be equal to $130,000 today. He hadn't planned on making such a large gift; but when necessity arose, he quickly did so.

So often, his thoughts ran to helping those in need.

Closer to Borden's abiding interest in China as a missionary, he found a way to contribute significant financial help, within a year of his passing, to reach Muslim peoples there. We see this in a letter to F. Herbert Rhodes of China Inland Mission, written early in 1913—

> I have been most interested in the efforts you have been making to arouse the missionary forces in China ... and am very anxious to do what I can to help you ... I have seen your letters to Mr Upson and to Dr Zwemer, and so have kept in touch with what you are doing ... It seems to me that you have some very good suggestions [for] the opening of a correspondence bureau, [and] issuing an appeal [for Christian aid on] behalf of the Moslems in China, etc.
>
> Wishing to further ... what is being done, I have taken some money entrusted to me and sent two hundred pounds to the Mission at Shanghai as a special gift, to be used for the purpose of all evangelical missionaries in China. I have suggested to Mr Stevenson[20] that he simply turn this over to you ... Then I have

---

19. See Taylor, *Borden of Yale* (1926), pp. 195-196. See also *The Continent* magazine, April 22, 1915, p. 514: 'A memorial tablet to the memory of William Whiting Borden was unveiled April [11, 1915] in the headquarters building of the National Bible Institute.' This marked the two-year anniversary of Borden's passing. This story was also covered on page 9 of the Monday, April 12, 1915 edition of *The New York Times*. 'A tablet was unveiled yesterday afternoon in the auditorium of the National Bible Institute, 214-216 West Thirty-Fifth Street, in memory of William Whiting Borden. It was presented by the Board of Directors of the Institute "in memory of their beloved associate and devoted fellow-worker, whose gifted, generous, spirit-filled life was lived out in quenchless passion for Jesus Christ." The memorial address was made by Hugh R. Munro, Treasurer of the Institute, and there was special singing by the chorus from Manhattan Gospel Hall.'

20. J. W. Stevenson, for nearly thirty years China Inland Mission's Deputy-Director in China.

also sent you, through Mr Upson, some Arabic literature from the Nile Mission Press, which I hope may be of service also.[21]

Borden's gift to F. H. Rhodes of £200 would be worth approximately £22,388 today, or some $30,000 in U.S. currency. He had yet to travel to China to take up his long-hoped-for service to the Muslim people of Kansu; but he found a way to be present there already in the gift sent to Rhodes and his fellow missionaries.

Based also on Samuel Zwemer's research, we know Borden's philanthropy 'began long before' he was twenty-one, when he received his inheritance, 'and the control of his investments.'

Walter Erdman saw a telling instance on the world tour he chaperoned from 1904-1905. On Borden's seventeenth birthday, Erdman recalled—

> [William] received by instructions from his father a liberal allowance of spending money, half of which he immediately turned over to the uses of the Y.M.C.A. in the city of Osaka, where we happened to be staying at the home of the General Secretary [Galen M. Fisher].[22] [During this time,] he was having his first opportunity of seeing for himself methods of [missionary] work among Japanese students in their hotels, and their English classes in the Y.M.C.A.[23]

Given these financial resources, Borden might have been tempted to become an impulsive donor. 'But the fact is,' said Dr Zwemer, 'his giving was careful and prayerful, and therefore often startlingly opportune.'[24] This is seen in one surviving letter, when Borden wrote to a friend, we may use 'Smith' as a surname, 'with large responsibilities:'

21. See Zwemer, *William Whiting Borden* (1913), p. 208.

22. See *The Record of Christian Work*, April 1904, page 295. Here, Fisher is named as 'National General Secretary' of the Y.M.C.A. in Japan.

23. See Zwemer, *William Whiting Borden* (1913), p. 204.

24. ibid., p. 202.

Dear Mr [Smith] –

Thinking you might like some money now, *and being in a position to contribute,* I take the opportunity of sending my check for $300.

    Praying God's blessing upon you and the work,

I remain, Very sincerely yours,

W. W. Borden[25]

Dr William Henry Sallmon, the President of Carleton College, and one-time Treasurer of the Yale Mission in Central China, related how from the very outset, Borden was a deeply interested and hearty supporter of that enterprise—

> I never received [William] Borden's check for that work in far-off China with which there was not a note of thanksgiving that he had the privilege of giving his money, and [words of] cheer, to the Treasurer who was bearing the burden of getting it in …
>
> Now, as I have been thinking over [William's] life, and the impression made upon me, there are three things that stand out …
>
> First of all, his transparent character. He made me think of the 1st Psalm, and the best of the Beatitudes. The second thing that impressed me was his conscientious sense of trusteeship. Every dollar, he felt, was entrusted to him: to be spent for the benefit of his fellowmen …
>
> [And third,] the official distinction we make here between Home and Foreign Missions had no lodgment in his mind; to him the field was the world of God's work. All men were brothers to him, and in placing his money … he tried to bring the best results … He gave here liberally in New Haven, and liberally over there in Central China – for the salvation of men whom he had never seen.[26]

---

25. ibid., p. 202.

26. ibid., pp. 203-204. '[William Borden] was an ardent supporter of Yale in China' – W. H. Sallmon (Yale, Class of 1894). See *The Missionary Review of the World*, August 1913, p. 571.

Weighing all these examples of Borden's generosity, there is ample reason for Samuel Zwemer to have written in September 1913—

'Probably no young man of the present generation has afforded such a clear and [noteworthy] example of Christian stewardship as William Borden.'[27]

---

27. ibid., pp. 197-198.

CHAPTER 14

The Autumn Tour

The very day he [took his] last examination at Princeton,
[Borden was] in New York with Dr John R. Mott, deep in plans
for the work he was to take up in the fall in connection with
the Student Volunteer Movement. A three months' schedule
[was arranged,] for visits to many colleges.[1]
– Geraldine Taylor (1926)

With such prominent coverage of Borden's ordination throughout
America, in *The New York Times, Chicago Tribune,* and William
Hearst's *Chicago Examiner,* with national fame also as the founder
and benefactor of the Yale Hope Mission, one can see why leaders
of the Student Volunteer Movement saw great promise in the idea
of his taking a fall tour of colleges and universities, to speak on
behalf of foreign missionary endeavor.

For his part, Borden was deeply grateful for the opportunity
to tell the story of his 'call from God to become a missionary,' as
he'd told *The Chicago Examiner.*[2] Perhaps others would hear the
call, just as he had.

---

1. See Taylor, *Borden of Yale* (1926), p. 208. Selection edited. See also D. O. Shelton's
recollection of Borden's autumn 1912 tour, from *The Princeton Seminary Bulletin,* May
1913, page 13: 'During his tour of the colleges he sent me on one occasion his itinerary.
At the bottom of his typewritten schedule of engagements was this sentence, "I intend
to add $1,000 to my regular contribution next week." So he was always doing more than
he said he would do.' This would be $25,000 today.

2. See 'Young Borden ... Tells of Call to Become Missionary,' in *The Chicago
Examiner* newspaper, September 21, 1912, p. 1.

So a daunting schedule was set, calling for thousands of miles' travel by train. Biographer Samuel Zwemer gave a thorough list of the settings Borden was to visit 'in rapid succession, between September 26 and December 10.'[3]

Included were five Ivy League schools (Yale, Harvard, Princeton, Cornell and Penn), as well as seven other schools in New York State: Union College, Hamilton College, Colgate University, Syracuse University, Rochester Theological Seminary, Hobart College, and Auburn Theological Seminary.[4]

Nine schools in Pennsylvania were on Borden's schedule: Moravian College, Lafayette College, two Philadelphia divinity schools, Crozer Theological Seminary, Franklin & Marshall College, Pennsylvania State Normal School, Pennsylvania College, and Lutheran Theological Seminary, in Gettysburg.[5]

Five Virginia schools were on the list as well: Protestant Episcopal Seminary, the University of Virginia, Union Theological Seminary, Richmond College, and Hampton Normal Institute (a pioneering and famous African-American school).

New Jersey was well represented also. Borden visited Rutgers College and its Theological Seminary, Drew Theological Seminary, and last, Princeton Theological Seminary. Visits to Massachusetts schools rounded out his tour schedule: Andover Theological Seminary, Boston University School of Theology, Episcopal Theological School of Boston, and Newton Theological Institution.[6]

In all, a roster of thirty-four schools in seventy-six days: it promised to be a rewarding and challenging tour, as Geraldine Taylor said:

---

3. See Zwemer, *William Whiting Borden* (1913), p. 146.

4. ibid., p. 146. Writing to H. W. Frost from Hamilton College, Oct. 1, 1912, Borden said: 'I came here from Union yesterday, and am having a pleasant and profitable visit here at Dr Erdman's old college.' A letter at The Billy Graham Center, Wheaton College.

5. ibid., p. 146.

6. ibid., p. 146.

SPECIAL!

WILLIAM W. BORDEN

Will Visit the American Colleges This Fall in

the Interest of the

William W. Borden **STUDENT VOLUNTEER MOVEMENT**

The nationally-publicized announcement for Borden's Fall 1912 tour
of American colleges on behalf of the Student Volunteer Movement
(from *The Christian Worker's Magazine*, August 1912).

Beginning at Schenectady, New York, [Borden toured many]
colleges and seminaries [by December 10th,] before sailing for
Egypt [on December 17th].

One to three days in a place gave [the] opportunity for
interviews as well as meetings; [but] his time was so filled that it
was with difficulty he got away on his 25th birthday, [November
1st,] to spend the evening with his mother.[7]

∽ ∽ ∽

Surviving accounts offer something like a mosaic, or travelogue,
of the places, people, and topics that made Borden's autumn tour
memorable.

Getting a sense of what Borden said during his talks are a
beginning.

Two articles from his pen shed light on this: 'The Origin of
the Student Volunteer Movement,' in the March 1913 issue of *The
Christian Workers Magazine*, and second, 'The Watchword of the
Student Volunteer Movement,' published in the April 1913 issue
of *The Christian Workers Magazine*.

Passages from these articles capture Borden's common turns
of phrase, and recurring themes of his talks from late September

---

7. See Taylor, *Borden of Yale* (1926), pp. 216-217; and Zwemer, *William Whiting
Borden* (1913), p. 145.

to early December 1912. Indeed, it's likely these articles grew directly out of notes he'd prepared for his talks.

This would have been natural, given the many demands on Borden's time. And since no actual transcript of a talk from this tour has survived, these articles closely approximate the content and themes he would have shared.

To start, the influence of D. L. Moody was something Borden often spoke of, as in this passage, which expressed a personal debt of gratitude—

> It was said to Mr Moody on one occasion, 'The world has yet to see what God can do with a fully surrendered man.' Mr Moody himself, and others, have shown us how God uses those who really surrender themselves to His service.[8]

If D. L. Moody was one guiding influence, J. R. Mott, the future Nobel Prize Laureate, was surely another. Borden would have spoken of him many times in his college and seminary tour, in words like these—

> To what, then, are we to rally?
>
> To use the phraseology of Mr Mott, we are to rally to the proposition, 'that all … should be given an adequate opportunity to know Jesus Christ as their Saviour, and to become His real disciples. This involves such a distribution of missionary agencies as will make the gospel accessible to all.'[9]

Crucially, one part of any talk Borden gave during his autumn tour was an appeal for students to prayerfully consider what role they might take in the cause of missionary endeavor. This theme, and the abiding call upon each Christian believer was centerstage, as when Borden said—

> By all means, some are to be saved. We have said that the work is to be done by the missionaries; but that brings up the question

---

8. See *The Christian Workers Magazine*, March 1913, p. 456.
9. See *The Christian Workers Magazine*, April 1913, p. 504.

as to who they really are, and when this work is to be done. *Obviously, if the people of this generation are to be reached, it must be done now, and by us, the people of today.* Those of past generations have gone: those that are to come will have no opportunity of reaching the generation that now is.

Moreover, this is our *only* opportunity. As Mr Mott has said, 'In the last analysis, if the world is to be evangelized in this, or in any generation, it will be because a sufficient number of individual Christians recognize and assume their personal obligation to the undertaking.'

We have then before us a rallying cry, which rests upon the assumption that all need Christ, and which, resting upon this assumption and the command of Christ—together with His promises—holds before us the duty and possibility of accomplishing a great task.[10]

What was this great task? For Borden it came down to something he learned from the life of J. Hudson Taylor. As he explained—

And so the word comes to us with regard to this task in very much the same way that it came to Hudson Taylor in regard to inland China, 'I am going to do this, and I will use you, if you will follow Me.'[11]

Then too, Borden was always careful to share reflections on the 'watchword' J. R. Mott and other leaders of the Student Volunteer Movement had so faithfully proclaimed since 1886: 'The Evangelization of the World in This Generation.'

As Borden saw it, what this watchword involved was—

thorough consecration in deciding the question of our own life work, study of missions, prayer and work toward its accomplishment, both by what we are able to do ourselves, and by urging the adoption of this watchword upon others.

[Won't] you, if you have not already done so, make this watchword *your watchword* – and seek to hasten the time when

---

10. ibid., p. 504. Italics added.
11. ibid., p. 505.

the knowledge of God shall cover the earth, as the waters cover the sea?[12]

And last, Borden spoke continually on his autumn tour of words he'd heard from his great friend and mentor Robert P. Wilder. Doubtless many times, as he did so, he thought back to his time with the Wilder family in Norway in 1910.

It likely brought a smile in recollection, as Borden said—

One of the questions which Mr Wilder often used in beginning a conversation with men whom he met in the colleges was this,

'Are you steering, or drifting?'

This opened up the whole question of a student's choice of his life work.

The dangers of drifting were of course, manifest, and if a man said he was steering, the next question might well be, 'What is your goal?' and 'Who is in the boat with you?' It would seem that this question might well be asked by all: 'Are we drifting, or steering?' And may each one of us be able to say that we are steering – and that He is not only on board, but at the helm.[13]

This passage, from Borden's article on 'The Origin of the Student Volunteer Movement,' bore fruit in the life of a young man who read it, even as Borden's talks during his tour bore fruit. It was yet another way that his labors on behalf of the Student Volunteer Movement had far-reaching influence.

The moving story behind this event, from 1914, ran as follows—

The last [issue] of 'The Moody Church Herald' contains the testimony of O. C. Olsen, a present student of [Moody Bible] Institute, who came [there] through the influence of the late William W. Borden. Mr Olsen says:

'I had become interested in the life of Mr Borden, and one day I read in *The Christian Workers Magazine* an article ... dealing with the early history of the Student Volunteer Movement. As I came to the words, "Are you steering, or drifting," something

---

12. ibid., pp. 504-505.

13. See *The Christian Workers Magazine*, March 1913, 456. Selection edited.

happened. I do not know what it was, but I was unable to finish the rest of the article. [Then,] alone with God in my room, I had a battle. The rudder was given into His almighty hand, and there was peace within.'[14]

Beyond this, another thing typical of Borden's autumn tour was sharing his testimony, as stated in the October 12, 1912 edition of *The Cornell Daily Sun*—

'Mr W. W. Borden,' the article began:

> traveling secretary of the Student Volunteer Movement, will speak in Barnes Hall tomorrow, immediately after the Vesper service in the Chapel.
>
> This will probably be at 4:30 p.m.
>
> Mr Borden will tell of the experiences he had on a trip around the world before he went to college, which influenced him to become a missionary. After a year in Egypt, studying Arabic, and a year in London, spent in studying medicine, Mr Borden will go to China and take up missionary work there.[15]

Following this, Borden went to Auburn Seminary in New York, where he had been invited to speak from October 15 to 16, as 'Minister-in-Residence,' making 'several addresses to the students in the Club House, and Willard Chapel.'[16]

As the *Auburn Seminary Catalogue* described this visit—

> For two days, October 15th and 16th, Rev. W. W. Borden was the guest of the Y.M.C.A. Mr Borden, who has come to be [widely] known as the 'millionaire missionary,' is for this fall and winter traveling among the colleges and seminaries in the interests of the Student Volunteer Movement.
>
> Last spring he graduated from Princeton Seminary. On September 21st he was ordained at The Moody Church in Chicago.

---

14. See *The Christian Workers Magazine*, July 1914, p. 762.

15. See 'W. W. Borden To Talk in Barnes Hall Tomorrow,' in *The Cornell Daily Sun*, Saturday, October 12, 1912, p. 6.

16. See *The Auburn Theological Seminary Catalogue, 1912–1913* (Auburn, New York: Auburn Theological Seminary, 1913), p. 46.

During his stay, Mr Borden lived in the dormitory and at the Club House with the men. It was a pleasure to know him, and profitable to discuss with him the missionary work, for his travels in the different mission fields and his interest in their work have given him an unusual understanding of the problems that face the missionary today.

On the first evening of his visit, he met with the Volunteers of the Seminary and on the second addressed a union prayer-meeting of the classes ... Mr Borden will be remembered for his earnest and consecrated spirit, and for the uplift we have felt from his visit among us.

After this year, he will go to Cairo, Egypt, and to London for the purpose of further [medical] study in preparation for his work [with] China Inland Mission in the Kanzu province, where he will be located.[17]

After the Auburn Seminary visit, the *Delaware County Daily Times* of Chester, Pennsylvania, ran a page one feature story on Borden's forthcoming visit to Crozer Theological Seminary, famous now as the seminary that Dr Martin Luther King, Jr attended. Describing a Y.M.C.A. gathering scheduled for Thursday, October 24, the *Daily Times* reported that a meeting was to be

conducted [on this evening] by William W. Borden, Travelling Secretary of the Student Volunteer Movement. Mr Borden is a graduate of Yale University, and is a consecrated Christian young man who has entered into his chosen line of life work with his whole being. All the friends of the seminary are cordially invited to attend the meeting. The public in general is also welcome.[18]

From this same part of Borden's autumn tour, his visit to Lafayette College, in Easton, Pennsylvania, was covered in a local press article, which reported—

---

17. ibid., pages 405-406.

18. See page 1 of the Thursday, October 24, 1912 edition of the *Delaware County Daily Times* from Chester, Pennsylvania.

[Mr Borden] visited here during the first term, previous to his sailing for Egypt. His short stay here gave many undergraduates an opportunity to meet him. All who came in contact with him were distinctly impressed by his strong personality and amiable qualities.[19]

Moving to early November, Borden's University of Virginia visit was widely publicized in the campus periodical *Madison Hall Notes,* which printed the following feature article on November 9th—

Mr W. W. Borden, Field Secretary of the Student Volunteer Movement, will be here Saturday, Sunday and Monday. He will not make an address, but will confer with all who wish to talk with him.

On Sunday evening, a dinner will be given at the Commons in his honor, to which [students] have been invited … who are deeply interested in Mission work. On Sunday he will meet with as many of the Bible Study Classes as do not conflict. Mr Borden is a college man; a graduate of Yale and of Princeton Theological Seminary. His preparation and experience have fitted him for a great work, and he is accomplishing much.

Borden's visit to Union Seminary in Richmond, Virginia, took place in close proximity to his University of Virginia appearance. This brief but compelling notice about it ran in the *Presbyterian of the South* newspaper—

'Mr Borden found at the Seminary a warm and active missionary spirit, and among the one hundred and seven students, he found twenty-six volunteers for the Foreign Field. It made a strong impression on him.'[20]

≈ ≈ ≈

Near the end of Borden's autumn tour, one good friend was present when he addressed the German department of the Rochester Theological Seminary.

---

19. See *The Princeton Seminary Bulletin,* May 1913, p. 11.

20. See page 441 of the May 14, 1913 edition of the *Presbyterian of the South* newspaper.

After his spirited address, this friend remembered:

[William] said that if there were any questions they cared to ask, though he would not promise to answer them all, he would be glad to try.

Many questions followed—wise and otherwise—and I marvelled at his unfailing patience, and complete lack of pride or self-consciousness, though he, the teacher, was probably the youngest of them all. During the months since I'd [last] seen him, a wonderful grace and sweetness had come into his life; but there was not one whit less of strength or humour.[21]

About the same time, and after the address Borden gave at New Brunswick Seminary, a Yale classmate who was present tried to draw him out on the subject of marriage. That question led to a memorable exchange, as follows—

At the end of November, when Bill was here to give a talk in the Seminary, he came to my room and lay down on the couch, having caught a feverish cold. We talked over many matters.

In a joking way, I asked him when he was going to marry. He replied seriously that he thought it was cruel for a man who was going into one of the most difficult of missionary fields to ask any girl to go with him.[22]

There was a context behind this statement, for as Geraldine Taylor has noted, Borden 'strongly approved the rule of the China Inland Mission with regard to out-going missionaries, whether men or women, that they should remain unmarried for the first two years in China, so as to give undivided attention to the study of the language and have the best opportunity of becoming acclimatized, and getting into touch with the people.'[23]

There was so much to adjust to and learn about in such a two-year period. And for Borden, readily as he agreed with the wisdom

21. See Taylor, *Borden of Yale* (1926), p. 219.

22. ibid., p. 219-220.

23. ibid., p. 220.

of China Inland Mission, it was really a matter of common sense and prudence. Compassion for a future wife warranted following this wise policy, and kindness guided his resolve.[24]

As with so many chapters of Borden's life, his great friend Charlie Campbell had a near view of the good things that resulted from Borden's autumn tour.

Campbell's account of the tour, especially Borden's time at the University of Virginia, catches something of the reception he had in so many settings—

For three months [Bill] traveled [on behalf] of the Student Volunteer Movement. The [roster] of colleges and universities which he visited occupies considerable space, [and later,] the secretary of the Y.M.C.A. of the University of Virginia [described] what must have [unfolded] at many of the other colleges ...

'Mr Borden has come and gone. His visit was an inspiring one. His deep spiritual life, his splendid preparation for service, and his absolute dedication to the missionary cause have made a lasting impression ...

In his quiet and unassuming way he met our men, presented the claims of a foreign field, and gave helpful counsel [to] the Missionary Committee. The most helpful and abiding feature of his visit, however, was the quiet, pervading influence of his personality, and of a life consecrated to the Master's cause. We know that our University has been blessed by having Borden in our midst ...'[25]

Here it seems fitting to offer another passage from Borden: one that shows the thorough consecration and purpose that guided his life. These words might well have been like one of his prayers with students during his autumn tour.

We do know it was a prayer he had made his own—

24. ibid., p. 220.
25. See Campbell, *William Whiting Borden* (1913), p. 25.

*I also pray that God will take my life into His hands
and use it for the furtherance of His Kingdom
as He sees best.
I feel sure that He will answer my prayer.*[26]

F. P. Turner, the General Secretary of the Student Volunteer Movement, penned an eloquent tribute about Borden's autumn tour:

> Those were fruitful months. William was used to lead students in many colleges and universities to give their lives to foreign missionary service. The last letter I received from him enclosed the 'declaration card' of a Student Volunteer who had signed it after his visit; and sent it on to him in Cairo.
>
> In years to come, there will be missionaries in many fields who owe their decision, under God, to William's unselfish service during his last months in this country.[27]

In closing this chapter, it seems best to let Borden himself have the last word, with a phrase of deep meaning. It's the kind of phrase that would have graced many talks during his fall tour of colleges and seminaries—

*How wonderful, that we have the
blessèd hope ...*[28]

---

26. See Taylor, *Borden of Yale* (1926), p. 69-70.

27. ibid., p. 221.

28. A letter from Borden in Hanover, Germany to Henry Weston Frost, Wed., July 20, 1910, housed at The Billy Graham Center, Wheaton College.

CHAPTER 15

The Banner of the Red Lion

Borden's whole soul was wrapped up in his desire to do the Lord's will and work ... With unusual natural gifts, [and] trained by an exceptional education ... it appeared that the Spirit of God was purposing to use him mightily ... Integrity, humility, [and] magnanimity were the three marked characteristics of [his] life ...[1]

– Erving Yale Woolley (June 1913)

But my preparation will take some time. In December, I will go to the school of Dr S. M. Zwemer in Cairo, Egypt. There I intend to study Arabic. I also will take a course in medicine in London before I go to China. The people in the Province of Kansu ... suffer from diseases that are easily curable.[2]

– William Borden from a page one interview
in *The Chicago Tribune*, Sept. 21, 1912

... realize the intrinsic value of the thing to be gained ... It is really nothing less than the abiding with us of a divine Person, to work in and through us ...[3]

– William Borden (October 1912)

---

1. Rev. Erving Yale Woolley, in *The Missionary Visitor*, June 1913, p. 197. Woolley served Moody Church as: Asst. Pastor, 1907–1913; Acting Pastor, 1913–1915; Assoc. Pastor, 1915. See *The Christian Workers* magazine, Feb. 1918, 482. Woolley (1866–1935), was a graduate of Brown University (1888).

2. Quoted in 'Young Millionaire Renounces World To Be Missionary,' from the 21 Sept. 1912 edition of *The Chicago Tribune*, page 1.

3. W. W. Borden, 'The Price of Power,' in *The Bible To-Day*, p. 141. A version of this ran in the Oct. 1912 issue of *China's Millions* magazine, pp. 117-118, confirming the time Borden wrote it.

Near the close of Borden's autumn tour on behalf of the Student Volunteer Movement, *The New York Times* reported on a happy event: his reunion with several close friends from Yale. On Thursday, November 28th, the *Times* reported—

> Louis Girard Audette was married ... to Miss Helen Argyll Campbell, daughter of James R. Campbell, Headmaster of the Kingsley School, Essex Fells, New Jersey. The ceremony was performed in the Assembly Room of the school by the Rev. Alfred K. Bates of Ithaca, New York.
>
> Miss Louise Campbell, sister of the bride, was Maid of Honor, and Charles Soutter Campbell acted as Best Man. The ushers included William Borden of Chicago, Joseph F. Jefferson of Lakeville, Connecticut; Malcolm B. Vilas of Cleveland, Ohio, and Frederick Gates of Montclair, New Jersey, all of whom were classmates of Mr Audette at Yale.[4]

Borden's friend Charlie Campbell well remembered this gathering—

'On November 28th, Bill was [an] usher at my sister's wedding to Louis G. Audette. Other Yale fellows were there. We had a jolly time, and Bill was in for all the fun. The wedding was an evening affair, after which Bill packed off to the city to be with his mother, as the days before he sailed [for Egypt] were few.'[5]

On December 10th, Borden's fall tour for the Student Volunteer Movement concluded, followed by a flurry of final preparations before sailing aboard the steam ship *Mauretania* for England. From there it was a journey to Cairo, to commence a study of Arabic, before a London course in medical training for service in China.

Here, Geraldine Taylor captured something more of the crowded hours and moments of Borden's remaining days in America.

'The last Sunday of all,' she said, December 15th, 'William spent quietly with his mother. They went to church together in

---

4. See page 84 of the Sunday, December 8, 1912 edition of *The New York Times*.

5. See Taylor, *Borden of Yale* (1926), p. 222.

the morning, little thinking it was for the last time, and on the following day,' Monday, December 16th, 'he took part in the meeting, held regularly in their home, [of] prayer for the Moslem world.'[6]

Later, several friends came for dinner at his mother's New York City home, among them Dr and Mrs Henry Weston Frost, and D. O. Shelton of the National Bible Institute.[7] Festive thoughts for the future were the order of the evening.

Borden was leaving the next day, and 'by common consent, the five or six [friends] with whom he [was] most closely associated in [Christian work] gathered in his room, for a last hour of prayer and fellowship.' As Shelton remembered—

> We prayed that our beloved friend [William] might be kept in safety throughout his long journey, and guided and upheld in all his ways. And then, he prayed for us, and for the work we represented. He was so strong and vigorous in body and mind that night; [and] we anticipated for him long and useful service ...[8]

Few moments of fellowship are sweeter than the eve of an ocean departure. Borden had this kind of keepsake, born of faith and the good words of his friends, to carry on the journey ahead.

∾ ∾ ∾

When the *R.M.S. Mauretania* pushed away from the pier in New York City, at six in the evening on Tuesday, December 17, 1912, it was a scene not unlike the departure of a great ocean liner like the *Queen Mary*. The *Mauretania* was some 792 feet long and she was a massive ship of 45,000 tons. She was also a fast ship; and set several Atlantic crossing records.

---

6. ibid., p. 223.

7. ibid., p. 223.

8. ibid., p. 223. See also *The Princeton Seminary Bulletin,* May 1913, pp. 13-14: Shelton recalled: 'I can never forget the seasons of prayer that I have had with William Borden ... I always discovered that he was a man of persistent and believing prayer. He visited us in the office in New York hundreds of times. Seldom did we [discuss] any important matter without his saying, *"Let us have a word of prayer about this."*'

Such a trip, especially for 'Christmas sailing,' as *The New York Times* phrased it, was a unique and fine experience. Festive décor was set about the Corinthian columns and the ornate marble hearth beneath the great atrium window of the *Mauretania's* reception room – and carol singing would be held at welcome intervals throughout the voyage. Outside, set over the stern, the *Mauretania* proudly flew the wide banner of a lion – set in scarlet. It moved regally in the wind.

The R.M.S. *Mauretania*, on which Borden sailed in December 1912
(from the author's photo collection, postcard circa 1910).

Yet this journey wasn't all excitement and anticipation. 'In spite of eagerness to get to his work,' Charlie Campbell said, 'it caused [Bill] real sorrow to leave his own country, friends, and especially his mother and [younger] sister [Joyce].'[9]

Yet at the same time, there was the feeling of deep satisfaction that at last, he was leaving to take up a task he'd been so long preparing for. Four years of college, and three years of graduate study at seminary: seven years in all. Now, he stood on the deck of the *Mauretania*, bidding farewell to family and friends.

The sight of Borden as he stood on the deck was one Charlie Campbell long remembered: '[Bill] never looked better,' he wrote, 'or more calm and peaceful.'[10]

---

9. See Campbell, *William Whiting Borden* (1913), p. 26.

10. ibid., p. 26.

The next day, December 18th, writing to Henry Weston Frost on stationary with the caption, 'On board the Cunard *R.M.S. Mauretania*,' Borden said—

Dear Mr Frost,

I am writing you now, at this early stage ... simply to thank you for your very kind letter assuring me of your continued prayers ... I was very glad that you and Mrs Frost could come over to New York [to bid farewell.]

I don't know how Mother told you that I was thinking of returning next summer, for I just barely mentioned it [as one] of the possible courses that were open at present to me. I realize that this, *and the question as to when I should go to China,* are very important steps.

What I want is the Lord's will, and I am confident that if I go ahead, honestly desiring to do that whatever it may mean, I will be sure of the next step when it comes time to make it ...

Everything is going smoothly [so far], and I am enjoying it all very much. [I'll] try to let you hear from me again from London.

> Very sincerely yours,
> William W. Borden[11]

The journey he'd embarked on was one of several stages. Once in England, he would spend Christmas with Robert Wilder and his family in London. Then it was a cross-Europe trip to Brindisi; thence to board a steamer for Port Said.[12]

But before these stages of his journey came, we have a glimpse from Borden's own pen of what it was like aboard the *Mauretania,* as the powerful vessel parted the waves. On Thursday, December 19th, 1912, Borden walked to his stateroom, past halls set with Christmas trimmings, turned the lamp on over his desk, and took up a familiar, well-used fountain pen, writing—

---

11. Borden to H. W. Frost, Wed., Dec. 18, 1912, call no. at The Billy Graham Center, Wheaton College: 'BCG CN215 Folder 3-80, William Borden.'

12. See Campbell, *William Whiting Borden* (1913), p. 26.

Dear Mother—

I hope you went straight home when you left me last night, or rather the night before last ...

The boat sailed quite promptly at 6:05. As I wrote you in the letter I sent ashore by the Pilot, the lights in lower New York were simply wonderful.

The light on the Metropolitan Tower stood out like an evening star, while the top of the Singer Tower looked like a veritable castle in the air; suspended as it was in the sky. As we passed [by] the Battery the light was different, but wonderful, and a lot of people were on the deck admiring it ...

I am taking some time each morning now, in addition to my usual Morning Watch, for study of the Christmas passages in the Bible. They are certainly wonderfully beautiful, are they not?

... the weather [here] continues very mild, as far as the temperature is concerned, though it has been a little rougher. Still as I thought, the vibration has not been at all bad, though it has been a little more noticeable than it was.

This morning, Sunday, we had service, conducted by the Purser. [Later,] I read Dr Stone's [book about Rev. Maltbie Babcock,] *Footsteps in a Parish* ...

I will be eagerly awaiting a first letter from you to know how things have been going. I hope for the best, believing that you will be sustained and helped daily by our Heavenly Father.

Lots and Lots of love,
William[13]

This letter, written at sea, has many virtues. Borden's vivid description of the lower New York City skyline—as it was in December 1912—is something of a gift in itself. It's an account from a bygone era, before the Empire State Building, and the iconic Chrysler Building, had been constructed. They were some twenty years in the future. To have Borden's description of this skyline, seen from an ocean liner, is a true, if slender, cultural

---

13. See Zwemer, *William Whiting Borden* (1913), pp. 171-172.

artifact. For he had a fine way with words, much as his sister Mary (who became a noted poet) did.

Then too, we've a glimpse in this shipboard letter of Borden's habits of the heart, or what people in his time called 'devotional life.' His Morning Watch had always been a time for prayer and Bible study. Now, he took special care to go to the very heart of Christianity's beginning, to trace telling passages in Scripture centered on the Christmas story. That this time of study deepened his sense of reverence for things of faith is a special insight from his writings.

And sometimes a fleeting reference, such as Borden's mention of J. T. Stone's memoir of scholar athlete Maltbie Davenport Babcock, author of the poem which became the hymn 'This Is My Father's World,' says a great deal.

For a start, the author of *Footsteps in a Parish* was none other than Dr John Timothy Stone, of Fourth Presbyterian Church, Chicago, who'd given the pastoral charge at Borden's ordination on September 21, 1912. There is every reason to think Borden's copy of *Footsteps in a Parish* was a gift of Dr Stone himself, perhaps an ordination service gift – so all the more welcome as a keepsake.

Further, Dr Stone's personal friendship with Maltbie Babcock, recounted in *Footsteps in a Parish,* held a close tie to The Hill School, the prestigious preparatory school Borden had attended.

How appreciative Borden must have been to read one particular passage by lamplight as the *Mauretania* crossed the Atlantic. There, Dr Stone said—

During those years which immediately followed [Babcock's] annual visit … students' rooms throughout the schools and colleges where he preached had his photograph [displayed]. This was especially true in room after room among the boys in the fifth and sixth forms at The Hill School … Here particularly, he seemed to have a hold upon their hearts, and frequently when I [visited] their rooms, a [student] would say, as I stopped before the photograph—

'He gave that to me himself.'

In speaking of The Hill School, memory goes back to the occasion of my first visit there during the winter of 1901 or 1902.

Many demands for outside work came to me [in] those first years [of my pastorate] in Baltimore, especially from the schools and colleges, and it was wise to decline most invitations.

But when the invitation came from The Hill School, I recalled a single remark [Dr Babcock] made on the night of my installation. His part was the charge to the pastor, but just before [the service], in his happy pleasantry of impulsive suggestion, he said, *Do not say "Yes" to all the invitations you get, but if they ask you to go up to preach to the boys at The Hill School, you go'*...

Those boys in the upper forms all remembered [Dr Babcock, and] during [my visit,] I referred to the personal wish he had expressed, as to them, if the invitation came to preach. [The students cherished] his affectionate, winsome personality, and many a hand-shake which was mine that day, I recognized as alive with the ambition and spirit he had created.[14]

In addition to storied memories of The Hill School, another recollection of Maltbie Babcock might well have resonated in a meaningful way with Borden.

J. T. Stone remembered that one friend had said of Babcock—

He opened every window of his soul toward Him who is love, Who 'went about doing good,' then turned [to all] that crossed his path, and light and warmth radiated from him to them ...

Little children that he met always received his cheery smile. Yes, it once pleased [Dr Babcock] that a common little English sparrow continued to drink when he had passed close to it. He knew the value of [seeming] trifles. It is out of littleness that greatness germinates. He realized that words and acts are seeds. Only God can estimate the harvest.[15]

---

14. See Dr John Timothy Stone, *Footsteps in a Parish* (New York: Scribner's, 1908), pp. 58-61.

15. ibid., p. 67.

Last of all, *Footsteps in a Parish* was a book that celebrated Babcock's pastoral ministry in the years after he'd been a standout athlete on the Syracuse University baseball team and trained for pastoral ministry at Auburn Theological Seminary.

Borden had visited Auburn Seminary during his long autumn tour for the Student Volunteer Movement. Babcock's memory was hallowed there, and indeed, this may be why Borden thought to read more of Babcock's story while sailing for England. It would have been fresh in his mind if Babcock was spoken of at Auburn, and also at Syracuse University. It's likely he was spoken of, in both places.

That Borden read of a fellow college athlete turned minister holds a special kind of symbolism. His life, in the reading of *Footsteps in a Parish,* touched the life of another gifted exemplar of faith. Borden and Babcock were kindred spirits.

Maltbie Babcock's story had inspired thousands of readers, and it likely held many moments of inspiration for Borden. So to know this was one of the books he read is meaningful. It had his book-plate, 'engraved after his own design,' showing an 'open door into regions beyond, over hills of difficulty.'[16] Over the door's lintel was the Scripture text so well known as 'the Great Commission'—

And He said unto them,
'Go ye into all the world, and preach the
gospel' (Mark 16:15)

Just after the *Mauretania* docked in England, Borden spent Christmas 'in the home of Mr Robert P. Wilder in London'[17] His fondness for the Wilder family was born of a friendship that had deepened in recent years, and as seen earlier, Wilder and his wife Hélène cherished the memory of Borden's visit with them in 1910.

---

16. See Zwemer, *William Whiting Borden* (1913), p. 133.

17. See Campbell, *William Borden* (1913), p. 26.

After Christmas with the Wilder family in England, Borden crossed Europe to Brindisi, where he took a steam ship to Port Said, a city in northeast Egypt.

From here, Borden's biographer Samuel Zwemer described those first days in the Land of the Pharaohs—

'On January first, Borden arrived in Cairo, and was ready to begin his final preparation in Arabic and Islamic study before going to China. On the day of his arrival, a friend who also hoped to work [among] Chinese Mohammedans, and was passing through Cairo, accompanied me to meet him at the station.'[18]

Borden could not have been more pleased to discover that a new friend who hoped to work in China had joined Dr Zwemer to greet him, and said as much in a letter written on January 5th—

I landed in Cairo about 5:30 p.m. [on January 1st,] and was met at the station by Dr Zwemer and a German missionary from China, a Mr Zeigler who had heard of me from [C. H.] Robertson of Tientsin, and had wanted very much to meet me.

It appears [Mr Zeigler] had become interested in the Moslems of China and decided to take up that work. He was with the Y.M.C.A., but affiliated with the German branch of the C.I.M. in a way. He is now on his way back to China, and stopped to see things here in Cairo a bit, especially with regard to work for Moslems. He went to the Ashar University ... and they found there a man from China. Mr Gairdner could speak with him in Arabic, and Mr Zeigler in Chinese.

It appears that he had been here two years and had not written home. In fact he couldn't write Chinese, and would have to write in Arabic to some priest in his hometown, which was in Kansu, who could then translate it to his family.

Another remarkable thing was that he hadn't heard of the revolution in China! With the help of Dr Zwemer I am going to try and get in touch with him, and see what can be done.[19]

---

18. See Zwemer, *William Whiting Borden* (1913), p. 173.
19. ibid., p. 173.

This turn of events held much excitement for Borden. He'd only just arrived in Egypt, and already, he'd met two people who had a direct connection to the work he hoped to undertake someday in China. It was a beginning rich with promise.

And one friend from Yale student days, Charlie Campbell, was grateful to receive letters and news from Borden once he'd arrived in Egypt.

Looking back on them, Campbell wrote: 'in Cairo, Bill settled down to study [and] hard work of many kinds. His classes were chiefly in Arabic, and in the study of Islam. Cairo, as the intellectual center of Islam, afforded splendid opportunities for just such work.'[20]

Moreover, as Samuel Zwemer observed, Borden 'had spent some time in the study of classical Arabic at Princeton,[21] and was therefore an apt and eager pupil at the Cairo Study Center, under the direction of the Rev. W. H. T. Gairdner, a leader in the work of the Church Missionary Society, with his staff of native teachers, and other missionaries.'[22]

William Henry Temple Gairdner, a widely-respected British missionary, long remembered how 'wholeheartedly' Borden undertook this formidable task—

> William Borden studied Arabic under my general superintendence all the time he was in Cairo; it was a pleasure to have to do with one so keen and able. His object was to acquire the classical language ... [begin] literary work among the Arabic-reading Mohammedans of China ... [and] read and decipher Arabic letters. [Once in China, he wished] generally to be available as [one well versed in] Arabic matters, in a land where it seems not a single Christian worker [is as familiar with them as needed] ...

20. See Campbell, *William Borden* (1913), p. 26.

21. At Princeton, Borden and A. B. Fowler had begun work on 'an Arabic Concordance of the Bible.' See Taylor, *Borden of Yale* (1926), p. 184.

22. See Zwemer, *William Whiting Borden* (1913), pp. 174-175.

I represented to him that this was a pretty [tall] order, and that such a knowledge of Arabic would certainly need more than a year at Cairo. He seemed quite unappalled by the idea, [so he undertook] lessons in the phonetics and pronunciation of Arabic ...

I soon saw he had a good ear and was quick [to note] sound differences ... He believed too that the oral use of classical Arabic might be directly useful in China. With the same broad view of the situation, he even aimed at using Egyptian colloquial, totally useless though it would have been to him from the moment he quitted Egypt. But he saw that without it, he would not be able to take advantage of the instruction in Arabic from the Sheikhs [in Cairo,] who do not know any other language.[23]

This passage from William Gairdner is revealing, for it shows Borden had a true gift for other languages and a very keen dedication to learning them. He was a scholar of languages – and an accomplished linguist.

To see this, it need only be remembered that he studied classical Arabic at Princeton, and Hebrew.[24] Greek had been part of his studies at Princeton, as it was at Yale. He'd also studied Greek and Latin at The Hill School, with a careful study of German in Berlin in 1910, and he was planning on learning Chinese. He was also fluent in French. And now, he looked to learn Egyptian also. In time, he would have achieved fluency in eight languages.

Borden's letters were full of his studies, and his ardor to learn. On February 26th, he'd written home to one friend—

You will be interested to know that I am reading a big French book on the Moslems in China with [my friend] Ibrahim. It is Dr Ollone's *Recharches sur les Mussulmans Chinois [Research on Chinese Muslims],* and as it has a good deal of Arabic sprinkled about in it, it is very convenient to have someone who knows Arabic, as well as French and English.

---

23. ibid., pp. 175-176.

24. See the *Catalogue of the Theological Seminary of the Presbyterian Church at Princeton* (Princeton: The Trustees of the Seminary, 1908), p. 39.

I have been going ahead at the Arabic, and making good progress on the whole, though it is slow of course; and while what I learned at Princeton has been a help, it was powerful small as to quantity, I discover.

I am using Thatcher's *Arabic Grammar* (in the Gaspey Otto Sauer series), going through that before attempting [more]. This is no small job ...

Then I am reading [the Gospel of] John, working out the translation, and then reading aloud in Arabic with a teacher ...

I am taking a bit of conversation [in Arabic], as I have opportunity. This is, of course, rather different from what those who are to be in Arabic speaking countries do; [but I think it] best. From the standpoint of missions to Moslems, Cairo is a great place to be; especially now the Study Center is in operation.[25]

As a respite from his studies, Borden took time for sports in his leisure hours at the Cairo Y.M.C.A. One special photo brings this facet of Borden's time in Egypt to life in a way that is at once very American, and very much a period piece of expatriate life in the early 1900s.[26]

Sixteen young men are shown in the photo. Borden is seated there among them – the second person on the left in the first row. Wearing an English cap, he has catcher's gear set out on the grass in front of him. A fine mitt, looking very much like a catcher's mitt today; a face-mask that also looks very much like a catcher's mask now; and a chest guard – much more 'old school,' torso shaped and about two inches thick, with a strap that allows it to be hung from a player's neck. It would offer some protection, but not much, for a fastball foul-tipped by a batter.

Borden, for his part, looks as though he was made to play catcher.

His physique at twenty-five evokes a pre-World War I era player who looked rather like Boston Red Sox catcher Carlton

---

25. See Zwemer, *William Whiting Borden* (1913), p. 176. Italics added.

26. This photo is housed in the Archives of The Billy Graham Center at Wheaton College.

Fisk in his youth. Athletic and quick on his feet, Borden had a strong arm, and one gets the sense that not many runners would try to steal second base on him. He also gave every indication on the hitting side that he would have hit for power, much as a player like Fisk did. Batting practice for this Y.M.C.A. Club must have been something to see.

Borden was one of several players wearing a uniform with Y.M.C.A. in initials across the chest. All in all, this is a remarkable photo, and it shows a scene where Borden was an on-field general for his team, as a quarterback would be in football. He called the pitches, barked out 'two away, one to go!' then stood in at the plate, perhaps batting clean-up for his team.

He would have been a deep ball threat, especially as he may have been hitting one of the new 'live' balls which were in use after the World Series of 1910.[27] He'd led teams to victory at Yale, and it seems likely that here, in Cairo, his team would have been a hard one to beat. Their games were welcome contests of skill.

Borden's arrival in Cairo was one well begun; a season rich with promise. He was a gifted, well-regarded missionary-in-training, savoring every moment in Egypt.

---

27. 'We used our newly patented cork center ball … in the 1910 World Series.' George Reach, in *The Chalmers Race*, (Lincoln: Univ. of Neb., 2014), p. 64.

CHAPTER 16

To the Home Above

When my spirit, clothed immortal,
Wings its flight to realms of day ...
– Fanny Crosby (1875)[1]

Lines from Samuel Zwemer's biography of Borden bring the busy days after his arrival in Cairo to life. One passage, in particular, highlights what Zwemer called Borden's 'ministry of friendship.'[2]

In this regard, Zwemer wrote, Borden was 'ever ready' to—

> show people their seats at the American Mission evening service, help at the Y.M.C.A., lead the Christian Endeavor meeting, or encourage Coptic young men in their society, 'Friends of the Bible.'
>
> His generosity found opportunities, on every hand, to lighten a missionary burden, or provide better equipment for workers. Yet it was his personality ... not his [financial wherewithal], that won hearts and deeply impressed native Egyptians and missionaries alike.[3]

In addition to what he saw of Borden in the company of others, Zwemer had a very close personal insight into the way Borden took up his task as a missionary. It would be at least a year before

---

1. Fanny Crosby, 'All the Way My Saviour Leads Me,' © 1875 by Biglow & Main. See *The Epworth Hymnal* (New York: Phillips & Hunt, 1885), p. 127.

2. See Zwemer, *William Whiting Borden* (1913), p. 179.

3. ibid., p. 179.

going to China, but during the time he had in Cairo, Borden was determined to make a real difference in sharing things of faith. 'I never saw,' Zwemer recalled—

> a man come to Egypt with eyes more open to see the kingdom of God. Other men come to see the dead Pharaohs, to study history, or join the great company of tourists all over the land; never once lifting their eyes to see the fields 'white unto harvest.' Borden had not been in Cairo two weeks before he organized the students of the theological seminary, to [begin] a house-to-house canvass with Christian literature for the whole city, with its eight hundred thousand people.[4]

And then there were the moments when Borden entered the Zwemer family circle. He'd become part of the family – almost from the first. Zwemer said that with 'the mind of a scholar, [and with] the grasp of a theologian as regards God's truth,' Borden was anything but full of himself, or such attainments. He was 'so tender in the relations of home-life that our children used to nestle upon his knee as if they had known him for years.'[5]

Trained at Princeton himself as a scholar, Dr Zwemer could appreciate what seven years' academic training at Yale and Princeton meant to Borden's life of the intellect; yet his kindness among the Zwemer children belied any staid notions of a 'proper reserve' among young ones. He hadn't any.

This said, the linguistic challenge Borden had given himself was formidable. Zwemer saw that also, and it made a deep impression—

> Knowing that he had to learn Chinese, [Borden] came to Cairo to perfect himself in Arabic. Some people shrink from the foreign field, questioning, 'Could I learn the language?'
> Here was a man who deliberately set before himself the task of learning not one, but two of the most difficult languages in

---

4. See Taylor, *Borden of Yale* (1926), p. 240.

5. ibid., p. 240.

the world – *before* entering upon his life-work of declaring the unsearchable riches of Christ to Chinese Mohammedans ... At Yale, at Princeton, in Cairo, we see him digging deep, thinking deep, and studying hard ...[6]

Noteworthy too was Borden's very obvious commitment to what we would now term 'mere Christianity.' Zwemer saw and heard Borden speak of his 'great convictions of the eternal truth of God,'[7] or the first things of evangelical faith. These were, as Charles Erdman of Princeton said, 'particularly precious to him.'[8]

And what were they? Dr Erdman said that these 'first things' were—

> the inspiration of the Bible, justification by faith, the regenerating power of the Holy Spirit, the grace of God in Christ, the spiritual union of all true believers of every denomination, and the personal, pre-millennial return of our Lord ... [William] was always ready to give a reason ... for the faith that was in him. These truths were the inspiration of his life, and the explanation of his career.[9]

Still more, Zwemer saw that when Borden lived in Cairo, he never evinced any tendency whatsoever to 'keep to himself,' or fellowship solely with those of his own particular faith tradition: he sought fellowship in other Christian settings also.

Zwemer watched his protégé become 'a friend to the Coptic Christians and the Armenian Christians. He was a brother to the American missionaries and to the British missionaries.'[10] He attended the Scottish church and the American church, and befriended 'all sorts and conditions of Christians.' Zwemer

---

6. ibid., pp. 240-241. Italics added.

7. ibid., p. 241.

8. C. R. Erdman, 'An Ideal Missionary Volunteer,' *The Missionary Review of the World*, Aug. 1913, p. 575.

9. ibid., p. 575.

10. See Taylor, *Borden of Yale* (1926), p. 241.

considered this to be both wise and winsome – something that ran to the heart of who Borden was.

Borden's generosity of spirit showed itself in other ways.

As Geraldine Taylor wrote: 'At the Y.M.C.A. [in Cairo,] he was in touch with men of various nationalities, whom he joined in sports as well as meetings.' As one Syrian friend, with whom Borden was reading French, recalled, 'he was a splendid young man – so healthy, mentally, morally and spiritually.'[11]

Borden's presence at Christian Endeavor Meetings was long remembered also, especially the evening when he spoke on the topic, 'Be a Christian: Why not?' It was a talk on 'apologetics,' or cogent reasons for the acceptance of Christian faith. He was a compelling, effective speaker; and though we've several of the fine articles he'd written, one wishes that a copy of this memorable address had survived.

Yet a good idea of Borden's presence as a speaker, and turns of phrase, rests in lines that do survive in his papers. Three representative passages catch the flavor of how he spoke: showing his wide knowledge of ancient history, his reading of classic novels, and the use of personal testimony. Plato and Charles Dickens were part of this, and the first selection from Borden's writings touches on a scene from the Sage of Athens. 'Many today,' Borden said—

> are spiritually blind and fail to see it. Such people are like those in 'The Allegory of the Cave,' who were expert in interpreting the shadows cast on the wall of their prison (for such it was), but were absolutely ignorant of the real life and light outside which made these shadows.
>
> Moreover, they were so contented that when one of their number had visited the outer world and returned to them with glowing accounts of it, they refused to believe him, or take the trouble to go and see for themselves.
>
> This, I say, is the attitude of many towards Christianity and Christians. Is it a reasonable attitude? Is it your attitude?

11. ibid., pp. 243-244.

If it is, be sure that you are cutting yourself off from a world of beauty of which you have no conception ...[12]

And when it came to Christian teaching – say the idea of Christ's atonement, Borden drew on a literary allusion to Charles Dickens' *A Tale of Two Cities*. His listeners would have been curious here, no doubt, to learn how a scene from the French Revolution could help them discern a key tenet of faith.

So Borden explained that while 'there is no true analogy to this wonderful provision of [Christ's] substitution; yet there are cases which illustrate it'[13]—

> I remember reading of a young Frenchman who was imprisoned in the Bastille during the time of the French Revolution. He had an English friend who was almost his twin brother in appearance.
>
> The Englishman managed to visit his friend and take his place, having the Frenchman, who was very weak and sick, removed. And the next day when the guillotine fell, it was upon the neck of the friend, and not on that of the one who had been condemned to die.[14]

Last of all, when it came to bearing testimony for one's faith, and thoughts in favor of belief, Borden pointed to something his friend Kenneth Latourette would have deeply appreciated: the flow of Christian history, as reflected in the lives of noteworthy believers. And here everyone, in reality, could share something of what Christ meant to them – in talking with others, as Borden stated—

> There are a great many different arguments for Christianity which weigh differently with different people. But probably no argument has greater weight or more universal effect than that from Christian experience.

---

12. W. W. Borden, *Gospel Addresses* (1914), p. 21.

13. ibid., p. 15.

14. ibid., p. 15. In *A Tale of Two Cities,* the novel by Charles Dickens, Englishman Sydney Carton offers to die in place of Charles Darnay. Carton is able to die in Darnay's place, switching places in prison, because the two resemble one another so greatly.

This is true of it in the larger sense, as we see it exhibited to us in the history of the Church, from the time of Christ on; but especially as wrought out in the life of the individual.[15]

Because of his keen interest and regard for Egyptian young people, Borden gave money 'to encourage the Egyptian Student Movement.' One gift to the ESM 'made possible the obtaining of much better quarters' for the group, 'including a room set apart for Bible study.' And so, 'the students of different institutions could [meet together], one school having one night, and another school another.'[16]

After Borden's passing, a young friend from the Egyptian Student Movement contacted a missionary who knew Borden well, 'asking for a picture of Mr Borden' for 'this Bible-room.' The student from the ESM said that Borden had been 'such a help to them; and his blessing is still with them in their work.'[17]

To better aid the study of Arabic, and at the urging of Dr William Gairdner, Borden decided to seek lodging in the family residence of Gamil Hassoon, a Syrian Christian. The idea was 'to get in closer touch with spoken Arabic, and so make more rapid progress.' This decided, Borden 'moved all his things from his rooms at the Y.M.C.A.' to the home of Mr Hassoon, a 'cultivated Christian in the Shubra Quarter,' near the Cairo Railway Station.[18]

Borden's moving day brought another noteworthy event, as Geraldine Taylor recounted in her biography:

> The day [Borden] moved to the Hassoons, he had 'put in some hard licks at Arabic,' as he wrote in his journal, [and he] called on Mr J. Pierpont Morgan at Shepheard's Hotel with Dr Zwemer …[19]

---

15. ibid., p. 18.

16. See Taylor, *Borden of Yale* (1926), p. 244.

17. ibid., p. 244.

18. See Zwemer, *William Whiting Borden* (1913), p. 179.

19. See Taylor, *Borden of Yale* (1926), p. 251.

Sadly, we are left with only this tantalizing reference to a call on J. P. Morgan, then America's great titan of finance. Ostensibly, Borden and Zwemer thought to seek a possible charitable contribution from Morgan. As a courtesy to Borden, who was a young man of Morgan's social standing, they were received, but it seems any such request for a financial gift was politely rebuffed – as no further mention of this visit appears anywhere in extant sources.

At any rate, it was worth trying, and any thought of this being a setback soon faded. Borden wrote to his mother about this time, telling her many details about his decision to take lodgings with the Hassoon family.

He was thoroughly enjoying it, as he told his mother on March 1, 1913:

> The work at the [Cairo] Study Center continues to be most interesting and instructive; and now that I am here in this family, I hope that my progress in Arabic will be more rapid. For while we do use a good deal of English, yet I hear [Arabic] constantly all around me, and am given lessons by the various members of the family at meals, and any other time I wish.
>
> The flat is on the third floor of a house in the Shubra Quarter, near the station and right by the tracks, but I do not mind that …
>
> I have a room facing the north, and looking over other houses, which are lower, so that I get quite a view. My room is rather small for what I have in it; but as I have the use of the dining room and library as well for study and writing, it does not much matter.[20]

It is easy to picture Borden in this setting, sitting and gazing out the window of his room at sunrise, the time for his Morning Watch. Both Samuel Zwemer and Gamil Hassoon saw this contemplative side of Borden first-hand. Their recollections of it were both vivid and revealing. Dr Zwemer wrote:

---

20. See Zwemer, *William Whiting Borden* (1913), p. 179.

[William] was a man of the Bible, as his Greek Testament and the Bibles he used for study and devotion show, and he was a man of prayer. Even in the smallest details of life, he looked up for wisdom and strength.[21]

And over many days in his home, Gamil Hassoon remembered that Borden

appointed a large portion of his time for reading the sacred Scriptures. His Bibles, and he had many of them, were all visited by his eyes.

Many were the remarks on their margins made in his handwriting, and the texts underlined: which showed that he had chosen them, and probably put them into memory. His reading the Scriptures was not in the order of a daily duty. He read them because he loved them.[22]

Moments of silent prayer, seeking context and nuance in moving passages of Scripture, seeing shades of meaning in the original Greek, writing lines in his diary, and growing deep in the things of faith – all these were facets of the great riches Borden believed his Morning Watch bestowed. And hearing a distant train whistle, as it drew closer to the station near his home – that was like the call to a pilgrim.

Another keepsake from this time comes from the pen of Gamil Hassoon. He wrote something of a brief memoir of Borden, and one of the things that stood out in his memory was the way Borden's 'life and deeds agreed' with the teachings of the Bible he cherished. '[William] loved everybody,' he stated, 'and as a rule, when you find one who loves like that, you may be sure of his love to God.'[23]

Borden's deep commitment to the Y.M.C.A. in Cairo was yet another thing that Hassoon remembered in vivid detail. Borden cherished the idea of its growth.

21. See Taylor, *Borden of Yale* (1926), p. 280.

22. ibid., pp. 254-255.

23. ibid., p. 255.

'In conversation with him,' Hassoon had written:

I found that he loved the Y.M.C.A. with a wonderful love, [and] I knew from him that he wanted to strengthen the Arabic branch by all the power he could: financially, morally, and mentally – so that it might attain a level with the greatest European [Y.M.C.A. branches], and surpass them …

Many times he expressed to me his pleasure in the progress this branch had taken, in the short time since it was organized …[24]

Borden also immersed himself in the home life and folkways of the Hassoon family, as his host remembered well.

That brought a memorable phrase, given in italics just below:

He loved to communicate, and *mix up himself with us,* and we with him, preferring to change his long-accustomed habits and acquire our ways, so that he might prepare himself with what would agree with the taste of [those] among whom he hoped to live … The kindness and sociability God endowed him with were very great.[25]

In addition to this, Gamil Hassoon saw something far more subtle: a piece of paper that Borden always carried with him. As Hassoon recalled, Borden 'had a special motto written on a paper in his pocket: "My Lord, enable me to conquer my will, and overcome my desires." And he had another motto [also]: "Not my will, but Thine be done."'[26]

These phrases, written out on paper, were something like a literary talisman. To carry them always meant the sentiments in them could never be very far from Borden's awareness. Each time he looked at them, his resolve for Christian service was renewed. They were like a draught of cool, clear water – drawn from the sacred fountain of faith. They were restoring and renewing, lending him strength.

---

24. ibid., p. 255.
25. ibid., p. 255.
26. ibid., p. 255.

~ ~ ~

A great love for Muslim people was, as Hassoon saw, set deeply in Borden's Christian faith. 'What impressed me most,' Hassoon said:

was [William's] strong faith. He did not think that there was anything impossible to do in the service of the Lord.

In the books [that] he and I read, we found that it [was] nearly impossible to enter into Tibet, or Afghanistan, to bring the gospel to the Mohammedans there. But that fact was not [one] to shake his faith ...

He was very fond of Mohammedans. Once he came home with a very pleased face.

'What is it makes you look so happy?' I asked.

He had met, he said, two Azhar Sheikhs, and stopped them by the way. They spoke to him in Arabic, something he could not understand.

But he did all he could, and led them a long distance to Dr Zwemer's house. Showing them the house, he said, '*Koll yom gomaa*' (every Friday). And he spent with them fifteen minutes by the roadside, using the few Arabic words he knew.

I asked him to repeat the Arabic he used, and we had great fun of it! But it was good enough to make those men understand that he wanted to gain them for Christ, and they parted with peace.

To my full belief, they [did indeed go] to Dr Zwemer's on Friday ...[27]

Gamil Hassoon's last recollections of William Borden mingled memories of what it was like to be his friend with a realization that while he was wealthy, it was something so seldom spoken of that Hassoon had no genuine idea of the extent of Borden's personal fortune. He lived modestly, and unpretentiously.

'William,' Hassoon also said, 'had a winning look and an attractive spirit. He was meek and kind.' The bonds of affection for him, Hassoon said, were 'very great, and I remember every

---

27. ibid., pp. 255-256.

movement of his [while in our home].'[28] In a word, Borden was
like family to his Syrian friend.

As for Hassoon's late discovery of Borden's wealth, he explained
how he had learned of this by saying—

> Although he was a rich man, [William] denied himself the
> privileges of rich people, and lived as simply as any missionary
> could live. He was following the footsteps of Jesus.
>
> Once a friend said to me: 'Your guest is a millionaire.'
>
> 'I do not know anything about his dollars,' I replied ...
>
> I [then] told [William] what I heard; but he did not confirm it.
> *'People often mistake us,'* he said, *'for the rich Condensed Milk
> firm that bears the name of Borden.'*
>
> This [led me to think] he was not so rich, and I kept on
> treating him as a brother – not as to please a millionaire.
>
> I am sure he liked it that way. He was perfectly at home
> [in a family like] mine, and we lived together with great peace
> and love.[29]

On Sunday, March 9th, 1913, Borden sent a letter home relating
sad news concerning one of the new and much-respected friends
he'd made in Cairo.

That friend was Dr Ernest Maynard Pain of the Church
Missionary Society. Borden spoke of him to Dr Inglis Frost, a
physician in New York City:

> An event here in Cairo has saddened us all, and made me realize
> anew the heroism of the doctor in his every-day work. I refer to
> the sudden death of Dr Pain of the C.M.S. here in Cairo, a man
> beloved by hundreds and filled with the spirit of Christ. I only
> met him twice, once soon after my arrival: and the next thing I
> knew, he was dead.
>
> I wish I could give you [all] the medical particulars, as you
> would be interested in them, I am sure, but as far as I could
> ascertain, he was attending a patient sick with meningitis.

28. ibid., p. 256.
29. ibid., p. 256.

The patient coughed in his face as he was examining him, and infection followed on this apparently.

It occurred on a Sunday, and the following Wednesday, about 5 a.m., he had gone on to the home above. His funeral [service], attended as it was by a great crowd of natives and Europeans, was a most eloquent testimonial of his loving faithfulness in serving the Master.[30]

There was something deeply poignant in this, beyond Borden's thoughts in tribute to a fallen friend. For twelve days after this letter about E. M. Pain had been posted, the time of Borden's own summons heavenward began.

Samuel Zwemer described it as 'the story of his sudden illness, his long fight against death in the hospital, and his homegoing.'[31]

Zwemer's account begins as follows—

The last time I saw [William] strong and well was on [Monday] March 17th at the railway station, when Mr C. T. Hooper and I were leaving on a journey to Jiddah and other Red Sea ports ... How well I recall his enthusiastic exclamation, *'Wish I could go with you!'* and his hearty farewell.

On March 19th he wrote in his diary: 'Wed. Played tennis again after my [Arabic] lesson, and [then I] went up to last part of a meeting celebrating the centenary of Livingstone. [To the] Y.M.C.A. in evening.'[32]

The centenary meeting to honor missionary pioneer David Livingstone was, as Samuel Zwemer said, 'the last public meeting [William Borden] ever attended,'[33] but it was something more: a true symbol in its way. Borden wished to be present for the memorial celebration of someone he'd heard of all his life, and his presence at the Livingstone Meeting seems deeply fitting, for

---

30. See Zwemer, *William Whiting Borden* (1913), p. 185.

31. ibid., pp. 187-188.

32. ibid., pp. 185-186.

33. ibid., p. 186.

it was one of the last things he did before his passing. One young missionary, honoring another from history.

Sometimes, moments converge in moving, meaningful ways.

~ ~ ~

Borden's final diary entry was written on March 20th. It read:

'Thursday. Arabic as usual. Arranged for conversational lessons with a converted sheikh of the Ashar. Went with Mr Straub to the Bulak Quarter in the evening to see the Mulid of Abu' Ilya. We didn't go into the mosque, which was packed, but saw one or two Zirks. One man collapsed.'[34]

These are likely the last words William Borden ever wrote. And as ever, he had been faithfully preparing for service among the Muslim peoples of China.

For, as Samuel Zwemer states: 'in the dense crowd of that Mulid, on the street, or in the mosque, Borden caught the infection of the deadly microbe which [claimed his life].'[35]

Unwittingly, his resolve had brought with it a great danger.

~ ~ ~

Recollections from Samuel Zwemer's wife Amy, a highly trained nurse, begin the story of Borden's last days, and his valiant struggle against a terrible illness.

On Friday, March 21st, as Amy Zwemer wrote, 'the Syrian family with whom [William] was living telephoned me that he was sick'—

> I went out and found him rather feverish, but not apparently very ill, a little headache and fever. He had seen a doctor, who had prescribed, and told him to go to bed.
>
> The next morning they telephoned again, saying that he was all right, no fever. I was thankful, and rather expected he would be out as usual to take dinner with us on Sunday (our home is

---

34. ibid., pp. 186 and 187: a Zirk is a kind of 'religious remembrance of God and His attributes.'

35. ibid., p. 187.

about two miles away from where he was staying, but he often came out).

The next day one of our missionaries went out, and was told that he had cerebro-spinal meningitis, which stunned us all.

I chased the doctor from place to place, and saw him personally Sunday evening ... He would not give any hope, [saying] only that Mr Borden was worse, and that he had injected serum into the spinal cord.[36]

During this time, as Samuel Zwemer wrote, 'Rev. W. H. T. Gairdner and the Rev. Dr John Giffen visited [William,] but he was unconscious most of the time.' Dr Giffen saw Borden twice, and remembered—

The first time, I found him sleeping, after the pain and fatigue caused by an injection of serum in the spinal column: so of course I did not awaken him. The day before yesterday afternoon, the nurse asked me if I would like to see him. The Doctor had told me that no one must see him, on account of the harm it might do to the patient; and also because of the danger of infection.

However when the nurse invited me, I felt that there was little danger of harm to him, as I understood that his mind was not very fully under his control, and so he would soon forget having seen me.

The nurse at his bed told me also so much, and that he would probably not recognize me at first. This proved to be the case. My speaking to him however seemed to call him to himself, and he knew me and he answered one or two questions. I told him that we at the Mission were all thinking about him much, and praying for him. He thanked me, and said he was just trying to get to us to help us. I asked him if he would like me to pray with him there. He replied, 'Yes,' so I prayed. He thanked me and I said, 'Goodbye, we'll not forget you,' and he put out his hand to me, and said, 'Goodbye.'[37]

---

36. ibid., p. 188. Amy Zwemer wrote this Wed., March 26, 1913.

37. ibid., pp. 188-189.

On Thursday, April 3rd, as Samuel Zwemer noted, 'there was still hope of [William's] recovery.' Zwemer's wife Amy, who was caring for Borden at the risk of her own life, sent word to those who had gathered for constant prayer, saying:

> Mr Borden is just hovering on the line, and is making a splendid fight, and we trust his heart will hold out. His temperature still keeps up, but his heart and lungs are doing their work all right, thus far.
>
> This morning he was not so well again … He is having restless nights lately, but seems to rest in the afternoon better. He is not unconscious, but drowsy from disease and [the] bromides. He can be recalled, and answers quite intelligently; but of course [he] cannot sustain conversation.
>
> His sister, Mrs [Mary] Turner, came from London yesterday. He knows she is here. He asks for his mother, and we hope she will reach here the first part of next week. I think he will feel more comfortable when she comes.
>
> The nurse thinks that [the loss of] his [missionary] work troubles him a good deal. He talks about it all the time, when delirious.[38]

As for Samuel Zwemer, he returned from his Red Sea trip on Wednesday, April 2nd, and immediately went to the hospital where Borden was.

Zwemer would later recall: '[William] was so greatly changed by the terrible effects of the disease that I scarcely recognized him. It was the fifteenth day since he was taken ill, and he was reported slightly better; although the doctor had expressed no hope for recovery that morning.'[39]

Touchingly, Gamil Hassoon came to Borden's bedside, risking infection to tend to his young friend. His recollections were:

> As I stepped into the room [William], in spite of his great suffering, gave me a wonderful smile, which is printed on my memory. He then sat up in bed, but very soon had to lay himself down again …

---

38. ibid., p. 189.
39. ibid., p. 189.

I sat by his bedside for a short time, and spoke to him with all [the composure] I could master at that critical moment. I was greatly astonished that all his sufferings did not hinder him from showing gratitude and love.

I passed my hand over his forehead, and wiped away the drops of sweat that stood there; and asked God to help and cure him.

He smiled again and held my hand in his, and pressed it very gently but warmly, in such a manner which made me feel his love. He was not so very able to speak much; but his eyes spoke, and transmitted to my heart all that was in his heart and mind. And thus I left him for the last time.[40]

On Tuesday, April 8th Samuel Zwemer went to Port Said to meet Borden's mother and his younger sister Joyce, who had been able to divert their travel from a long-planned stop in Europe to rush to the hospital where Borden was.[41]

The following day, Wednesday, April 9th, Zwemer met the Bordens for a train ride of several hours from Port Said to Cairo. On the way constant 'Marconi messages' gave news of William's condition, and a first message brought news that his health was 'not more alarming than before.'[42]

But then, halfway to Cairo, 'a telegram came that it was all over.'[43]

≈ ≈ ≈

Amid the shocking news, the pain it brought was heightened by the tragic fact that Mary and Joyce Borden reached William's bedside just four hours after his passing. They had no moment to bid him farewell, while he lived.

They'd reached Cairo at 1 p.m. and William had passed away at 9 a.m.[44]

---

40. See Taylor, *Borden of Yale* (1926), p. 261.

41. See Zwemer, *William Whiting Borden* (1913), p. 190.

42. ibid., p. 190.

43. ibid., p. 190.

44. See Taylor, *Borden of Yale* (1926), p. 263.

It was heartbreaking; for Borden knew his mother and sister were doing all they could to reach him. As Geraldine Taylor had written poignantly—

'He knew that his mother was expected.'[45]

Borden's best friend from Yale, Charlie Campbell, described the funeral that followed, and offered a tribute of plainspoken eloquence—

> The funeral was simple. The burial service and the 16th Psalm were read, after which two American missionaries offered prayer.
>
> The hymns sung were, 'We Have Heard A Joyful Sound,' 'Jesus Saves,' and 'Face To face With Christ My Saviour.'
>
> *Face to face I shall behold Him,*
> *Far beyond the starry sky;*
> *Face to face in all His glory,*
> *I shall see Him by and by ...*[46]

At the age of twenty-five, Bill had gone home – to be with Christ his Savior.

... years before, he had seen Jesus Christ in the Grand Hall on the Strand, London, and had given his life to Him. [And] for seven years, he had faithfully walked with his Master in conse-crated service.

Detail of the original stone memorial placed at William Borden's grave in Cairo (photo from River Valley Church, used with kind permission).

All over the world were [so many people] whose lives had been blessed and strengthened – because Bill Borden had lived.[47]

---

45. ibid., p. 261.

46. Carrie Elizabeth Breck, in *New Songs of the Gospel* (Philadelphia: Hall-Mack Co., 1900), p. 34.

47. See Campbell, *William Borden* (1913), p. 28. Borden was buried in the American Mission Cemetery, Cairo. See the *Princeton Theological Seminary Bulletin Necrological Report,* August 1914, p. 321.

'All over the world' – this was the theme that leaders of The Moody Church in Chicago conveyed as they spoke of William Borden's legacy. It was the church of his youth, the setting where he stood as a boy for R. A. Torrey's invitation to live a life for Christ. And though in recent years his education and work had often taken him far from his native Chicago, his thoughts had always been with them.

William Borden, they said—

never lost his heart-interest in the work of the Lord in this place. His frequent letters, and visits, and his constant gifts bore witness to that ...

[Like D. L. Moody,] he inaugurated and supported in this church the largest Daily Vacation Bible School in Chicago, which brought more street children into our Sunday School, and services, than any other [endeavor] ...

He was the largest giver to our Fresh Air Work, our Sunday School and the general expenses of the church during the last years of his life, and he left this church one hundred thousand dollars, realizing the wonderful opportunity it has as a downtown church [for all] within the reach of its influence ... this teeming city of thirty different nationalities ...

[And William] believed this church could do a great foreign missionary work here at home – but he did not stop at that. During his lifetime he made use of his money in a world-wide ministry, yet so quietly that his left hand knew not what his right hand did.

After his [passing,] his statesmanlike grasp of the problem of the evangelization of the world in this generation became apparent, for he bequeathed practically the whole of his inheritance, about one million dollars,[48] in four nearly equal parts, all for the purpose of preaching Christ: one-fourth to be used in Chicago, another quarter [elsewhere in America], the third portion in China, and the remainder in other foreign countries ...

---

48. i.e. $25 million today. See https://www.usinflationcalculator.com

This was [William] Borden: quiet but powerful; saying little but doing much; rich but self-denying; humble in spirit a general in organization, but always willing to be a private in service.

He declined our urgent invitation to preach in The Moody Church, on the ground that he was not capable [enough, just then,] but he was not ashamed to tell of his faith in Jesus on the street corner.

His heart went out to the [Muslim people] of Kansu, but he did not overlook the worthy widow, orphan and cripple in the back streets of Chicago, as some of us [saw first-hand] ...

He was intent upon seeking to win for Christ and His service the young men of our colleges and universities ... To this end the last months of his life in America were given, but that did not prevent his thinking of, praying for, and giving to the care of [children] and the agèd.[49]

Still other tributes came ...

'There could scarcely a greater loss befall us than this', said Robert E. Speer in the first shock of grief. 'William Borden was one among a million. There was no better among the younger men who have gone out from our colleges in the last ten years ... It seems impossible that all that strength and devotion can have been taken away from the work of the Church down here.'[50]

Henry Weston Frost of China Inland Mission, the family friend who had so often been a mentor, stated: 'William Borden has lived two lives in one; for he has done more in twenty-five years than many men accomplish in fifty.'[51]

And with a deep, fatherly affection, Samuel Zwemer remembered 'our own William Borden, who laid down his life for China in Cairo.'[52]

---

49. See Taylor, *Borden of Yale* (1926), pp. 228-229. Edited for clarity.

50. ibid., p. 267.

51. H. W. Frost, quoted in *The Bible To-Day* magazine, June 1913, p. 133.

52. See *The Missionary Review of the World*, March 1914, p. 185.

Thoughts from Professor William Brenton Greene of Princeton Theological Seminary were like so many brushstrokes on a canvas of memory – pictures in prose.

Dr Greene remembered this of Borden—

I used to think when I would see him, from my study window, dashing down Library Place on his bicycle to the early morning recitation, 'That man is so strong, and is so sane, that his prospect of life on earth is better than that of any student in our Seminary' ...

His memory was as wax to receive an impression, and as marble to retain it. His judgment was characteristically broad and just. He had a singularly happy faculty of seeing at once the point of a question and of going straight to the point. Yet he never relied on this power; on the contrary, he used every means at his command. Rarely, if ever, was he absent from the classes. I cannot recall an instance of inattention on his part. As might have been expected, he attained the natural result. He became distinguished as a scholar ...

It is my practice to hold written tests at intervals, and to decide the standing of those who take these tests; and as I remember, with but a single exception, Mr Borden was among the first two or three. I distinctly remember my deep regret, the feeling of positive loss, when I read his last paper, at the time of his graduation, that I should never read another paper from him ...

But of course, it was as the missionary that we think of him; and it was as the missionary that his influence was ... strongest, most strikingly unique. He did not develop the missionary spirit as other men usually [do]. *We are accustomed to associate sacrifice with the missionary life ...*

But he taught us another lesson.

We had learned from others the duty of consecration: he taught us the blessedness of it.[53]

---

53. W. B. Greene, quoted in *The Bible To-Day* magazine, June 1913, p. 133.

Sherwood Day, the fellow Yale alumnus whose family had enjoyed so many days of hospitality with Borden at Camden, Maine, and Lake George, New York, penned one brief but telling phrase:

'How Bill's life stands out! A splendid mind – and a great soul.'[54]

Many searched for 'reasons why' in the wake of Borden's passing. Professor Benjamin W. Bacon of Yale was one of them.[55] During the memorial service held for Borden at Yale Hope Mission on Sunday, April 20, 1913, Dr Bacon said:

> To many of us I am sure, the death of this young heroic missionary, just entering on his field of labor, will seem [an] example of unmitigated loss, and disappointment to the cause of the Kingdom.
>
> It is a loss as seemingly complete as we are likely to meet with in life, or ever come in close connection with. It is not often you find a young man of such thorough consecration ... a splendid, engaging figure, attractive in demeanor, a friendly fellow, honorable and high-minded ... in his conduct, and a leader of his class in scholarship ... giving himself up whole-heartedly to the work of Christ where most needed.

The William Borden Bronze Memorial Fountain at Yale (photo by Vienna Hinkson, used with kind permission).

---

54. See Taylor, *Borden of Yale* (1926), p. 267. See also page 60 of *China's Millions*, May 1913, which states: 'Mr Borden was an exceptional man ... may thanks be given to God for all the winsomeness of [his] life.'

55. See the *Obituary Record of Graduates of Yale University* (1915), p. 476: 'Special services in [Borden's] memory were held in Cairo, New York, Philadelphia, Chicago, New Haven, and Princeton. His classmate Parry [wrote] in his memory a play called *The Flower of Assisi*.'

We do not see such things more than once in a generation ... [56]

Much like this, *The New Haven Register* stated: 'Yale today is mourning the loss of one of her most cherished sons, William W. Borden, the founder of the Yale Hope Mission.'[57] And Princeton Seminary said: 'the death of no recent alumnus has occasioned such sorrow, or called forth such expressions of deep regret.'[58]

The Memorial Plaque for William Borden in The Hill School Chapel (photo by Louis Jeffries, used with kind permission).

Borden's good friend from Princeton days, Francis Shunk Downs, penned these words of tribute: 'He accepted Christ's values of life; and gave his own life for the highest things to the utmost.'[59]

From the town of Princeton itself, a poignant tribute came from the pastor Borden worked with in 'parts of two winters

56. See *The Bible To-Day* magazine, June 1913, p. 135.

57. See page 1 of the 10th April 1913 edition of the *New Haven Register* newspaper. See also page 171 of *The Missionary Herald* magazine (Boston: Thomas Todd Company, 1927); 'When the death of William Borden was cabled from Egypt (April, 1913), it seemed as though a wave of sorrow went around the world. There was scarcely a newspaper in the United States that did not publish some account ... and letters from many lands attested the influence of [Borden's] high ideals and unselfish service.'

58. See the May 1913 issue of *The Princeton Seminary Bulletin*, p. 8.

59. See *The Princeton Theological Review*, July 1927, p. 518.

when he was in Princeton Seminary.' There, in Mt Pisgah African Methodist Church, Borden taught Sunday School for children who returned his affection. As the pastor wrote to Borden's mother: 'We had a little memorial service for [William],' and he then stated, our memories of 'his deep consecration, and unassuming, Christ-like life,' will live on.[60]

A tribute was given as well in *The Crisis* magazine, edited by W. E. B. Du Bois, and published in New York City by the National Association for the Advancement of Colored People (NAACP). Here, Borden's love for the people of Africa took center stage, as *The Crisis* described: 'William W. Borden, a young graduate of Princeton Theological Seminary, died in Cairo a short time ago, and left a bequest of $50,000 for mission work in Africa. Mr Borden was a man of great wealth, and had, in the course of his life, done much for missions.'[61]

'God took William to his side,'[62] Borden's mother read in a letter from his Japanese friend, Mobuta Iyima. And a Chinese student from Yale, Shaowen James Chuan, told her of the moving Memorial Service held for Borden at New Haven.

'I had the honor to speak on behalf of China,' Shaowen stated, in a service 'that will always remain in my fond memory of him. We Chinese Christians hope sincerely that another man will soon come forth to take up his unbegun task.'[63]

---

60. See Zwemer, *William Whiting Borden* (1913), p. 226. See also Taylor, *Borden of Yale* (1926), pp. 270-271. This church was Mt Pisgah African Methodist Episcopal (AME) Church, 172 Witherspoon Street, Princeton.

61. See *The Crisis* magazine, Jan. 1914, conducted by W. E. B. Du Bois (New York: the National Association for the Advancement of Colored People, 1914), p. 116. $50,000 in 1914 would be worth $1.25 million now. See also page 7 of the Saturday, Nov. 15, 1913 edition of *The Washington Times* newspaper: 'William W. Borden, a young graduate of Yale and of Princeton Theological Seminary ... made a bequest of $50,000 for mission work of his church in Africa.' See also page 726 of *The Missionary Survey*, July 1913: 'Mr Borden made [a] bequest ... of $50,000 for [the Presbyterian Church's] work in Africa and Japan.'

62. See Zwemer, *William Whiting Borden* (1913), p. 223.

63. ibid., p. 234. See also *The Princeton Theological Review*, July 1927, p. 518. F. S. Downs said of his Princeton Seminary friend: 'Borden honored the Word of God, its

Geraldine Taylor, in reading over these many tributes, observed—

> A volume in itself might be made of the letters [that paid tribute to William Borden's memory,] letters from leaders in the front rank of Christian activity, as well as from fellow-students and friends of his own age.[64]
>
> From the National Parliament in Peking,[65] and the House of Commons in London – from great city churches, oriental universities, and lonely mission stations came the same testimony.
>
> 'Mr Borden has become a national character in his life and influence,' said a leading man in Chicago.
>
> 'It gratified me to hear him speak as he did,' wrote Dr J. T. Stone, 'because he is careful as to what he says, and views everything with a broad and real justice.' From the Fifth Avenue Presbyterian Church in New York City, Rev. Dr [J. Henry] Jowett wrote: 'His life just now is standing before the American people ... Thousands of people are looking at it ...'[66]

Nobel Laureate J. R. Mott sent a tribute by letter to Borden's mother—

> My association with William has given me a keen appreciation of the value of the service which he accomplished for Christ and His kingdom by his life, by his witness, by his gifts, and by his activities.

---

integrity, its messages, its claims, and God honored the man who honored Him. He yielded his life to God. He kept nothing back ... He was a steward found faithful ... [He was] a strong man, who built his life upon the Rock of Ages.'

64. See also *The Princeton Theological Review*, July 1927, p. 516. Borden's close friend and fellow student at Princeton Seminary, F. S. Downs, has written: 'But Borden's love for souls was constant. [As Hugh Munro has stated:] "He had that unique thing, an abiding passion for the souls of men ... it seemed never absent from his mind."' For Munro's tribute in full, see Taylor, *Borden of Yale* (1926), pp. 211-212.

65. In January 1912, Borden's close friend from Yale, C. T. Wang, was elected a member of the Provisional Legislature of the new Chinese Republic and chosen its Deputy Speaker. He would have been the prime mover behind this letter of tribute to Borden's memory.

66. See Taylor, *Borden of Yale* (1926), pp. 274-275. See also Zwemer, *William Whiting Borden* (1913), p. 169.

It has been on my mind, for some time, to write you to express my personal conviction as to the marked contribution which he made to his generation, within the sphere of his influence.

He exerted a great influence, in the direction of the conservation and expansion of the spiritual life of our colleges. This he did through his constant and helpful work in the [Y.M.C.A.] and Volunteer Movement during his student days, as well as in his many personal relationships ...

He did as much as any young man whom I knew to help realize the watchword of the Volunteer Movement: 'The Evangelization of the World in this Generation.'[67]

Then, following a trip to Asia, J. R. Mott wrote again to Borden's mother. Geraldine Taylor described that letter and other kindred tributes that came—

On his return from Asia [after Borden's passing in 1913], Dr Mott said that missionaries in every part of the world bore testimony to the influence of the life of William Borden: and that at the Student Conferences that summer, no appeal was used with such power as the story of his consecration.

'Many young men live stronger, purer, more yielded lives', wrote a [college] student, 'because of the life your [son] lived, and because of the death he died. You cannot hear of them all. *You will know someday.*'

The name of William Borden was more used than any other during [a] great Convention in Kansas City [about this time].

---

67. See Taylor, *Borden of Yale* (1926), pp. 232-233. When Mott spoke before 5,000 students at a Student Volunteer Missions Conference a few months after Borden's death it was said: 'the name most lovingly mentioned by many speakers was that of William Borden, the young volunteer who [dedicated] himself to the cause of Christ and laid down his life in Cairo.' See page 105 of the February 1914 issue of *The Missionary Review of the World.* See also Jayson Casper, 'The Forgotten Final Resting Place of William Borden,' in *Christianity Today,* February 24, 2017: 'The 1913 Student Volunteer Movement conferences all honored his memory; John Mott called them the "most powerful appeal for missionary service ever."'

Students [stated] that the investment of life as Borden invested it was the greatest of all investments.[68]

Samuel Zwemer, who had guided and befriended Borden in Cairo, recalled Borden's visionary heart and deep spiritual commitment. His young friend, he said, 'had the spirit of a pioneer, and the soul of an apostle.'[69]

S. D. Gordon, the author Borden so admired, told readers how Borden had 'laid down his life in Egypt.' And further on, in *Quiet Talks on Following the Christ* (published later in 1913), Gordon spoke poignantly of the Christian gifts mirrored in the life of 'that young friend of the Lord Jesus, William Whiting Borden.'[70]

So too, Erving Yale Woolley – the Brown University alumnus and pastor of The Moody Church who presided at Borden's ordination in Chicago, recalled:

> Generous in his nature, and broad in his sympathies, head and heart combined [in William Borden] to give – whether it was [charitable gifts] for the children of the city slums, or for [the people] of Africa.
>
> Every case of need … appealed to him, and enlisted his support.[71]

With a fondness born of many years' friendship, Dr James Martin Gray, of Moody Bible Institute, remembered 'the preparation this beloved brother had for His holy service, and the ardent desire of his soul to enter upon it.' Nor have they, he said, 'come to naught,' William's life has taught us so many lessons.[72]

Professor Charles Erdman of Princeton, who'd known Borden so well, said:

---

68. See Taylor, *Borden of Yale* (1926), p. 276. Italics added. This convention ran from Wed. afternoon, Dec. 31, 1913 to Sunday evening, Jan. 4, 1914. See *The Association Monthly*, Oct. 1913, p. 382.

69. See Zwemer, *William Whiting Borden* (1913), p. 234.

70. See S. D. Gordon, *Quiet Talks on Following the Christ* (New York: Revell, 1913), p. 69-70.

71. Erving Yale Woolley, in *The Missionary Visitor* magazine, June 1913, p. 196-197.

72. Dr James Martin Gray, in *The Missionary Visitor* magazine, June 1913, p. 197.

'Apart from Christ, there is no explanation of such a life.'[73]

These words adorn Borden's gravesite memorial in Cairo: a moving epitaph, and a living tribute, much remembered down the years.

And down to the present also.

For in spring 2009, one hundred years after Borden's graduation from Yale, 'the echo of his testimony' inspired a Yale graduate 'to pursue a life of dedication and service.' After reading a gift copy of *Borden of Yale*, this graduating senior said:

'I'm excited to follow in Borden's footsteps, and spread God's word to Asia.'[74]

Often, at great Urbana gatherings of collegians, Rev. Billy Graham quoted a six-word phrase attributed to William Borden. At Urbana 1981, Dr Graham said:

'There are a thousand things you can do with your life; a thousand ways you can spend it. But how many of them will enable you to say at the end of your life, "no reserves, no retreat, no regrets"?'[75]

Dr Graham drew deep, enduring inspiration from these words.[76]

But were they Borden's words?

Therein lies a story.

In truth, these famous words have come to us from Geraldine Taylor, in her biography of William Borden. They're partly inspired by a poem Borden knew; but the words and phrasing are hers, beyond doubt.

---

73. See Taylor, *Borden of Yale* (1926), p. 275. 'A service in memory of William Whiting Borden,' p. 12, 'was held in Miller Chapel on Friday, April 18, at 5 p.m. The President of the Seminary presided and opened the service with prayer.' See the May 1913 issue of *The Princeton Seminary Bulletin*, p. 9.

74. See page 12 of the Fall 2009 issue of *The Ivy League Christian Observer* magazine.

75. Billy Graham, quoted in *Confessing Christ as Lord*, ed. by J. W. Alexander (Downers Grove: InterVarsity Press, 1982), p. 130.

76. Dr Graham once spoke of Borden in close connection with 1950s missionary martyr, Jim Elliot. See *Decision Magazine*, May 5, 2005.

We begin with the poem, sent to him by his mother on 'sheet paper,' – lines of verse in her handwriting, sent to him in Japan to help mark his 17th birthday, November 1st, 1904 – a birthday he spent so far from home.

As Geraldine Taylor noted: 'All through college and seminary years he kept it. It was among his special papers to the last.' The poem read, in part:

> *Just as I am, Thine own to be,*
> *Friend of the young, who lovest me,*
> *To consecrate myself to Thee—*
> *O Jesus Christ, I come.*
>
> *In the glad morning of my day,*
> *My life to give, my vows to pay,*
> *With* **no reserve** *and no delay—*
> *With all my heart, I come.*[77]
>
> – Marianne Farningham

Recalling this poem, and the phrase 'no reserve,' Geraldine Taylor thought back to Borden's last days in Cairo, as he fought 'the bravest fight of all his life.'

She believed that during 'those Easter days, as he lay there, he could not but think of the young doctor-missionary [Dr E. Maynard Pain,] whose sudden call had come just in the same way.'[78]

Only days before, she knew, Borden 'had stood by that new-made grave. What if, for himself too, the call had come?' So reflecting it was here, in this place, Geraldine Taylor gave a great phrase to history, for she took up her pen and wrote—

> *No reserve, no retreat, no regrets*
> *had any place in Borden's consecration to God.*[79]

---

77. See Taylor, *Borden of Yale* (1926), p. 70. The full text of Farningham's hymn is in *Hymns of Faith and Life* (Glasgow: Maclehose & Sons, 1896), p. 640.

78. ibid., p. 260.

79. Despite diligent attempts, and inquiries with all manuscript repositories of Borden papers, no Bible that belonged to William Borden has come to light, and there's

Here is the true story of the stirring words many people, in numerous places, have cherished down though the years. They were written by a gifted biographer.

But the twelve words Borden had known, and treasured, and kept among his 'special papers' were these:

> *With no reserve and no delay,*
> *With all my heart, I come …*

These were the words his mother forwarded by letter: words she had quoted from poet Marianne Farningham.

And they helped to inspire Borden's deep dedication to serve God.

∾ ∾ ∾

Near the end of his life, as seen above, Borden had written to his good friend Inglis Frost in New York, with sad news to tell about Dr E. M. Pain.

'He passed to the home above,'[80] Borden said with thoughtful grace.

To be sure, he mourned his good friend. Yet Borden's words looked also to a living hope: a hope waiting beyond this life. It was his phrase for heaven.

'To the home above,' – the place where faith beckoned for him.

---

no indication of any kind that there was ever a Bible with the words Geraldine Taylor published written in Borden's hand inside it. She surely would have said these words were from a Bible of Borden's, if they were written there. For she had access, within a few years of his passing, to all family papers. Also, if this had been a phrase from Borden's diary, Taylor would have said so. She quoted from the diary many times in *Borden of Yale*, always with attribution. Further, Samuel Zwemer, who published his biography of Borden in Sept. 1913, with complete access to Borden's papers, says nothing of any phrase from Borden's Bible, and he doesn't quote anything said to have come from such a source.

80. See Taylor, *Borden of Yale* (1926), p. 254.

The Sterling Torch

I heard His call, 'Come, follow' …
[and] my gold grew dim: my soul went after Him.[1]
– William Reed Newell

The question of 'Why?' when it comes to William Borden's passing is one many wrestled with in his time – and others have, in all the years since.

Someone who knows first-hand what it is like to wrestle with a grievous loss like William Borden's passing is Olympic great and China missionary Eric Liddell's daughter Maureen. Millions today know him as the heroic young athlete portrayed in the film *Chariots of Fire*. But for Maureen, and for all of her life, he was the father she never knew. He died in a Japanese work camp in 1945, without ever having had the chance to meet her – not even as a babe in arms.

Her reflections when visiting her father's memorial in China in 2007 are at once discerning and deeply moving. Standing there with her elder sisters Patricia and Heather, they held hands in what their mother used to call the 'magic circle' of family. 'I felt so close to him,' she said afterward, 'and, more than ever, I realized

---

1. See Dr Grace Hamilton King, *An Anthology of Christian Literature* (Santa Barbara: Westmont College, 1948), p. 219. King gives the poem's first line as: 'I heard His call, "Come follow."' This is authoritative, for King states: 'Used by kind permission of the author.'

what his life had been for. It all made sense. What happened allowed him to touch so many lives as a consequence.'[2]

Closer to William Borden's time, indeed, within a year after his passing, J. R. Mott (of the Student Volunteer Movement) penned a phrase which seems as though it came from the same well of wisdom Maureen Liddell Moore found.

'Sometimes,' he said, 'we have a brief biography, as that of William Borden, which stirs the hearts of young and old alike to their depths.'[3] It's a moving phrase, from a Nobel Prize Laureate, for a friend whose life was an abiding inspiration.

Mott understood what his friend Borden had given the world.

Though his life was brief, he had lived steadfastly, generously and well. His faith, devotion, and philanthropy made heaven's hope real.

Countless readers, well into the millions, have since discovered this.

Ultimately, it is true, many have searched for reasons why William Borden's story seemingly ended too soon. But then, it may be his story has never really ended.

For this story, as Borden's great friend Kenneth Latourette said, has 'had a profound influence on successive generations.'[4]

His story is born anew in its touch on the lives of others.

And this may be said also: for the sake of the gospel he loved—and others, whom he hoped would love the gospel—William Borden chose to give his life.

The sterling torch of his sacrifice, and compassion, will always be alight.

---

2. See Duncan Hamilton, 'Olympic champion Eric Liddell's tale of glory and sacrifice,' in *The Toronto Star*, May 14, 2016.

3. J. R. Mott, in *The Missionary Review of the World*, within an advertisement after the Table of Contents in *The Homiletic Review*, June 1914.

4. K. S. Latourette, *Beyond the Ranges* (Grand Rapids: Eerdmans, 1967), p. 36.

Such thoughts suggest poetry in keeping with the tenor of William Borden's life, as in these lines from John Keats that summon moments of sunrise—

> … before the morning gates of heaven.
>
> – 'Endymion,' Book II

The Bible holds poetry too, citing 'the wisdom found in many counselors.'[5] So it is that many times, friends lend an insight we might otherwise have missed.

Thinking about William Borden, the gifted young scholar and missionary, I thought for a time of what an appreciable challenge it would be to commend a life that ended in 1913 to a modern audience, with slight living memory of who he was. He was only twenty-five when he died, a skeptic might say, and though he graduated from Yale and Princeton after leaving his mark there, what does a life that ended so prematurely have to teach us?

And all these years later, what could be so noteworthy about it?

Here is where I, as an author, owe a debt to Louis Jeffries—an archivist with amazing depth of knowledge regarding the history of The Hill School in Pottstown, Pennsylvania—the prestigious school William Borden attended for two years before going up to Yale. In correspondence regarding the early events and span of Borden's life, Louis offered his reflections on his reading of Harvard scholar Walter Jackson Bate's biography of the poet John Keats.

'That biography is over 700 pages long,' Louis observed, 'and this shows how an individual who lived a short life could make a lasting impact.'[6]

Reading this, the metaphor of ripples on a pond came to mind. At daybreak, perhaps, they start—and we seem to see where some of them go; but the journey of others is more subtle—as though they ask that we take time to follow them.

---

5. Proverbs 11:14.

6. Email correspondence with Louis Jeffries, Archivist at The Hill School: Monday, 5 February 2018.

In the same way, who would have thought that a poet's life of just twenty-five years, like Keats', might yield such a rich, detailed and revealing text?

Few books run to the length Dr Bate invested in his telling of Keats' life; but the wise lesson Louis Jeffries pointed me to remains. To paraphrase:

'An individual who lived a short life can make a lasting impact.'

The why of that, regarding William Borden, was the reason for the writing of this book – for a host of telling, important things marked his life.

> *Qui sequitur justitiam et misericordiam ...*
> *inveniet vitam et justitiam et gloriam.*
>
> He who follows righteousness and mercy ...
> finds life, righteousness, and honor (Prov. 21:21).

Here, one more word may serve ...

The memories set in the pages above are like photographs in an album, or the sound of scenes from long ago. If we take the time to look at them, or listen, we may know something of William Borden's world—hear something of the voices and scenes he knew—and maybe, we can hear something of his voice.

Faith spoke to him, and he did his best to speak of faith—to live its tenets—and show something of the light he'd found to others. What he left, in the impress of his life on others, is worth remembering. There are things he can teach us about what it means to live a life of devotion for God. To strive, and hallow, each day.

His story brings those lessons to us.

And for all the time that he had, he was vibrantly alive.

A Found Poem

(lines written by William Borden,
gathered and set together from his writings)

*but I believe it is true,
the might and the glory,
if we would but fix our eyes*

*His loving faithfulness,
as the waters cover the sea,
what a wonderful Redeemer*

The Princeton Seminary Prayer

The Prayer Offered by Dr C. R. Erdman
at the close of the Memorial Service held for
William Borden on Friday, April 18, 1913 in Miller Chapel,
Princeton Theological Seminary

Father of mercies, God of all comfort, we render to Thee hearty thanks for all those bright spirits which have come into our lives, and have made it more easy for us to believe in virtue, and faith, and holiness, and heaven, and Thee.

Especially do we thank Thee for Thy servant, whom we hold in loving remembrance at this hour. For all his strength and beauty of character, for the inspiration of his friendship, for the fidelity of his service, we praise Thee.

Send us forth to follow the Master in more of his spirit of love and devotion. Remember most graciously the bereaved mother, and the family circle, and grant the comfort of Thy presence, the strength of Thy sustaining grace. Vouchsafe a new spirit of consecration to all upon whom this shadow has fallen, and give to them the light of Christian hope.

We pray for the Moslem world for which this life has been laid down. Raise up new heralds, to take the place made vacant.

Prosper the proclamation of Thy Gospel in all lands. Hasten the fulfilment of Thy promises, and the coming glory of the King.

And while we wait the consummation, may we set our affections more upon things above, where Christ is seated at Thy right hand; and may we experience now something of the peace, and joy, and comfort of Immanuel's land.

And unto Thee be all the praise and glory, now and ever more. Amen.[1]

---

1. Dr C. R. Erdman, in *The Princeton Seminary Bulletin*, May 1913, p. 14.

Final Gifts

The Philanthropic Bequests Made in William Borden's Will

With the exception of keepsake gifts for family members, Borden's entire fortune of nearly $1,000,000 was left to religious and missionary work. It was a complete deed of gift, without any legal restrictions.

The Moody Church and Moody Bible Institute, each $100,000; the National Bible Institute, New York, $100,000; China Inland Mission, $250,000; the various departments of Presbyterian foreign missions, $150,000; the Princeton Theological Seminary, $50,000; Chicago Hebrew Mission, $50,000; the Chicago Tract Society and American Bible Society, each $25,000; African Inland Mission and the Nile Mission Press, in Cairo, Egypt, $25,000 each.[1]

In modern dollar amounts, Borden's bequests are as follows:

The Moody Church and the Moody Bible Institute $2,500,000; the National Bible Institute, $2,500,000; China Inland Mission, $6,250,000; Presbyterian foreign missions work, $3,750,000; Princeton Theological Seminary, $1,250,000; Chicago Hebrew Mission, $1,250,000; Chicago Tract Society and American Bible Society, each $625,000; African Inland Mission and the Nile Mission Press, $625,000.

These bequests would total some $22,500,000 now.

---

1. See *Mission Studies*, June 1913, p. 162.

Of this legacy, one that continues to this day, Dr C. R. Erdman wrote—

William Borden, in addition to the other abiding influences of his life and service, has bequeathed for the evangelizing of the world a larger sum than any man of equal years, in the entire history of the Christian Church.[2]

---

2. See *The Missionary Review of the World*, August 1913, p. 568.

Also available from Christian Focus Publications...

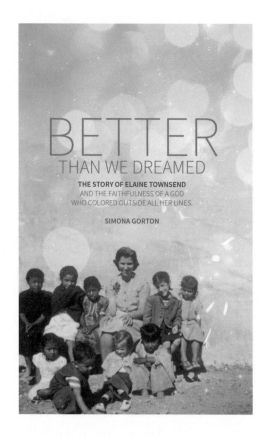

BETTER
THAN WE DREAMED

THE STORY OF ELAINE TOWNSEND
AND THE FAITHFULNESS OF A GOD
WHO COLORED OUTSIDE ALL HER LINES.

SIMONA GORTON

ISBN 978-1-5271-0266-8

Better Than We Dreamed
The Story of Elaine Townsend
SIMONA GORTON

Read the story of a life lived safely within the lines, that God turned upside down. From social star of 1930's Chicago to a Wycliffe missionary in South America and the USSR, Elaine Townsend's life was far from boring. Meet the woman who became Cameron Townsend's wife, and discover how a life can be filled with adventure, by simply saying 'yes' to God.

Through each stage of Elaine's life her trust and dependence on her Saviour shines as an example to believers everywhere, yet there are also weaknesses with which we can all identify. This account of her struggles and successes is filled with stories gathered from those who knew Elaine best, as well as insights into the mission work that renewed a generation's passion for Bible translation.

Both encouraging and challenging, this thorough biography leads the reader to rightly recognise Elaine Townsend as one of the great Christian women of the 20th century – a demonstration of what God can do with a willing heart.

This delightfully written and meticulously researched narrative traces her footsteps around the globe, recalling her life of devotion to Cameron and her indefatigable zeal in proclaiming the mission of God to the world. May her earnestness and joy be an encouragement to all.

Stephen J. Nichols
President, Reformation Bible College, CAO Ligonier Ministries,
Sanford, Florida

GEORGE MÜLLER

DELIGHTED IN GOD
Roger Steer

ISBN 978-1-8455-0120-4

George Müller
Delighted in God
ROGER STEER

George Müller's life is a powerful answer to modern scepticism.
His name has become a by-word for faith throughout the world.
In the early 1830s he embarked upon an extraordinary adventure.
Disturbed by the faithlessness of the Church in general, he longed
to have something to point to as 'visible proof that our God and
Father is the same faithful creator as he ever was'. He was more
successful than anyone could have believed possible and is as
much an example to our generation, as he was to his.

Uncovers the man from the myth ... a first class piece of work.
Evangelical Times

*Steer has penned a very readable volume that reminds the reader of
the greatness and generosity of God and the importance of prayer
in the believer's life.*
T. E. Byron Snapp, PCA News

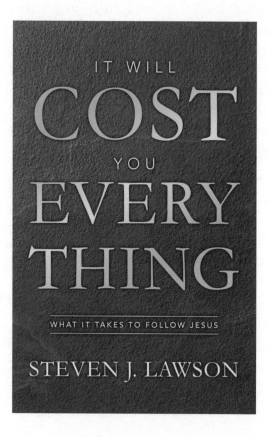

ISBN 978-1-5271-0703-8

It Will Cost You Everything
What it Takes to Follow Jesus
Steven J. Lawson

Nestled in a few verses in Luke's Gospel is a Jesus who would not have been tolerated today: He was not politically correct and He certainly did not try to save people's feelings. Steven Lawson unpacks these few verses, looking at the unashamed honesty, passion, and urgency with which Jesus explains the life-long cost involved in choosing to follow Him. True Christianity is the biggest sacrifice any person ever makes … but it is in pursuit of the most precious prize ever glimpsed.

Like a master builder Steve Lawson gives us the foundation of Jesus' own words to erect a frame showing the cost, demands, gains and losses of following Christ. In doing so, Dr. Lawson gives us a strong and firm edifice that brings glory to Him and His truth.

R. C. Sproul (1939 – 2017)
Founder & Chairman of Ligonier Ministries, Orlando, Florida

A fickle or indifferent disciple is a contradiction. Here is a book every Christian ought to read and seriously take to heart.

John MacArthur
Chancellor Emeritus, The Master's University and Seminary and Pastor–Teacher, Grace Community Church, Sun Valley, California

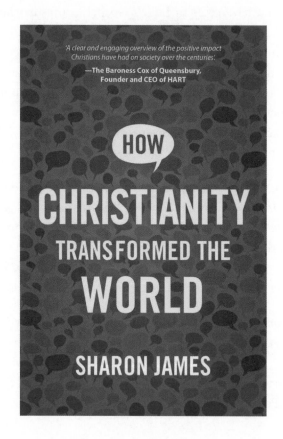

'A clear and engaging overview of the positive impact
Christians have had on society over the centuries.'

—The Baroness Cox of Queensbury,
Founder and CEO of HART

HOW

CHRISTIANITY
TRANSFORMED THE
WORLD

SHARON JAMES

ISBN 978-1-5271-0647-5

How Christianity Transformed the World

Sharon James

Many people today would say that Christianity has done more harm than good to our world. Sharon James argues, however, in seeking to love their neighbour and reflect God's moral character the followers of Jesus have had a largely positive impact on our society. James takes a number of areas – education, healthcare, justice, human dignity – and traces the ways in which these benefits have spread with the gospel.

… if you've been influenced to believe that the Christian gospel is a virulent intellectual infection that should be eradicated, that it robs people of joy and freedom, that it oppresses women and makes its heavenly-minded adherents of little earthly good, then you very much need to read this book.

Jon Bloom
President, Desiring God, Minneapolis, Minnesota

This brilliant little book … beautifully demonstrates the way that all that we treasure in Western civilisation – such as human rights, equality under the law, democratic government, science, healthcare, education and literature – has its roots in a Christian worldview which values human beings as special creations made in the image of God who are called by God to demonstrate His justice, creativity and character.

Peter Saunders
Chief Executive, International Christian Medical and Dental Association (ICMDA)

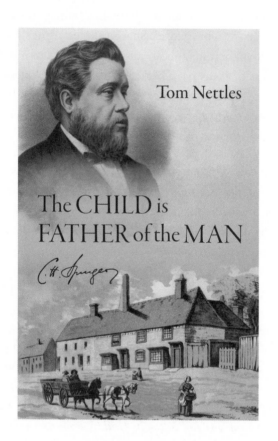

Tom Nettles

The CHILD is
FATHER of the MAN

ISBN 978-1-5271-0648-2

The Child is Father of the Man
C. H. Spurgeon
Tom Nettles

Tom Nettles examines the life of one of the world's most famous preachers. He isolates key convictions that appear in Spurgeon's life either before or immediately after his conversion, and traces them through his life as he develops into the charming, interesting, confident, humble, spiritual–minded man and pastor whose work and witness dominated evangelicalism in the last half of the nineteenth century.

... brilliantly focusses on ten key moments, convictions really, that shaped the larger-than-life Charles Haddon Spurgeon. These convictions steeled Spurgeon to weather controversy, depression, and setbacks. Through it all, Spurgeon's exuberant love for God, the gospel, and for the church shines through.

Stephen J. Nichols
President, Reformation Bible College, CAO Ligonier Ministries,
Sanford, Florida

... shows how the remarkable fruitfulness of Spurgeon's ministry developed from tiny seeds sown in his childhood and youth. Readers will enjoy the remarkable insights from a writer who is not only a Spurgeon scholar, but a man who has served the church as a professor of historical theology for more than forty years.

Donald S Whitney
Professor of Biblical Spirituality, The Southern Baptist
Theological Seminary, Louisville, Kentucky

Christian Focus Publications

Our mission statement —

STAYING FAITHFUL

In dependence upon God we seek to impact the world through literature faithful to His infallible Word, the Bible. Our aim is to ensure that the Lord Jesus Christ is presented as the only hope to obtain forgiveness of sin, live a useful life and look forward to heaven with Him.

Our books are published in four imprints:

CHRISTIAN
FOCUS

Popular works including biographies, commentaries, basic doctrine and Christian living.

CHRISTIAN
HERITAGE

Books representing some of the best material from the rich heritage of the church.

MENTOR

Books written at a level suitable for Bible College and seminary students, pastors, and other serious readers. The imprint includes commentaries, doctrinal studies, examination of current issues and church history.

CF4•K

Children's books for quality Bible teaching and for all age groups: Sunday school curriculum, puzzle and activity books; personal and family devotional titles, biographies and inspirational stories — because you are never too young to know Jesus!

Christian Focus Publications Ltd,
Geanies House, Fearn, Ross-shire,
IV20 1TW, Scotland, United Kingdom.
www.christianfocus.com
blog.christianfocus.com